Criminology and Criminal Justice in Russia

Though criminology took root in Russia in the early 1800s and has gone through various stages of maturation—paralleling developments of the discipline in Europe and North America over the last two centuries—its contributions and presence in the field is hardly noticeable in the English-speaking world. The objective of this book is by no means to fill that void but rather to bring together the recent developments in Russia, keeping in context its rich history of criminological legacies, its traditions, and its current experiences and growth since the restructuring of the Soviet Union.

The chapters in this book were originally published as a special issue of the *International Journal of Comparative and Applied Criminal Justice.*

Anna Gurinskaya is Associate Professor in the Department of Liberal Arts and Sciences at St. Petersburg State University, Russia.

Mahesh K. Nalla is Professor in the School of Criminal Justice at Michigan State University, USA.

Criminology and Criminal Justice in Russia

Past Legacies and Present Challenges

Edited by
Anna Gurinskaya and Mahesh K. Nalla

LONDON AND NEW YORK

First published 2018
by Routledge
2 Park Square, Milton Park, Abingdon, Oxon, OX14 4RN, UK

and by Routledge
711 Third Avenue, New York, NY 10017, USA

Routledge is an imprint of the Taylor & Francis Group, an informa business

Introduction, Chapters 1–3, 5–9 © 2017 School of Criminal Justice, Michigan State University
Chapter 4 © 2004 Taylor and Francis

All rights reserved. No part of this book may be reprinted or reproduced or utilised in any form or by any electronic, mechanical, or other means, now known or hereafter invented, including photocopying and recording, or in any information storage or retrieval system, without permission in writing from the publishers.

Trademark notice: Product or corporate names may be trademarks or registered trademarks, and are used only for identification and explanation without intent to infringe.

British Library Cataloguing-in-Publication Data
A catalogue record for this book is available from the British Library

ISBN13: 978-1-138-49137-3

Typeset in Minion Pro
by codeMantra

Publisher's Note
The publisher accepts responsibility for any inconsistencies that may have arisen during the conversion of this book from journal articles to book chapters, namely the possible inclusion of journal terminology.

Disclaimer
Every effort has been made to contact copyright holders for their permission to reprint material in this book. The publishers would be grateful to hear from any copyright holder who is not here acknowledged and will undertake to rectify any errors or omissions in future editions of this book.

Contents

Citation Information		vii
Notes on Contributors		ix
	Introduction	1
	Anna Gurinskaya and Mahesh K. Nalla	
1	Russian criminology as "Terra Incognita": legacies of the past and challenges of the present	5
	Anna Gurinskaya	
2	Soviet and post-Soviet Russian criminology – an insider's reflections	26
	Yakov Gilinskiy	
3	Social values and delinquency of Russian youth	36
	Olga Siegmunt and Peter Wetzels	
4	State and the Multilateralization of Policing in Post-Soviet Russia	56
	Gilles Favarel-Garrigues & Anne Le Huérou	
5	Pretrial detention in Russian criminal courts: a statistical analysis	74
	Kirill D. Titaev	
6	Plea bargaining in Russia: the role of defence attorneys and the problem of asymmetry	91
	Ekaterina Moiseeva	
7	The Restriction of Judicial Investigative Remand in Russia: the Role of Cultural Values in Citizen Acceptance and Perceived Fairness	113
	Olga B. Semukhina and K. Michael Reynolds	

CONTENTS

8   Severity and leniency in criminal sentencing in Russia: the effects of gender
    and family ties   140
    Iryna Chatsverykova

9   Female criminality in Russia: a research note from a penal colony   165
    Oksana Kaplun

    Index   175

Citation Information

The following chapters were originally published in the *International Journal of Comparative and Applied Criminal Justice*, volume 41, issue 3 (August 2017). When citing this material, please use the original page numbering for each article, as follows:

Chapter 1
Russian criminology as "Terra Incognita": legacies of the past and challenges of the present
Anna Gurinskaya
International Journal of Comparative and Applied Criminal Justice, volume 41, issue 3 (August 2017) pp. 123–143

Chapter 2
Soviet and post-Soviet Russian criminology – an insider's reflections
Yakov Gilinskiy
International Journal of Comparative and Applied Criminal Justice, volume 41, issue 3 (August 2017) pp. 113–122

Chapter 3
Social values and delinquency of Russian youth
Olga Siegmunt and Peter Wetzels
International Journal of Comparative and Applied Criminal Justice, volume 41, issue 3 (August 2017) pp. 211–230

Chapter 5
Pretrial detention in Russian criminal courts: a statistical analysis
Kirill D. Titaev
International Journal of Comparative and Applied Criminal Justice, volume 41, issue 3 (August 2017) pp. 145–161

Chapter 6
Plea bargaining in Russia: the role of defence attorneys and the problem of asymmetry
Ekaterina Moiseeva
International Journal of Comparative and Applied Criminal Justice, volume 41, issue 3 (August 2017) pp. 163–184

CITATION INFORMATION

Chapter 8

Severity and leniency in criminal sentencing in Russia: the effects of gender and family ties
Iryna Chatsverykova
International Journal of Comparative and Applied Criminal Justice, volume 41, issue 3 (August 2017) pp. 185–209

Chapter 9

Female criminality in Russia: a research note from a penal colony
Oksana Kaplun
International Journal of Comparative and Applied Criminal Justice, volume 41, issue 3 (August 2017) pp. 231–240

The following chapter was originally published in the *International Journal of Comparative and Applied Criminal Justice*, volume 34, issue 1 (Spring 2010). When citing this material, please use the original page numbering for each article, as follows:

Chapter 7

The Restriction of Judicial Investigative Remand in Russia: The Role of Cultural Values in Citizen Acceptance and Perceived Fairness
Olga B. Semukhina and K. Michael Reynolds
International Journal of Comparative and Applied Criminal Justice, volume 34, issue 1 (Spring 2010) pp. 173–199

The following chapter was originally published in *Policing & Society*, volume 14, issue 1 (March 2004). When citing this material, please use the original page numbering for each article, as follows:

Chapter 4

State and the Multilateralization of Policing in Post-Soviet Russia
Gilles Favarel-Garrigues and Anne Le Huérou
Policing & Society, volume 14, issue 1 (March 2004) pp. 13–30

For any permission-related enquiries please visit:
http://www.tandfonline.com/page/help/permissions

Notes on Contributors

Iryna Chatsverykova is a Junior Researcher in the Institute for the Rule of Law at the European University, St. Petersburg, Russia.

Gilles Favarel-Garrigues is a CNRS Researcher in the Centre de recherches internationals at Sciences-Po, Paris, France.

Yakov Gilinskiy is Professor and Chair of the Criminal Law Department at Russian State Pedagogical University of Herzen, St. Petersburg, Russia.

Anna Gurinskaya is Associate Professor in the Department of Liberal Arts and Sciences at St. Petersburg State University, Russia.

Oksana Kaplun is an Associate Professor in the School of Humanity at the Far Eastern Federal University, Vladivostok, Russia.

Anne Le Huérou is Professor at the Paris Ouest Nanterre La Défense University and Research Associate at the Centre for Russian, Caucasian and East-European Studies Paris, France.

Ekaterina Moiseeva is a Researcher at the Institute for the Rule of Law at the European University, St. Petersburg, Russia.

Mahesh K. Nalla is Professor in the School of Criminal Justice at Michigan State University, USA.

K. Michael Reynolds is Associate Professor in the Department of Criminal Justice and Legal Studies at the University of Central Florida, USA.

Olga B. Semukhina is Associate Professor in Social and Cultural Sciences at Marquette University, Milwaukee, USA.

Olga Siegmunt is a Lecturer and Project Leader at the Siberian Federal University, Krasnoyarsk, Russia, and a Consultant for Criminological Research Methods at the State Office for Criminal Investigation of Lower Saxony, Hanover, Germany.

Kirill D. Titaev is Senior Researcher at the Institute for the Rule of Law at the European University, St. Petersburg, Russia.

Peter Wetzels is a Professor for Criminology at the University of Hamburg, Germany.

Introduction

Anna Gurinskaya and Mahesh K. Nalla

More than 25 years have passed since the breakdown of the Union of Soviet Socialist Republics and the launching of the major political, economic, and social reforms. Both crime and its governance have also changed dramatically. The criminal justice system was gradually dismantled and reassembled on distinctive constitutional grounds that recognized the importance of international human rights standards and the due process requirements that sustain these standards. The new Criminal Code and Criminal Procedure Code were adopted, judicial reform was launched, and policing and law enforcement agencies were restructured. The transformations continue to be ongoing, and Russia is still in transition—some reforms that were initially adopted with great enthusiasm seem to be put on hold or amended. New ideas continue to emerge and result in decisions to downsize the police and cut down the prison population, and introduce numerous and often incongruous amendments to the Criminal Code. The nature and types of crimes have also been evolving in the rapidly transforming renewed state: crime rates skyrocketed in the 1990s and then began dropping with an equal magnitude in 2006, following the similar crime drop patterns that were observable in other countries. Russia, with all these fascinating crime and policy trends, represents a unique and fascinating case for those who want to understand more about crime, not just locally but globally.

The Soviet Union, before the breakup, was a unique country—politically, economically, and crime-wise. However, due to ideological and political reasons, not much was known to the outside world about how crime in this country was determined, how it was dealt with, and how it was analyzed. Surprisingly, not much has changed in the past quarter of a century: Russia is still almost absent from the non-Russian-language discursive space that engages with questions related to crime. This edited volume is aimed at filling this void by bringing to the forefront of international criminology discussions on contemporary Russian criminology and criminal justice perspectives of both Western- and Russian-based scholars, who for the most part were educated and hold academic positions in Russia. Making audible the voices of the latter group is especially important to us as they are rarely heard in the global criminological choir.

Why should anyone be interested in reading this volume? This collection of articles does not discuss the topics that are typically associated with the scholarly pursuits of issues of crime and justice in Russia—organized crime, corruption, being the second-largest prison system in the world, etc. Nor does it attempt to provide a systematic general overview of the crime rates; outline unique features of violent, property, and drug crimes in Russia; or address the complexity of the crime control apparatus. In that sense, this effort is not to outline a comprehensive introduction into criminology and criminal justice in Russia. It is, rather, a collection of articles that provide answers to a number of pertinent and puzzling questions, such as: if crime is such a pressing issue in Russia, why is almost nothing known about it to the outside world? Does criminology as a field even exist in this country, and if it does, how is it different from the other "criminologies" out there in the world? How is crime controlled? Has policing in Russia undergone a process of pluralization, as witnessed in recent decades in many other parts of the world? How does law behave in Russia? Do the gender or socioeconomic characteristics of the offenders influence judges' pretrial decisions, sentencing, and life in a penal colony? Do citizens approve of the criminal justice system reforms? How have social transformations influenced people's value systems? How does it affect their decisions to engage in criminal behavior? How does it affect acceptance of such state reforms as limitation of the judge's remand authority or engagement in pretrial negotiations and plea bargaining?

This volume is broadly divided into three sections. The articles in the first section cover discussions on the scope and development of the field of criminology in Russia. In the first article, Gurinskaya explores the early developments of criminology in pre-Soviet times and expands the scope of her inquiry in the post-Soviet era, leading up to the present time. Keeping in context the advances experienced in other social sciences, Gurinskaya identifies a range of ideological, institutional, and economic pressures shaping Russian criminology over the past century. Drawing data from a survey of Russian criminology educators, she finds support for her narrative on the nature and the transformation that occurred in Russia since the fall of the Soviet Union. She examines the legacies and the foundations of contemporary theoretical criminology to address two key questions: why has Russian criminology remained fairly static since its revival in the second half of the 20th century, and how has it managed to remain isolated from the international community? In her conclusion, she reflects on the current controversies of Russian criminology and suggests obstacles the discipline has to overcome for it to be accepted and integrated into global criminology.

In the second article, Giliniskiy traces the history of criminology, spanning nearly a century of Soviet and post-Soviet Russia, and identifies the key phases of the development of the field, with particular emphasis on the time period since the late 1960s, integrating the narrative with reflections from his personal experiences from the time. He identifies four critical areas of development in criminology. These areas include research in criminology; the academic status of the field of criminology (topics that are considered important by Russian criminologists for empirical research); exposure to international scholarship and networking; and, finally, criminology course offerings in Russian law schools.

In the third article, Siegmunt and Wetzels investigate delinquency among Russian youth from Volgograd in southwestern Russia. Grounding their work on Durkheim's anomie and Messner and Rosenfeld's institutional anomie theories, Siegmunt and Wetzels test the relationship between social values and participation in violent criminal behavior among 1,747 ninth-grade students. Of the three latent groups they identify (i.e., indifferent, competitor-centered, and tradition-centered), the authors find that competitor-centered youth have greater criminal propensity to engage in violent behavior relative to traditional-centered youth, who appeared the least criminal.

The second set of articles explores topics related to criminal justice processes in post-Soviet Russia. In the fourth article, Favarel-Garrigues and Huérou analyze the developments in policing in post-Soviet Russia. More specifically, the authors address the issue of the "multilaterization" of policing, as has been happening in many of the market-oriented democracies, and whether these developments have occurred in post-Soviet Russia, with its "unilateral all-state" authoritarian past. Favarel-Garrigues and Huérou argue that, contrary to the imagery of the state-centric police state, policing in the Soviet Union did not represent a "homogenous" authority of police but consisted of many levels of state and citizen groups orchestrating social control, making it virtually impossible to draw a distinction between public and private policing functions. The demand for policing increased in the latter half of the 1980s and particularly in the 1990s because of the increase in crime rates, massive reductions in the military and policing organizations, the dramatic exodus of law enforcement personnel to the private sector, and a resurgence in the self-policing mechanisms adopted both inside and outside factories. These developments of "informal multilateralization" were no different than what existed prior to the breakdown of the Soviet Union.

In the fifth article, Titaev focuses on pretrial detention in the Russian criminal justice system. He examines the factors that influence the likelihood of pretrial detention in the Russian courts and to what extent pretrial detention influences case dismissal, type of punishment, and length of incarceration. Data for this research were drawn from over 10,000 coded decisions of Russian criminal courts. Controlling for demographic characteristics, such as gender, employment status, criminal history, and procedural characteristics of the case, Titaev shows that unemployment status, informal criminal records, and the nonconfession of guilt are the key predictors of the probability of pretrial detention. Additionally, he demonstrates that the occurrence of pretrial detention significantly influences the probability of the nondismissal of case detention, though no significant connection between pretrial detention and length of imprisonment was established.

The focus of the sixth article, by Moiseeva, is plea bargaining and the role of defense attorneys in pretrial and trial negotiations in Russia's criminal justice system. While describing the organizational contexts of how lawyers dispense with justice, she argues that, as in other countries, defense attorneys are a weaker professional group in Russia, and they leverage their skills to play on the weaknesses of law enforcement agencies to balance their bargaining positions. Drawing data from semi-structured interviews with advocates, judges, and law enforcement officers, and hours of observations of criminal trials in the district courts of St. Petersburg, Moiseeva concludes that the "shady" practices of defenders are the result of the accusatory bias of the Russian criminal justice process, the managerial problems in law enforcement agencies, and ineffective regulation of the appointed counsel system. She also notes the overreliance of defense attorneys on law enforcement in the judicial process, highlighting the notion of "pocket defense attorneys," while appointed counsels work more in the interest of the state than defendants.

In the seventh article, Semukhina and Reynolds examine fairness in judicial investigative remand in Russia from the citizens' point of view. Following up on a major reform relating to the revocation of trial judges' authority to remand a case for additional investigation, the authors examine citizens' support for limiting judges' remand authority. More specifically, they examine if citizens' value systems, that is, collectively oriented versus individually oriented, respond positively to these reform measures. Data for this study come from a survey of 1,640 respondents drawn from 50 of the 89 Russian regions, with a sampling frame conducted in five stages. Semukhina and Reynolds find that Russia continues to be a country predominantly guided by collective cultural values, with citizens supporting the adversarial criminal justice reforms, but they caution that individualistic values are gaining ground.

The eighth article in this issue, by Chatsverykova, deals with severity and leniency in sentencing in Russian courts, focusing on gender and family ties. More specifically, the author examines the effects of gender, marital, and parental statuses on influencing sentencing decisions. The article demonstrates that gender order, as well as the cultural and legal contexts of a particular society, has a moderating effect on gender disparity in sentencing. Chatsverykova presents her findings from a large data set of over five million defendants prosecuted in Russian criminal courts from 2009 to 2013 and suggests that women face a significantly lower likelihood of being incarcerated and receive shorter sentences compared to men, with the exception of for drug-related crimes. She also notes that marital status influences the probability of incarceration. For instance, having children, as a factor, has little effect on whether they receive "in/out or sentence length decisions." When defendants face prison sentences, childcare responsibilities can increase sentence length, especially for females, highlighting the significance of gender as a moderator in sentencing.

In the last article, Kaplun presents a case study of crime trends among female offenders in modern Russia. In a review of prisoner data consisting of 212 women between ages 18 and 64 from a penal colony in Vladivostok, a city in the Russian Far East, Kaplun examines factors that influence female criminality. She notes that of the 13 kinds of punishments specified in the Criminal Code of the Russian Federation, incarceration was the most widely used punishment for women. Further, most female offenders were incarcerated for violent and drug-related offenses. The findings from this research also suggest that lower education and alcoholism are among the factors strongly associated with female violent crime and punishment.

This volume is the result of the toil and efforts of many individuals. We are grateful to the contributors for responding to our call with enthusiasm and responding in a timely manner! The findings from various contributions in this special issue shed light on the current state of Russian criminology that so far has remained primarily invisible in Western academia. All the contributors have pointed out policy implications, and we hope that these efforts will spur and spark more systematic exploration of topics on Russian crime and justice in the English language. They also reveal the processes occurring in the criminal justice system in Russia, pointing to the similarities and differences relative to scholarship from other parts of the world, adding to our current knowledge of comparative and global criminology.

Russian criminology as "Terra Incognita": legacies of the past and challenges of the present

Anna Gurinskaya

ABSTRACT

In this article, we outline the place of Russian criminology on the world criminological map during the pre-Soviet, Soviet, and post-Soviet eras. We examine the external institutional and economic pressures experienced by the field of criminology in past decades and assess its current development against the backdrop of other social sciences in Russia. Further, we interface these arguments with data drawn off Russian academics' perceptions on whether criminology as a discipline has significantly transformed in Russia after the breakdown of the Soviet Union; how relevant Russian criminology is for the practice of law-enforcement and state crime control policy; and whether criminology has appropriate placement within law schools which serve as primary residence for the discipline. Finally, we conclude with some reflection on the current state of Russian criminology and the future directions of the discipline.

Introduction

The development of criminology as an academic discipline in recent decades has demonstrated "a remarkable success story" (Garland, 2011, p. 298). Indeed, the field has expanded significantly both in terms of the programmes and courses offered, the scope of problems that it tries to address as well as the range of methodologies that it is equipped with. However, this story of success becomes less obvious if we shift our gaze from the North to the South, from the West to the East or, in Wallerstein's (2004) world systems theory terminology, from the "core" to the "periphery". Cohen (1988) noted that the voices and problems of the criminological periphery are often neglected by the core. Despite more recent trends in the internationalisation of the discipline (Barberet, 2007), growth of interest in comparative studies (Bennett, 2004; Crawford, 2011; Nelken, 2010), and calls for developing more democratic epistemologies (Aas, 2012, 2013), criminology still primarily remains the discipline of the North (Lee & Laidler, 2013, p. 141). Theories, concepts, and methods developed in the global North are privileged over those that are rooted in the experience of the other parts of the world (see Carrington, Hogg, & Sozzo, 2016). However, a proper application of Western theories and "translation" of policies is impossible without a thorough account for cultural differences as well as political, economical, and societal changes in the peripheral geographies (Shepticky, 2008). Scholars also warn that inappropriate use of Western criminological discourse and neglect of the non-Western experience is capable of producing a negative impact on the non-Western societies (Agozino, 2004; Cain, 2000). Global division of labour in social sciences and academic imperialism (Alatas, 2003) as well as social and economic inequalities (Medina, 2011) perpetuate dependency of the non-core scholars on the institutions and ideas of the West and hinder academic progress in the peripheral and semi-peripheral countries. It should be noted though that progress (or the lack of it) is not equally distributed among non-core countries. While recently some regions of the global South became much more visible on the world knowledge map national criminologies of other countries still remain "terra incognita."

The focus of this article is Russian criminology, a discipline that has existed, thrived, and survived in a world that throughout the most of the twentieth century remained unknown, unseen, and untouched by Western scholars and readers (as exceptions see Berman & Burgess, 1937; Connor, 1970; Shelley, 1979a, 1979b; Solomon, 1974, 1978). Crime and crime control in the post-Soviet region and specifically Russia once-in-a-while does attract some interest from the outside (see Botchkovar & Broidy, 2013; Piacentini, 2012; Pridemore, 2005; Slade & Light, 2015). However, voices of indigenous Russian criminologists are barely distinguishable even in the not so large choir of scholars who devote their work to the region and approach it with the Western set of tools and concepts. Are there any criminologists in Russia? Does the discipline even exist and, if it does, what prevents it from engaging in meaningful dialogue with rest of the world? Is Russian criminology capable of providing unique and significant contributions that would be seen as crucial for understanding crime and its control globally?

One would be surprised to find out that the origins of Russian criminology date as far back as 1801. Since then it has undergone dramatic changes: from gradual maturing to complete abandonment; from rebirth on the new theoretical ground to losing these grounds and sliding down towards slow decline. Doing criminology in contemporary Russia means facing a range of intellectual, institutional, and economic challenges. One of the biggest challenges is rethinking and adapting the legacy of the sophisticated Soviet criminology to current social conditions – a project that has not advanced much in the past 25 years. The scope of this article is rather limited. It should be viewed as a starting point in exploring the terrain of contemporary Russian criminology, tracing its history, and identifying its key features. Our aim is to outline the place of Russian criminology on the global map of criminological knowledge and introduce it to the academic community that has paid particularly little attention to the criminologies of the former Eastern Bloc countries that are "out of mind, sight and consciousness" of the criminologists in the English language hemisphere (Płatek, 2016).

This article addresses the current state of affairs in Russian criminology through the lens of its past achievements. In the first section, the article will briefly describe the origins and several stages of the history of the discipline, paying attention to the Soviet theory of crime causation grounded in the cornerstones of the Marxian philosophy – dialectic and historical materialism. The second section addresses the question of whether the legacy of the Soviet past is still present in the current criminological theory, and whether it can be seen as an internal impediment for the growth of the field. The final section examines the problem of isolationism of Russian criminology. It also looks at external institutional and economic pressures that were put on criminology in past decades and assesses its current development against the backdrop of other social sciences in Russia. Further, we interface these arguments with data drawn off Russian academics' perceptions on whether criminology as a discipline has significantly transformed in Russia after the breakdown of the Soviet Union; how relevant Russian criminology is for the practice of law-enforcement and state crime control policy; and whether criminology has appropriate placement within law schools. The article concludes with some reflection on the current state of criminological knowledge in Russian and the future directions of the discipline.

The history of criminology in Russia

Emergence and demise of criminology: 1801–1933. Since its emergence in the early nineteenth century, Russian criminology has followed a path similar to that of the European criminology: The initial fascination with the possibility of gathering crime statistics and its potential in analysing crime trends and patterns in the first decades of the nineteenth century (Herrmann, 1824; Radishev, 1801/2005). By the end of the century, it had developed into a science that aimed to provide anthropological and sociological explanations of crime assessing the relevance of the European theories in the Russian context (see Dril, 2013). The advances of Russian criminology of the nineteenth century in the seminal historical work of Ivanov and Ilyina (1991) are attributed to the anti-regime spirit of the time coupled with the crisis of the classical school of criminal law and disenchantment of some scholars with its ideas. Young criminal law professors were eager to challenge traditional views about crime as an expression of free will alone. They blamed the state for not creating proper conditions for social development and pointed out the need to examine social conditions of crime (Dukhovskoj, 1872). The question remained whether new findings about the nature of criminal behaviour should be laid in the foundation of the sociological school of criminal law (Fojnitskij, 1873) or if this knowledge should find its place outside of the legal domain (Sergeevskij, 1879; Tagantsev, 1902). The debate aimed at reconciling the "free will" paradigm with determinism continued throughout the next century and at least partially determined the current placement of criminology in the legal arena.

The major judicial reform launched by the Tzar Alexander II in 1864 contributed to the development of criminology in Russia (Kowalsky, 2016). The reform was aimed at creating a completely new system of the judiciary, promoting independence of judges and introducing adversarial jury trials. New defence attorneys employed a defence strategy that shifted the jury's attention from the crime to the offender. The latter was viewed as a "hostage" of the environment created by the oppressive state that had made the offender incapable of exerting free will (McReynolds, 2013). The scientific approach had to be brought to the courtroom to provide evidence of this determinism. And, the Russian case was no different from the European where determinism brought about the first schools of criminology (Radzinowicz, 1965). Kowalsky (2016) describes that in 1903, Russian criminologists participated in the Brussels meeting of the International Union of Criminologists where they could boast that criminology as an occupation had success in Russia. Its expertise was highly demanded by the courts, it was taught in universities, influenced legal policy, and was integrated in the European intellectual field without losing sight of the particular Russian conditions (Kowalsky, 2016, p. 416). Over the next three decades, criminological research in Russia was not only diverse, competent, and sophisticated (Shelley, 1979a), but also equal to if not surpassing the intellectual ideas of the criminologists from the West (Shelley, 1979b).

The Russian Revolution of 1917 brought dramatic political and economic shifts that were coupled with the Russian civil war. However, this did not impede the development of criminology in Russia. On the contrary, criminologists received substantial support from the newly established Bolshevik government. In 1918, the government established new centres for the study of crime (*kabinety*) in a number of Russian cities – the first one in Petrograd (now St. Petersburg), followed by Saratov, Moscow, Rostov-on-Don, and in the new republics of the USSR (Ukrainian, Belarussian, and Transcaucasian (that united Azerbaijan, Armenia, and Georgia)) (Ivanov & Ilyina, 1991). The centres had very diverse research agendas, used a variety of empirical methods (surveys, study of court cases, clinical examinations, compiling criminal-diagnostic cards, etc.), brought together specialists from different fields, and contributed to the policy and everyday action of the crime control agencies. Ivanov and Ilyina (1991) also noted that in 1925, a central State Institute for the Study of Crime and Criminal was established in Moscow that took upon the administration of the dispersed centres whose projects were ambitious in scope and policy-relevant: a minimum length of imprisonment of 1 year was introduced after the Institute's report had pointed out the ineffectiveness of the short-term prison sentences. Overall, criminology was not affected much by the political changes and continued the tradition established in the previous century combining various approaches to studying crime and developing empirical methods.

This "golden age" for Russian/Soviet criminology lasted until 1929. Solomon (1974) describes in details how criminologists were first accused by the scholars of the Communist academy (a mouthpiece of the Marxist-Leninist ideology) of excessively using biopsychological and biosocial explanations of crime. The biological view over the nature of crime was said to lead to conclusions of crime being an a-historical, eternal phenomenon (Ivanov & Ilyina, 1991). This was an impossible deviation from Marxist historicism and social determinism – dominant premises of all sciences in the new Soviet country. Criminologists were accused of "Lombrosianism" (generalising about physical or psychological traits of the criminals) and "positivism" (adherence to "bourgeois" objective social science) (Solomon, 1974). These accusations were not a part of the innocent scientific debate about the accuracy of the research methodology – by 1933 they had a deadly impact on the discipline of criminology, and affected personal life trajectories of criminologists employed by the Institute and local research centres: at best, they lost their jobs, but some of them also found themselves in prison camps (Gilinskiy, 2014). Research agenda became a political matter. Initial attempts to defend criminology on the grounds of its utility for prisons and the administration of justice (Solomon, 1974) turned it into a very applied science serving the purposes of the judicial administration (Shelley, 1979b). In 1933, the Institute was reorganised into All-Union Institute of Juridical Sciences. Any theoretical study of crime was labelled as ideologically wrong – under Marxist-Leninist ideology, crime was seen as a phenomenon destined to disappear; therefore, its study was redundant (Solomon, 1974). Some research work was carried out in the next decades, but it was limited to studying historical aspects of crime and penal institutions (Gernet, 1951–1956). It is possible to argue that the tradition of the diverse research that shared the same scientific language with the European colleagues was abruptly terminated and has never been re-established despite the re-emergence of criminology as a discipline 30 years later.

Criminology of "developed socialism": 1956–1991. Criminology's revival began on completely different theoretical grounds after the Stalin's cult of personality was publicly denounced in 1956 and the subsequent Khrushev's "thaw" began associated with the relative liberalisation of political climate. The study of crime was brought back, but only as "the governmental project" (Garland, 2002): the very purpose of the new discipline of criminology was to serve the aspirations of the communist party to put an end to disruptions of public order and deviance that accompanied the processes of industrialisation and urbanisation. This governmental, administrative nature of the newly emerging criminology becomes evident when one looks at the new Agenda of the Communist Party of the USSR adopted at the XXII General Assembly in 1961 (Kommunisticheskaja Partija Sovetskogo Sojuza [Communist Party of the Soviet Union], 1961). This document created the necessary conditions for the development of the discipline. First, it explicitly established the goal of the complete elimination of crime and its causes in Soviet society. Priority was given to crime prevention and strict punishment of not just criminals, but also of other rule-breakers and idlers (Kommunisticheskaja Partija Sovetskogo Sojuza. [Communist Party of the Soviet Union], 1961). Secondly, it criticised the overly dogmatic approach of legal science and insisted on enriching the legal field with sociological and philosophical perspectives aimed at deeper understanding of the law's development and its social role (Alekseyev, 1962). In addition, the new Criminal Procedure Code (CPC) adopted in 1960 required investigators, prosecutors and judges to discover the causes and conditions of each crime and undertake measures for their elimination (Ugolovno-protsessualnij kodeks RSFSR [Criminal Procedure Code of RSFSR], 1961, article 21). Therefore, legal training of these professionals was to be supplemented with topics related to crime causation. Utility of criminology for the state was, as Solomon (1974) noted, the condition upon which the discipline was brought back to existence – the Marxist principle of bridging theory and practice required sciences to provide theoretical ground for policy solutions. In addition, he observed that criminology's mission was to fight on the forefront of the ideological Cold War, demonstrating the successes of the Soviet system of dealing with crime and making the Soviet situation look favourable compared to capitalist countries.

In 1964, a course titled "The essentials of the Soviet criminology" was introduced at the Law Department of Moscow State University and Sverdlovsk (now Ekaterinenburg) Law Institute (Ostroumov & Kuznetsova, 1964). Soon, other law schools offered courses and the first criminology textbooks were developed (Gertsenzon, 1965; Gertsenzon, Karpets, & Kudrjavtsev, 1966). Despite aspirations for intellectual independence (Utevskij, 1964 [as cited in Gertsenzon, 1970, p. 42]), institutionally criminology was firmly grounded within law departments with criminal law becoming its "master" (Gertsenzon, 1970, p. 49). Research was concentrated in research institutes that functioned under the auspices of law enforcement agencies, a tradition that still exists today. In 1963, the All-Union Institute for the study of causes of crime and developing measures of crime prevention was opened in Moscow and took the lead in developing the field of criminology. A handful of publications of Soviet scholars appeared in English-language journals (e.g., Kuznetsova, 1972; Kuznetsova & Shupilov, 1982; Ostroumov & Kuznetsova, 1968). However, these journals specialised in Soviet studies and not criminology, which made the scholarship unlikely to reach the eyes of criminologists. Even radical and conflict theorists, and other scholars who work within the Marxist paradigm are not familiar with Soviet interpretation of the Marx's ideas (see Cowling, 2008; Greenberg, 1993; Lynch & Groves, 1989). Although Soviet theoretical criminology for decades did not engage in any dialogue with the West, it had certainly been exerting strong theoretical influence over criminologies of the countries of the Soviet Union [see for Estonia (Saar, 2004), Lithuania (Dobryninas & Sakalauskas, 2011), Ukraine (Foglesong & Solomon, 2001)] and more moderate influence over the countries of the Eastern Bloc that enthusiastically embarked on other approaches when Soviet ideology began losing its power in the late years of the Soviet Union (for Poland see Krajewski (2004); for Hungary – Kerezsi and Levay (2008); for Slovenia – Meško and Jere (2012), for a general overview of the influence over the socialist countries, see Frankowski (1980)). Institutionally criminology became very well established, and intellectually it managed to develop a coherent explanation of why crime occurs and suggest an ambitious programme to fight it.

Soviet theory of crime: Theoretical development of the Soviet criminology after its revival in the 1960s was severely constrained by ideology. Criminologists were explaining crime in the USSR using historical and dialectical materialism – the only acceptable methodological approaches of Marxist theory. "Bourgeois" criminology was condemned as alien to the Soviet scientific methodology (Kuznetsova, 1974). Its major flaw, as identified by Soviet criminologists, was ideological blindness and mechanical theoretical eclecticism (Korobejnikov, Kuznetsova, & Minkovskij, 1988). Western criminology was said to have failed to produce a general conceptual theory that would explain crime and its causes in the capitalist society (Nikiforov, 1966, p. 13). Also, criminology in the West was said to be sponsored by and produced in the interests of the ruling class of "imperial monopolists". It meant to provide a semblance of a thorough research that allowed it to hide behind the unbiased scientific procedures the true nature of crime in the capitalist society (Gelfer, Grishaev, & Zdravomyslov, 1967; Reshetnikov, 1965). Its main function was justification of the bourgeois legality and legal order (Fedotov, 1973). Even critical ideas developed by Quinney (1970, 1977), Chambliss (1975), Chambliss and Seidman (1971), Turk (1977), and by the New Criminology of Taylor, Walton, and Young (1973) were regarded by Soviet criminologists to be only moderately progressive. The critique that these scholars had provided was seen as democratic and humanistic, whereas their policy recommendations were regarded as "flawed by the positivist methodology" for not proposing the destruction of the capitalist system (Korobejnikov et al., 1988, pp. 217–219). It is necessary to mention that the access to foreign scholarship among Soviet criminologists was limited and regulated. Even when few works were available the access to those volumes was tightly controlled. Those who managed to gain access and wished to cite these works were expected to critique Western perspectives purely on ideological grounds. Essentially, Soviet criminologists were familiar with the major developments of the discipline in the West, but the substance was irrelevant for the ideological project of portraying not just the capitalist society as incurably flawed but also the sciences that studied this society as irrelevant for the Soviet conditions. Soviet criminologists did not engage in any argument with the Western colleagues over the substance of the Western theories. They rejected all those views as false by default and inapplicable to the socialist economic system. Soviet theory did not develop as a response to the foreign theories. It took its own completely independent track, which ran parallel to the criminology of the capitalist world and developed its theoretical propositions from scratch, without taking into consideration neither its own century-long tradition of development, nor any western trends of the time.

Soviet criminologists did not dare to openly oppose the Party's directions and argued that socialist system had eliminated the "root cause" of crime, i.e. exploitation. Therefore, crime was supposed to cease to exist. The Soviet Union was not crime free only because of the criminogenic effects of the "residuals of the past" or "birth marks" of capitalism that were embedded in the social and individual consciousness – individualistic traditions, habits, interests, and motivations (Kudrjavtsev, Karpetz, & Korobejnikov, 1985; Kuznetsova, 1984). Developed socialism was also said to have crime because of the existence of crime-producing conditions. One of those external conditions was the influence of the "imperialist surrounding" that was aimed at disrupting economic and social relations in the Soviet Union (Karpets, 1966).

Eventually the adoption of the Marxist approach by criminologists led to the development of a very abstract integrative theory that was intended to be capable of explaining crime at macro, micro, and individual levels. Conceptually, it was grounded in the approach of dialectic materialism with its three fundamental laws (for discussion of the influence of Marxist philosophy upon development of sciences in Soviet Union see Graham, 1987). Macro-social explanations of crime in Soviet criminology were rooted in the second law of dialectical materialism – "the law of unity and struggle of the opposites," according to which all natural and societal processes, including crime, are driven by the contradictory, mutually exclusive, opposite tendencies or "contradictions" (Zhigarev, 2013). The concept of contradictions allowed criminologists to provide a solid critique of crime in the capitalist world and also to account for crime incidence in the Soviet Union. Criminologists agreed that the nature of these contradictions was different in capitalist and socialist settings, but debated whether they serve as an "objective" source of crime (Dolgova, 2005; Nomokonov, 1985) or are necessarily mediated by human consciousness (Kuznetsova, 1984; Volzhenkin, 1975; see also Prozumentov & Shesler, 2014; for discussion of the debate).

While the macro-level theory of social contradictions is unique to Soviet criminology, other ideas although developed independently seem to be in line with Western explanations of criminal behaviour (a fact that had never been reflected upon or acknowledged by Soviet criminologists). Soviet theory combined deterministic ideas with the rational choice explanations. It viewed the individual as a product of social relations (Karpetz, 1969) who was also capable of exerting free will (Yakovlev, 1976). The degree of the offender's "social dangerousness", a main trait of the offender's personality, was determined by the depth, stability, and prevalence of the individualistic, as opposed to collectivist, anti-social predispositions (Sakharov, 1961) that were a result of their interaction with the social environment (Kudrjavtsev, 1968). Crime was described as an act of conscious wilful activity: the offender was said to be able to calculate positive and negative outcomes of their behaviour, consider non-criminal alternatives, and make a decision on each stage of executing the act (Kudrjavtsev, 1968; Sakharov, 1995). In addition, the lack of self-control was linked to criminal behaviour (Kuznetsova & Luneev, 2005). Criminologists pointed out the importance of the immediate situation in the mechanism of crime causation. Situation was said to have both an objective content and the subjective meaning for the offender; it could serve as the source for a crime motive, create opportunities to satisfy the motive, become a trigger for committing a crime, ease or impede the desired outcome (Kudrjavtsev & Eminov, 2016). What those theoretical explanations lacked was extensive empirical testing. 1977).

Unlike Western criminology that only recently became engaged with the idea that criminology has to adapt itself to the preventive logic and to the challenges of pre-crime and security (Zedner, 2007), Soviet criminology has always been forward looking. As early as the

1960s, criminologist claimed that criminology is a science about crime prevention (Kudrjavtsev, 1967) and any criminology textbook had large sections on crime prevention and crime forecasting. Criminologists have also claimed to have developed a theory of crime prevention – its foundation was the Soviet theory of crime causation (Zvirbul, Klochkov, & Minkovskij, 1977). Suggested prevention measures ranged from general, i.e. aimed at improving social conditions, to specific, e.g. treatment programmes for high-risk offenders. Those measures were to be carefully planned in advance on the state level based on the scientific predictions about crime (Orekhov, 1972) and implemented by a wide range of the state and non-state actors (civil volunteers to protect public order ("*druzhinniki*"), workers' teams, youth organisations, etc.). Since the 1960s, Soviet criminologists have been developing classifications of offenders based on the degree of their social dangerousness and estimating the risk that they pose to the general society as well as the probability of their future offending. This served as a basis for suggesting appropriate control measures including the type of correctional institution as well as the length of imprisonment and the post-punishment control (Burlakov, 2006). These ideas were expressed before modern Western society was said to be a society of risk (Beck, 1992), the Western criminal justice system embraced risk-based actuarial approaches (Feeley & Simon, 1992; O'Malley, 2004) and acknowledged the fact that non-state providers of security outnumber the state (Shearing & Stenning, 1981) became evident.

Overall, by the late 1970s and in the 1980s, theoretical criminology in the Soviet Union was a flourishing field. One mainstream approach still prevailed, but scholars began engaging with Western scholarship in a constructive and substantial way (see Yakovlev, 1985). As Gilinskiy (2017) observes, new areas of research emerged – from family violence and juvenile delinquency to geography of crime and prison studies. He further suggests that as the iron curtain had risen the flow of information from abroad and joint conferences with foreign colleagues became possible. Finally, he notes that as a result of Gorbachev's "perestroika", all ideological pressures were removed from social sciences. This gave hope for further development of the field through its engagement with Western knowledge and re-establishing the forgotten Russian criminologies of the 1920s.

Criminology in Russia today: "consigned to oblivion"?

The transition of Russia to the market economy brought about not just long-awaited political freedoms, but also disorder, social inequality, and insecurity. It was not the dissolution of the Soviet Union in 1991 that put a final end to the ambitious goal of the Communist Party to eliminate all crime in the socialist society – crime rates had already been on a constant rise from 1968 and doubled in the 1980s (Gilinskiy, 2006). Likewise, it was not only the increase in the total amount of crime that criminologists in the new country had to deal with. Crime became more violent, its organised forms proliferated, and law-enforcement agencies struggled to fight back. One could have expected that the increase in the crime problems should have brought about new opportunities for criminologists and eventually promote criminological development. However, under the new economic conditions, crime flourished, but criminology did not. Having survived totalitarian ideological pressures, criminology appeared to be helpless in front of the neoliberal capitalist economic conditions. The story of post-Soviet criminology is very much like the stories of the peripheral countries where this discipline suffers from the lack of institutional recognition, underfunding, and neglect on behalf of the core countries (Medina, 2011). As the President of the Russian Criminological Association (RCA) has stated: "[c]riminology in the country is again being consigned to oblivion as an independent science and a teaching discipline. And the question of its revival is once again on the agenda" (Dolgova, 2016; translated from Russian by the author). This statement reveals a very deep concern about the current state of criminology in Russia despite the fact that the situation does not look that pessimistic at first glance.

When one accounts for the number of criminologists, defended dissertations, and schools where criminology courses are being offered, it appears that the discipline bears semblance of a relatively stable and even growing area of knowledge. Criminology remains a part of the legal programme where it is usually taught within the departments of criminal law. The number of law schools has grown from 52 during Soviet times to 1211 in 2009 (Popova, 2014, p. 46). An independent programme in criminology has never been established but sociology departments offer some courses on deviance and social control. There are a great number of the Russian language textbooks and several publishing houses have divisions that specialise in criminal law and criminology scholarship. In the period between 1989 and 2013 as many as 1566 dissertations were defended that discussed exclusively criminology topics (Zhmurov, 2013). A number of professional organisations were established – both country-wide and regional. The RCA established in 1991 is a flagship of criminological community in Russia. It claims to have more than 1300 active members (Russian Criminological Association, 2017). This number matches the membership level of the European Society of Criminology in which Russia is surprisingly represented by five members only (Aebi & Kronicz, 2016). The Union of Forensic and Criminology Scholars, St. Petersburg International Criminology Club, Saratov Centre for the Study of Organized Crime and Corruption facilitate research, academic meetings and publishing activity. Currently there are four state-funded federal research institutes that have criminology divisions. Three periodical specialised criminology journals and a number of law journals provide venue for publications.

On the surface and for the outside observer the field looks diverse and even blossoming. However, Russian scholars have a different opinion about the state of the discipline. They characterise it as being "in crisis" (Zhalinskiy, 2011), "stagnant" (Matskevitch, 2011; Zhigarev, 2012), "frozen" (Nagornaja & Pogosova, 2011), and "trivial" (Samovichev, 2011). Empirical research is primarily limited to examining non-verified official crime and demographic statistics or survey data drawn from small samples of citizens (Zhalinskiy, 2007, pp. 97–98). Examination of criminology journals reveals the fact that authors commit themselves to descriptive analyses of different crime types or broad critique of policy initiatives. The quality of teaching and textbooks is also said to be declining (Dolgova, 2016). Legislators ignore the opinion of criminologists even when major amendments to the Criminal Code are discussed (Kuznetsova & Luneev, 2005).

While empirical support for the broad range of criticisms about the state of criminology identified in Russian literature raised above are lacking, we attempted to assess the perceptions of Russian Academics engaged in teaching Criminology courses about some of these assertions. More specifically, we were interested in understanding the views of these academics in the relevance of criminology in crime control policy and legislation: specifically, its impact on law making, policymaking, and crime prevention. Data on various dimensions of the criminology as a discipline was gathered from Russian academics engaged in teaching criminology and who attended a national criminology conference in Moscow, Russia in May 2016. The survey was primarily developed to capture academics' perceptions about the current state of the discipline of criminology in Russia. Responses were gathered on a 7-point Likert scale where 1 represented absolutely disagree and 7 fully agree. In particular, the survey was designed to assess their opinions on whether the discipline in Russia has significantly undergone changes in the post-Soviet era and its relevance to the practices of law enforcement and crime control. In addition, their views regarding the contribution of Russian criminology to the world knowledge and general perception of the adequacy of the Western theories for analysing crime in Russia were assessed. Of the 200 surveys distributed to the participants who attended the conference, 110 useable surveys were returned representing a 55% response rate. Respondent characteristics are presented in Appendix 1.

Gender distribution was fairly equal with 52% being male and 48% female. The majority of the respondents (70%) held a degree of candidate or doctor of sciences. About 16% were assistant professors, 31% docents (equivalent to associate professors), and 31% full professors. The rest were PhD students. Nearly half of all the respondents (48%) were from Moscow and St. Petersburg with the remaining from other regions of Russia. All respondents taught either criminal law, criminology or criminal-corrective law, or a combination of these core courses or related electives. Thirty four per cent considered criminology as their primary area of teaching and research. The majority of the respondents were teaching at state universities (46%), followed by professional law-enforcement universities (32%). The rest taught at small private universities. About 66% had more than five years of teaching experience, and 10 people (9%) had been teaching criminology since before 1991. Many respondents had prior experience working for law-enforcement agencies (66%) and 26% claimed that they authored or co-authored a criminology textbook. Although the sample size is relatively small, the survey used the obtained results to illustrate some ideas discussed in this article. The survey questions and distribution of the responses are presented in Appendix 2.

A majority of the criminology professors do not believe that criminology has any impact on law making, policy making, and crime prevention. For instance, only 15% believe criminologists' opinions are taken into account when crafting and adopting new laws. Thirty seven per cent also claimed that the findings of criminological research are relevant for the law-enforcement practitioners. In addition, the respondents were asked if a specialisation in criminology is on high demand on the job market. Only 17% of the respondents agreed with this statement. The lack of state interest in the development of criminology is evident from the fact that in 2010, the Ministry of Education and Science introduced a new Russian State Educational Standard that does not any longer mention criminology as a required discipline for the law curriculum. As a result, university administrative bodies now have the discretion to remove criminology completely or retain it as an elective only discipline. RCA undertook several attempts to restore the status of the field appealing directly to the President of Russia and heads of the law-enforcement agencies (Dolgova, 2016). But to this day, the institutional perspectives of the criminology in the universities remain unclear.

A characteristic of theoretical criminology in Russia as being at the dead end, and empirical research in the embryonic stage requires further clarification and explanation. As Magun (2010, p. 160) suggests the abandonment of Marxism as the dominant paradigm and the widespread import of Western theories has led to "spectacular ideological disorientation" of social science scholars and the collapse of existing theoretical schools. In criminology, the situation was different. Although not many admit explicitly (for exception, see Milyukov, 2005, p. 104), the tradition that was originally grounded in dialectic materialism is often retained as a frame of analysis in current Russian scholarship. However, as Zhigarev (2012) warns, this approach is often used without much reflection and is interpreted in a very loose manner that distorts the original Marxist theory or even directly contradicts it. The theory of social contradictions that manifest themselves in inequality and injustices, poverty and capitalist exploitation, capitalist greed, ethnic conflicts, and low morale remains the central explanatory frame for thinking about crime causes at the macro-level (see, for example, Avanesov, 2012; Kudrjavtsev & Eminov, 2016; Kuznetsova & Luneev, 2005; Luneev, 2011; Milyukov, 2005; Shestakov, 2006). There is a strong belief that this approach is capable of explaining crime in any society and not just socialist one (Khokhryakov, 2002).

The initial disorientation that social science scholars have experienced in about a decade was followed by a conservative turn that again led to the "ideologization" of science (Gudkov, 2010) and its "indigenization" (Solovyov, 2015). Domestic social science scholars tend to view Russia as an exception, a specific historical case that requires unique, and necessarily non-western approaches to analysis (irrespective of what one considers to be western) (for discussion see Gelman, 2015; Solovyov, 2015). The attitude of Russian criminologists towards western theories appears to be ambiguous. As the responses from our survey demonstrate, 43% of respondents feel that foreign theories cannot adequately explain crime in Russia. Yet, at the same time the majority (65%) believe that crime is caused by similar factors in all modern market economies. These two numbers taken together might suggest that criminologists in Russia believe in the ability of Soviet theory in its post-Soviet modification to explain crime not only in Russia, but elsewhere. The first number points out to the stronger belief in explanatory power of the Russian concepts. However, only 42% of the respondents believe that Russian criminology managed to fit into the world criminology. Very illustrative of the process of indigenisation of the Russian science about crime is the suggestion of some scholars to develop and use a new vocabulary for criminology that introduces authentic Slavic words instead of words that have Latin origin (*prestupnostievedenie* instead of *kriminologija*) (see Shestakov, 2015, p. 3).

However, it would be wrong to suggest that a "conservative turn" in the field of criminology was of the same magnitude as in other social sciences. As argued above, Russian criminology has never departed too far from its Soviet past. This statement might seem contradictory to the findings of our survey: 59% of respondents believe that Russian criminology has changed a lot in terms of the topics that animate scholars, and 64% believe that it has been significantly transformed in terms of the contents. A thorough research is needed to trace the legacies of Soviet criminology in contemporary scholarship. But at least there are several signs for the lack of transformation that are evident even for the naked eye – popularity of the "social contradictions" theory as the main explanatory framework, limited engagement with any criminological ideas outside of Russia, and lack of thorough empirical research. Unlike in Eastern Europe where the breakdown of the socialist system had practically erased all the legacy of the socialist past from the criminology books so that even the old list of cited sources became instantly different (De Nike, Ewald & Nowlin, 1995), Russian criminology represents a continuation of the Soviet tradition. The fact that scholars have abandoned the Soviet idea of the possibility to eliminate crime or are engaging with the new topics such as globalisation and transnational organised crime do not suggest that they have abandoned the methodological tools developed in the 1960s through 1980s.

Isolationism of criminology in Russia: the unexplored west and the unlikely interdisciplinary dialogue

What is peculiar for the case of criminology compared to other social sciences is that the import of Western ideas was much more limited. Almost none of the works that are considered in the West to be "seminal" for criminological research (for lists of these works, see Gabbidon & Martin, 2010; Thornberry, 1990) were translated in Russian. Western theoretical approaches and practices of crime control were brought to the attention of scholars by a number of criminologists and sociologists (Gilinskiy, 2014, Inshakov, 1997; Kleymenov, 2012; Komlev, 2014; Shipunova, 2012; Smorgunova, 2005) but were never fully integrated into the mainstream criminology textbooks. As a very common example, in a popular 800-page Criminology textbook by Kudrjavtsev and Eminov (2016), foreign theories are discussed on the six pages of the "history of criminology" section. References to foreign sources are minimal both in textbooks as well as in research articles, which comes as no surprise given that only 52% of our respondents claimed that the library of their universities has access to journal databases. Coupled with a low level of proficiency in foreign languages [only 30% of Russians who have higher education have some command of foreign language (Levada-Center, 2008)] lack of access to the world knowledge contributes to the isolationism of Russian science about crime. Also, given the increasing level of methodological sophistication of articles published in the leading world criminology journals and the admittedly basic level of the methods development in Russia (Zhalinskiy, 2007), it is quite possible that Russian criminologists do not find scholarly output produced by the foreign colleagues relevant to their work.

Russian criminology is not only isolated from the West, it also maintains weak contacts with other social science disciplines within Russia. But it is not uncommon for criminology in other countries as well to have close ties with the criminal law – in many European countries the discipline is institutionally placed exclusively or predominantly in the legal departments (Baars-

Schuyt, 2001). The legal field does have its own approach to doing research that has much to offer for the criminal justice and criminology (Nolasco, Vaughn, & Del Carmen, 2010). Scholars from our sample strongly believed in the importance of not losing strong ties between criminal law and criminology. Eighty three per cent reported that they believe the knowledge of criminal law is indispensable for understanding criminology problems and, vice versa: a good specialist in criminal law must be familiar with criminological ideas. Russian criminologists produce critiques of criminal legislation, identifying gaps and proposing changes and grounding their arguments in legal debates and knowledge of the practice of the law enforcement (i.e. Lopashenko, 2009; Milyukov, 2000). However, devotion of criminology to the legal field in Russia limits the capacity for other types of research – social science research methods are not a part of the legal curriculum; the explanation of quantitative methods does not go beyond correlation analysis (Luneev, 2004). A way out of this situation was proposed in bridging the gap between criminology and other social sciences through joint work on the research projects (see Matskevitch, 2011). The majority (64%) of scholars in our sample believed that criminology is a multidisciplinary science and should be introduced not just for the law students. As much as the idea of engaging in such cooperation and strengthening interdisciplinary ties looks natural and tempting, its realisation is impeded by a variety of factors.

First of all, the institutional setting that provides incentives for the specialists from different areas to take upon joint research (or teaching) projects is missing. Also, the current state of affairs in the social sciences in Russia does not look particularly bright. After the breakdown of the Soviet Union sociology and economics underwent major transformations trying to familiarise themselves with and adapt Western knowledge to the Russian conditions (for sociology see Radaev, 2000; for economics – Suspitsyna, 2016). Political science emerged as a completely new discipline. However, these new or transformed social sciences are described by a great number of scholars as being atheoretical or pseudo theoretical, isolated from international scholarly trends, heavily normative, and lacking the knowledge of the up-to-date research tools, especially sophisticated quantitative methods (Gelman, 2015; Gudkov, 2010; Kirtchik, 2012; Libman & Zweynert, 2014; Lokshin, 2009; Radaev, 2008; Sokolov, 2009, 2012; Solovyov, 2015). The definition of contemporary sociology as a "poor" science (Sokolov, 2009) captures not just the difficult economic situation in higher education, but also the overall poor quality of produced scholarship. It is very doubtful that the meeting of "stagnant" criminology with "poor" sociology can produce a healthy offspring. The wheel of neoliberal reforms coupled with the crisis of the belief system rolled over all academic fields putting them in the position where their struggle for survival makes any meaningful intellectual dialogues unlikely (for discussion, see Magun, 2010).

Neoliberal educational reform of the recent decade has followed years of the state's neglect of the problems of education system. The reform was aimed at introducing the Bologna standards of education, increasing competition among universities and improving their positions on the international arena through introduction of a set of bureaucratic means of assuring the quality of teaching and research. So far it has instead led to the enormous over-regulation and bureau-cratisation of the educational process that is seen by instructors as more harmful for academia than complete neglect (Gilinskiy, 2015). One of the reform measures was meant for improving the quality of scholarship. It introduced the requirement for publishing in highly ranked indexed journals to the scholars' contracts with the universities. However, it was coupled with the creation of the "protectionist" (Magun, 2010) national system of academic ratings aimed at maintaining status quo in existing academia, allowing it to continue the inefficient practices of the last decades. It is quite unlikely that it will allow for much improvement of the quality of scholarly work.

Discussion and conclusion

Our review of the rich history and current state of criminology in Russia points to the fact that it failed to take advantage of the opportunities that the downfall of totalitarian regime and the opening of the borders had brought. When criminologists began experiencing the pressures of the new economic conditions that had put scholars in the position in which economic survival and not the advancement of scholarship became the top priority. Initial enthusiasm about the possibility of traveling abroad, exchanging ideas, and becoming members of the international criminological community had gradually vanished. This is due in part to the fact that this international community did not express much interest in Russian criminology (Aas, 2012). Perhaps such a lack of interest was partially a result of the strong belief that all socialist knowledge was hopelessly infected by ideological requirements and, therefore, does not even deserve to be called knowledge and definitely cannot be generalised to explain crime in other contexts.

In the former socialist countries of the Eastern and Central Europe, criminology collapsed shortly after the breakdown of the socialist system, leaving criminologists uprooted and in the position of either developing a new theory from scratch or adopting existing western theories (De Nike, Ewald & Nowlin, 1995). In contrast, post-Soviet criminology appeared to be very reluctant to discard the legacy of the Soviet times and not without a reason. During the Soviet era, theories were developed that were drawn on the assumptions of rationality of the offender, lack of self-control, importance of the situational factors, and acknowledgement of the victim's role in the mechanism of criminal behaviour – the very ideas that have also shaped "criminologies of everyday life" that became so influential for the policy of crime control in the West in recent decades (Garland, 2001, p. 16). The "official" discourse about "birthmarks of capitalism" was retained in the textbooks of the late Soviet years (see Korobejnikov et al., 1988), but it was not the only way of theorising. It is wrong to view Soviet criminology just as a monolithic product of ideological pressures that have strangled all original thought (see also Gilinskiy, 2017). It was unique, relatively diverse in the last years of the Soviet Union, and capable of influencing crime control policy (Solomon, 1978). That is why the total rejection of the Soviet legacy was not even considered as a direction for criminology's development.

The question remains why Russia does not express much interest in joining the global academic community (whether such community exists or not). On the contrary, "self-exclusion and intellectual revanchism" (Tlostanova, 2015, p. 50) are characteristic of the Russian academic discourse. This tendency is said to be the product of Russia's position of a "subaltern empire" (Morozov, 2015; Tlostanova, 2008) – retaining imperial ambitions but no longer treated by the West as an equal. In social sciences, it results in the reproduction of outdated discourses, rejection of the universality of Western knowledge, and the creation of indigenous theories that are irrelevant in the global context (for a thoughtful discussion of this phenomenon as it relates to the discipline of International Relations see Makarychev & Morozov, 2013). It must be noted though that this tendency for revanchism is not as evident in criminology as in other social sciences. It is quite likely, however, that the nonexistence of the current (as opposed to the Soviet) debate about the advantage of the Russian theories compared to the Western might itself be regarded as an alarming sign that the discipline is in crisis. It is questionable whether the lack of intellectual dependency on the discourses of the Global North might in the end result in producing original knowledge. There is hope, however, that criminology will not get into the trap of "isolating narcissism" (Magun, 2010, p. 168), common among social sciences, and will engage in revisiting both the Soviet legacy and whatever the outside world has to offer – not limiting itself to Western knowledge only but staying open to the non-core discourses as well.

The story of Russian criminology demonstrates the dependency of the discipline on the state's willingness to support it. From the very beginning, Russian criminology has aspired to provide solutions for crime control and was trying to prove its utility for the state (Solomon, 1974). However, in the post-Soviet period it has gradually lost all of its influence and is now viewed by the state as a redundant luxury in the academic process constrained by budgetary considerations. Two explanations can be suggested. The first one has to do with the epistemological orientation of the Russian criminology that is a legacy of the Soviet times and is shared with the other Russian social sciences in general. Radaev (2000; [as cited in Gelman, 2015, p. 30]) argues that social scientists in Russia view theories not as competitive toolboxes for empirical research, but rather as all-encompassing worldviews that are capable of explaining their objects in all times, at all places once and for all. In the case of criminology, this noble aspiration to find "the Theory" of crime might be one of the reasons that had contributed to criminology's current irrelevance for the law enforcement practice and politics of crime control. These attempts to discover "the laws [...] that guide crime in all of its manifestations" (Dolgova, 2016; translated from Russian by the author) have resulted in the creation of the theories of the very high intricacy. Empirical analysis of these theories appears to be too complicated and unwieldy. Trying to avoid incompleteness of theoretical propositions and decontextualise the conclusions, Russian criminology is becoming too abstract and far removed from the flesh of the real crime. As a result, all controversies, paradoxes, and inconsistencies that permeate this flesh can neither be spotted nor explained.

The second explanation of why criminology has become irrelevant for the state has to do with a peculiar theoretical twist that occurred after the breakdown of the Soviet Union. As mentioned, Soviet criminology was grounded in the Marxist tradition and it has been applied to describe the causes of crime in the capitalist society. When Russia became market-oriented, the same arguments were used to explain crime in the process of transition. The state was to be blamed for promoting or at least not addressing adequately such problems as inequality, exploitation, poverty, and moral degradation, for introducing new flawed legislation, and having deficient crime control policy. Oligarchs, large businesses, corrupt civil servants all became targets of Russian criminologists' criticism. Instead of remaining "administrative" (like it was in the Soviet times), that is blind to the societal "root causes" of crime and providing only those explanations that would justify the crime control policy of the state (Hope, 2011), Russian scholars became critical criminologists. And those who did not become critical in the Marxist sense tend to adhere to social constructivist view (Gilinskiy, 2014) that also does not have immediate solutions for crime control policy. Naturally, the state does not find much use in the new criminology but provides limited funding for a few research and teaching units that are based under the auspices of the law-enforcement agencies. It should be noted, however, that the state underestimates the importance of all social sciences and humanities in Russia and not just that of criminology (Pipiya, 2010). Criminology is one among many disciplines that currently do not have much voice in deciding the government policy.

It should be acknowledged that Russian concerns about the development of criminology are not unique. Scholars from different non-core countries point to the similar difficulties (for Latin America see Olmo, 1999; for Asia – Lee & Laidler, 2013; for Balkan region – Petrović & Muratbegović, 2010; Getoš Kalac & Bezić, 2017). Especially familiar is the situation in China – lack of interdisciplinarity due to the placement of criminology as a subfield of law, lack of financial support for empirical research, and shortage of the social science research skills (Jou, Hebenton, & Cao, 2014). Criminology's revival in Russia and its appearance on the world criminological map is contingent on the extent that it will be able to overcome the impediments for development that these factors are causing. The way out of the crisis is possible only through broadening theoretical horizons, bridging the gap with reality through engaging in empirical work, and aspiring to become more policy relevant. All steps in these directions should be welcomed – be it the revival of the pre-revolutionary and early Soviet scholarship, development of the Soviet ideas, strengthening theoretical and empirical base through interdisciplinary collaboration, attention to the scholarship of the global North and global South, and cooperation with governmental agencies and NGOs. Western criminological theory has the privilege of complaining about the diversity of epistemological positions that results in the overwhelming number of theories of crime causation and contributes to the fuzzy state of the discipline (Bruinsma, 2016). It can allow itself to express concerns that criminology is governmental (Garland, 2011) and government's attention to or support for research can lead to politicisation of science (Savelsberg, King, & Cleveland, 2002). Criminologists of the core can make arguments that empirical criminological research does not have much explanatory power (Weisburd & Piquero, 2008). Russian criminology should be aware of these tensions and challenges. However, epistemological diversity, cooperation with the state and non-state providers of security, and building empirical research skills are crucial for its survival under the austere conditions of the neoliberal academia.

Russian criminology has gone through various stages in its history. While the pace of its development matched that of European criminology in its early phases it was not able to survive the ideological pressures of the new Marxist approach to science that considered "positivist" methods of criminology to be false and irrelevant for the communist project. The revival of the discipline in the 1960s appeared to be a result of the aspiration of the Communist party to put an end to crime through contributions of criminology. The new crime science also served an ideological function showing the advantages of the socialist system and revealing the deficiencies of the capitalist society and its crime control. From a theoretical standpoint, criminology faced a difficult challenge – it had to explain the persistence of crime in the socioeconomic system that was supposed to be crime-free according to the cannons of Marxist thought. Within three decades, criminology matured to a highly policy-relevant discipline, relatively monolithic theoretically and grounded in the methodology of the dialectic materialism. The demise of the Soviet Union in 1991 brought about a major ideological shift away from Marxism in social sciences. But it barely affected criminology. Although not admitting it overtly 25 years later, Russian criminologists have not abandoned major conceptual approaches of the Soviet past related to the question of crime causation. Its progress was impeded by its isolationism, inability to accomplish an institutional transfer and establish intellectual independence from the legal field, as well as by problems associated to underfunding and neoliberal educational reforms. Currently, Russian criminology finds itself in need for a substantial theoretical and methodological upgrade.

References

Aas, K. F. (2012). 'The Earth is one but the world is not': Criminological theory and its geopolitical divisions. *Theoretical Criminology*, *16*, 5–20. doi:10.1177/1362480611433433

Aas, K. F. (2013). *Globalization and crime*. London: SAGE Publications Limited.

Aebi, M., & Kronicz, G. (2016). ESC executive secretariat annual report 2015. *Newsletter of the European Society of Criminology. Criminology in Europe*, *15*(2), 8–12.

Agozino, B. (2004). Imperialism, crime and criminology. *Crime, Law and Social Change*, *41*, 343–358. doi:10.1023/B:CRIS.0000025766.99876.4c

Alatas, S. F. (2003). Academic dependency and the global division of labour in the social sciences. *Current Sociology*, *51*(6), 599–613. doi:10.1177/00113921030516003

Alekseyev, S. S. (1962). Tendencii razvitija sovetskoj juridicheskoj nauki v period razvernutogo stroitelstva kommunizma [Tendencies of development of the Soviet legal science during the full-scale building of communism]. *Pravovedenie*, *2*, 3–11.

Avanesov, G. A. (Ed.). (2012). *Kriminologija* [Criminology]. Moscow: Juniti-Dana.

Baars-Schuyt, A. (2001). Overview of criminology in Europe. *European Journal on Criminal Policy and Research*, *9* (3), 301–313. doi:10.1023/A:1011612826382

Barberet, R. (2007). The internationalization of criminology? A content analysis of presentations at American Society Of Criminology Conferences. *Journal of Criminal Justice Education*, *18*, 406–427. doi:10.1080/10511250701705362

Beck, U. (1992). *Risk society: Towards a new modernity*. London: Sage.

CRIMINOLOGY AND CRIMINAL JUSTICE IN RUSSIA

Bennett, R. (2004). Comparative criminology and criminal justice research: The state of our knowledge. *Justice Quarterly, 21*, 1–21. doi:10.1080/07418820400095721

Berman, N., & Burgess, E. (1937). The development of criminological research in the Soviet Union. *American Sociological Review, 2*(2), 213–222. doi:10.2307/2083475

Botchkovar, E., & Broidy, L. (2013). Accumulated strain, negative emotions, and crime: A test of general strain theory in Russia. *Crime & Delinquency, 59*(6), 837–860. doi:10.1177/0011128710382346

Bruinsma, G. (2016). Proliferation of crime causation theories in an era of fragmentation: Reflections on the current state of criminological theory. *European Journal of Criminology, 13*(6), 659–676. doi:10.1177/1477370816667884

Burlakov, V. N. (2006). *Ugolovnoe pravo i lichnost prestupnika* [Criminal law and personality of the offender]. St. Petersburg: St.Petersburg State University Press.

Cain, M. (2000). Orientalism, occidentalism and the sociology of crime. *British Journal of Criminology, 40*, 239–260. doi:10.1093/bjc/40.2.239

Carrington, K., Hogg, R., & Sozzo, M. (2016). Southern criminology. *British Journal of Criminology, 56*, 1–20. doi:10.1093/bjc/azv083

Chambliss, W. J. (1975). Toward a political economy of crime. *Theory and Society, 2*(1), 149–170. doi:10.1007/BF00212732

Chambliss, W. J., & Seidman, R. B. (1971). *Law, order, and power* (pp. 3). Reading, MA: Addison-Wesley.

Cohen, S. (1988). *Against criminology*. New Brunswick, NJ: Transaction.

Connor, W. D. (1970). Deviant behavior in capitalist society. The Soviet image. *The Journal of Criminal Law, Criminology, and Police Science, 61*(4), 554–564. doi:10.2307/1142044

Cowling, M. (2008). *Marxism and criminological theory: A critique and a toolkit*. New York: Palgrave Macmillan.

Crawford, A. (Ed.). (2011). *International and comparative criminal justice and urban governance: Convergence and divergence in global, national and local settings*. Cambridge: Cambridge University Press.

De Nike, H.S., Ewald, U., & Nowlin, C. J. (1995). *Crime in East Europe: Recent reflections from the eastern academy*. Bonn: Forum Verlag Godesberg.

Dobryninas, A., & Sakalauskas, G. (2011). Country survey: Criminology, crime and criminal justice in Lithuania. *European Journal of Criminology, 8*(5), 421–434. doi:10.1177/1477370811414267

Dolgova, A. I. (Ed.). (2005). *Kriminologija* [Criminology]. Moscow: Norma: INFRA-M.

Dolgova, A. I. (2016). *Nuzhna li kriminologija I kriminologicheskij vzglyad na prestupnost* [Is there a need for criminology and criminological opinion about crime] (Article published on the website of the Russian Criminological Association). Retrieved from http://crimas.ru/?p=3441

Dril, D. A. (2013). *Prestupnost i prestupniki; Uchenie o prestupnosti i merakh borby s neju: Sbornik trudov* [Crime and criminals; Studies on crime and on measures of fighting it: Collected volume]. Moscow: INFRA-M (Original works published 1895 and 1912).

Dukhovskoj, M. V. (1872). *Zadacha nauki ugolovnogo prava* [The task of criminal law science]. Yaroslavl: Tipografija Gubernskogo Pravlenija.

Fedotov, O. K. (1973). *Kritika sovremennoj burzhuaznoj kriminologii* [Critique of the contemporary bourgeois criminology]. Moscow: Znanie.

Feeley, M. M., & Simon, J. (1992). The new penology: Notes on the emerging strategy of corrections and its implications. *Criminology, 30*(4), 449–474. doi:10.1111/crim.1992.30.issue-4

Foglesong, T. S., & Solomon, P. H., Jr. (2001). *Crime, criminal justice and criminology in post-Soviet Ukraine series: Issues in international crime*. Washington, D.C.: National Institute of Justice.

Fojnitskij, I. Y. (1873). Vlijanie vremen goda na raspredelenie prestuplenij: opit sotsialnogo diagnosa prestuplenija [The impact of seasons on crime distribution: The experience of the social diagnosis of crime]. *Sudebnij jurnal*, 1- 2, 22–76.

Frankowski, S. (1980). Causes of criminality in socialist countries as perceived by socialist scholars. *Tijdschrift voor criminologie, 22*, 36–44.

Gabbidon, S. L., & Martin, F. (2010). An Era-Based exploration of the most significant books in criminology/criminal justice: A research note. *Journal of Criminal Justice Education, 21*(3), 348–369. doi:10.1080/10511253.2010.487833

Garland, D. (2001). *The culture of control*. Oxford: Oxford University Press.

Garland, D. (2011). Criminology's place in the academic field. In M. Bosworth & C. Hoyle (Eds.), *What is criminology?* (pp. 298–317). Oxford: Oxford University Press.

Garland, D. (2002). Of crimes and criminals: The development of criminology in Britain. In M. Maguire, R. Morgan, & R. Reiner (Eds.), *The Oxford handbook of criminology* (3rd ed., pp. 7–50). Oxford, UK: Oxford University Press.

Gelfer, M. A., Grishaev, P. I., & Zdravomyslov, B. V. (1967). *Sovetskaja kriminologija* [Soviet criminology]. Moscow: All-Union Juridical Distance-Learning Institute.

Gelman, V. (2015). Political Science in Russia: Scholarship without research? *European Political Science, 14*, 28–36. doi:10.1057/eps.2014.33

Gernet, M. N. (1951–1956). *Istoriya tsarskoj tjurmi* [The history of tsarist prison] (Vol. 5). Moscow: Gosjurizdat.

Gertsenzon, A. A. (1965). *Vvedenie v sovetskuju kriminologiju* [Introduction in the Soviet criminology]. Moscow: Juridicheskaja Literatura.

Gertsenzon, A. A. (1970). *Ugolovnoe pravo i sotsiologija (Problemi sotsiologii ugolovnogo prava I ugolovnoj politiki)*. Moscow: Juridicheskaja Literatura.

Gertsenzon, A. A., Karpets, I. I., & Kudrjavtsev, V. N. (Eds.). (1966). *Sovetskaja kriminologija* [Soviet criminology]. Moscow: Juridicheskaja Literatura.

Getoš Kalac, A. M., & Bezić, R. (2017). Criminology, crime and criminal justice in Croatia. *European Journal of Criminology, 14*(2), 242–266. doi:10.1177/1477370816648523

Gilinskiy, Y. (2006). Crime in contemporary Russia. *European Journal of Criminology, 3*(3), 259–292. doi:10.1177/ 1477370806065583

Gilinskiy, Y. (2014). *Kriminologija: Teorija, istorija, empiricheskaya basa, sotsialnij control* [Criminology: Theory, history, empirical basis, social control]. St. Petersburg: Alef-Press.

Gilinskiy, Y. (2015). Intellektualnaja antimobilnost sovremennikh rossijskikh obshestvovedov [Intellectual anti-mobility of the contemporary Russia social scientists]. Problemy dejatelnosti uchenogo I nauchnikh kollektiviv. *Mezhdunarodnij ezhegodnik, 1*(31), 58–62.

Gilinskiy, Y. (2017). Soviet and Post-Soviet Criminology: An Insider's Reflections. *International Journal of Comparative and Applied Criminal Justice, 41*(3), 113–122.

Graham, L. R. (1987). *Science, philosophy, and human behavior in the Soviet Union.* New York: Columbia University Press.

Greenberg, D. F. (1993). *Crime and capitalism.* Philadelphia, PA: Temple University Press.

Gudkov, L. D. (2010). Est li osnovanija u teoreticheskoj sotsiologii v Rossii? [Is there a foundation for theoretical sociology in Russia?]. *Sotsiologicheskij zhurnal, 1,* 104–125.

Herrmann, C. T. (1824).Recherches sur le nombre des suicides et des homicides, commis en Russie pendant les années 1819 et 1820 [Research on the number of suicides and homicides committed in Russia during the years 1819 and 1820]. In *Memoires de L'Academie Imperiale des Sciences de St. Petersbourg.* VI Serie. Sciences Politique, Historie et Philologie. Tome I.

Hope, T. (2011). Official criminology and the new crime sciences. In M. Bosworth & C. Hoyle (Eds.), *What is criminology?* (pp. 456–474). Oxford: Oxford University Press.

Inshakov, S. M. (1997). *Zarubejnaja kriminologija* [Foreign criminology]. Moscow: Norma.

Ivanov, L. O., & Ilyina, L. V. (1991). *Puti i sudbi otechestvennoj criminologii* [Paths and destinies of domestic criminology]. Moscow: Nauka.

Jou, S., Hebenton, B., & Cao, L. (2014). The development of criminology in modern China: A state-based enterprise. In L. Cao, I. Y. Sun, & B. Hebenton (Eds.), *The Routledge handbook of Chinese criminology.* Oxon: Routledge.

Karpets, I. I. (1966). O prirode i prichinah prestupnosti v SSSR [On the nature and causes of crime in USSR]. *Sovetskoje gosudarstvo i pravo, 4,* 82–84.

Karpetz, I. I. (1969). *Problema prestupnosti* [Problem of crime]. Moscow: Juridicheskaya literature.

Kerezsi, K., & Levay, M. (2008). Criminology, crime and criminal justice in Hungary. *European Journal of Criminology, 5*(2), 239–260. doi:10.1177/1477370807087646

Khokhryakov, G. F. (2002). *Kriminologija* [Criminology]. Moscow: Jurist.

Kirtchik, O. (2012). Limits and strategies for the internationalization of russian economic science: Sociological interpretation of bibliometric data. *Laboratirium, 4*(1), 19–44.

Kleymenov, I.M. (2012). *Sravnitelnaja kriminologija* [Comparative criminology]. Moscow: Norma.

Komlev, Y. Y. (2014). *Teorii deviantnogo povedenija* [Theories of deviant behavior]. St.Petersburg: Alef-Press.

Kommunisticheskaja Partija Sovetskogo Sojuza. [Communist Party of the Soviet Union] (1961). *Programma Communisticheskoj Partii Sovetskogo Sojuza* [Agenda of the Communist Party of the Soviet Union]. Moscow: Gospolitizdat.

Korobejnikov, B. V., Kuznetsova, N. F., & Minkovskij, G. M. (Eds.). (1988). *Kriminologija.* Moscow: Juridicheskaja literatura.

Kowalsky, S. A. (2016). Continuity and Change. Russian and early soviet criminology and the criminal woman. In Knepper, P., & Johansen, A. (Eds.) *The Oxford handbook of the history of crime and criminal justice* (pp. 416–432). Oxford, UK: Oxford University Press

Krajewski, K. (2004). Crime and criminal justice in Poland. *European Journal of Criminology, 1*(3), 377–407. doi:10.1177/1477370804044006

Kudrjavtsev, V. N. (1967). *Sovetskaja kriminologija - nauka o preduprezhdenii prestuplenij* [Soviet criminology – a science about crime prevention]. Moscow: Znanie.

Kudrjavtsev, V. N. (1968). *Prichinnaia sviaz v kriminologii* [Causation in criminology]. Moscow: Iuridicheskaia literature.

Kudrjavtsev, V. N., & Eminov, V. E. (Eds.). (2016). *Kriminologija* [Criminology]. Moscow: Norma.

CRIMINOLOGY AND CRIMINAL JUSTICE IN RUSSIA

Kudrjavtsev, V. N., Karpetz, I. I., & Korobejnikov, B. V. (1985). *Kurs sovetskoj kriminologii: Predmet, metodologija, prestupnost i ee prichini, prestupnik* [The course of the Soviet criminology.: Subject, methodology, crime and its causes, offender]. Moscow: Juridicheskaja literatura.

Kuznetsova, N. (1972). A comparative criminological study of crime in Moscow (1923 and 1968–69). *Soviet Law and Government, 11*(2), 177–186.

Kuznetsova, N. F. (1974). *Sovremennaja burzhuaznaja kriminologija* [Contemporary bourgeoise criminology]. Moscow: Moscow University Press.

Kuznetsova, N. F. (1984). *Problemi kriminologicheskoj determinatsii* [Problems of criminological determination]. Moscow: Izdatelstvo Moskovskogo universitetata.

Kuznetsova, N. F., & Luneev, V. V. (2005). *Kriminologija* [Criminology]. Moscow: Walters Kluwer.

Kuznetsova, N. F., & Shupilov, V. P. (1982). Western Sovietologists on the fight against crime in the USSR. *Soviet Law and Government, 21*(2), 11–20.

Lee, M., & Laidler, K. J. (2013). Doing criminology from the periphery: Crime and punishment in Asia. *Theoretical Criminology, 17*, 141–156. doi:10.1177/1362480613476790

Levada-Center. (2008). *Znanie inostrannikh jazikov v Rossii* [Knowledge of foreign languages in Russia]. Retrieved from http://www.levada.ru/2008/09/15/znanie-inostrannyh-yazykov-v-rossii/

Libman, A., & Zweynert, J. (2014). *Ceremonial science: The state of Russian economics seen through the lens of the work of 'doctor of science' candidates* (Institute for East and Southeast European Studies Working Paper No. 337). Retrieved from http://econpapers.repec.org/article/eeeecosys/v_3a38_3ay_3a2014_3ai_3a3_3ap_3a360-378.htm

Lokshin, M. (2009). A survey of poverty research in Russia: Does it follow the scientific method? *Economic Systems, 33*(3), 191–212. doi:10.1016/j.ecosys.2009.05.002

Lopashenko, N. (2009). *Ugolovnaja politika* [Penal politics]. Moscow: Wolters Kluwer Russia.

Luneev, V. V. (2004). *Juridicheskaja statististika* [Juridical statistics]. Moscow: Jurist.

Luneev, V. V. (2011). *Kurs mirovoj i rossijskoj kriminologii* [The course of the global and Russian criminology]. Moscow: Jurait.

Lynch, M. J., & Groves, W. B. (1989). *A primer in radical criminology.* New York: Harrow and Heston.

Magun, A. (2010). Higher education in Russia: Is there a way out of a neoliberal impasse? In B. Rehbein (Ed.), *Globalization and inequality in emerging societies* (pp. 148–175). New York: Palgrave Macmillan.

Makarychev, A., & Morozov, V. (2013). Is "Non-Western Theory" possible? The idea of multipolarity and the trap of epistemological relativism in Russian IR. *International Studies Review, 15*(3), 328–350. doi:10.1111/misr.2013.15.issue-3

Matskevitch, I. M. (2011). Sovremennaja kriminologija: Preodolenie krizisa [Contemporary criminology: Overcoming Crisis]. *Rossijskij kriminologicheskij vzglyad, 2,* 192–197.

McReynolds, L. (2013). *Murder most Russian: True crime and punishment in late imperial Russia.* Ithaca: Cornell University Press.

Medina, J. (2011). Doing criminology in the 'semi-periphery' and the 'periphery' in search of a post colonial criminology. In C. Smith, S. Zhan, & R. Barberet (Eds.), *Routledge handbook of international criminology* (pp. 13–24). Oxon: Routledge.

Meško, G., & Jere, M. (2012). Crime, criminal justice and criminology in Slovenia. *European Journal of Criminology, 9*(3), 323–334. doi:10.1177/1477370812440064

Milyukov, S. F. (2000). *Ugolovnoe zakonodatelstvo: Opit kriticheskogo analiza* [Criminal legislation: An experience of critical analysis]. St.Petersburg: SPbIVESEP.

Milyukov, S. F. (2005). Prichiny prestupnosti [Causes of crime]. In V. N. Burlakov & N. M. Kropachev (Eds.), *Kriminologija* [Criminology]. St.petersburg: St.Petersburg University Press.

Morozov, V. (2015). *Russia's postcolonial identity: A Subaltern empire in a eurocentric world.* New York: Palgrave Macmillan.

Nagornaja, I. I., & Pogosova, Z. M. (2011). Kakaja kriminologija segodnja nuzhna strane? Problemi prepodavanija i prakticheskogo primenenija [What kind of criminology does the country need today? Problems of teaching and practical application]. *Rossijskij kriminologicheskij vzglyad, 2,* 31–35.

Nelken, D. (2010). *Comparative criminal justice: Making sense of difference.* London: SAGE.

Nikiforov, B. S. (Ed.). (1966). *Sotsiologija prestupnosti. Sovremennie burzhuaznie teorii: Sbornik statej* [Sociology of crime. Contemporary bourgeois theory: Collection of essays] (A.S. Nikiforov, A.M.Yakovlev, Trans.). Moscow: Progress.

Nolasco, C. A. R., Vaughn, M. S., & Del Carmen, R. V. (2010). Toward a new methodology for legal research in criminal justice. *Journal of Criminal Justice Education, 21*(1), 1–23. doi:10.1080/10511250903518944

Nomokonov, V. A. (1985). Opredelenie i klassifikatsija prichin konkretnih prestuplenij [Definition and classification of the causes of concrete crimes]. *Pravovedenie, 6,* 39–46.

O'Malley, P. (2004). The uncertain promise of risk. *Australian & New Zealand Journal of Criminology, 37*(3), 323–343. doi:10.1375/acri.37.3.323

Olmo, R. (1999). The development of criminology in Latin America. *Social Justice, 26*(2,76), 19–45.

CRIMINOLOGY AND CRIMINAL JUSTICE IN RUSSIA

Orekhov, V. V. (1972). *Sotsialnoe planirovanie i voprosy borby s prestupnostju* [Social planning and the questions of fighting with crime]. Leningrad: Leningrad State University Publishing House.

Ostroumov, S., & Kuznetsova, N. (1968). The subject of soviet criminology. *Soviet Law and Government, 7*(3), 36–44.

Ostroumov, S. S., & Kuznetsova, N. F. (1964). O prepodavanii sovetskoj kriminologii [On teaching soviet criminology]. *Sovetskoe gosudarstvo i pravo, 11,* 92–97.

Petrović, B., & Muratbegović, E. (2010). Criminology in Bosnia and Herzegovina: History, recent trends and research. *Varstvoslovje /Journal of Criminal Justice and Security, 2,* 353–368.

Piacentini, L. (2012). *Surviving Russian Prisons.* Oxon: Routledge.

Pipiya, L. (2010). The status of social sciences in the Russian Federation. In Caillods, F. (Ed.) *World social science report.* (pp. 87–91). Paris: UNESCO. Retrieved from http://unesdoc.unesco.org/images/0018/001883/188333e.pdf

Płatek, M. (2016). Review of the book: criminality and criminal justice in contemporary Poland: Sociopolitical perspectives K. Buczkowski, B. Czarnecka-Dzialuk, W. Klaus, A. Kossowska, I. Rzeplińska, P. Wiktorska, D. Woźniakowska-Fajst and D. Wójcik. Farnham: Ashgate (2015) 195pp. *The Howard Journal of Crime and Justice, 55*(3), 367–368.

Popova, I. P. (2014). Nevostrebovannaja "vostrebovannaja professija" v karjerah vypusknikov juristov [Unwanted 'wanted occupation' in the careers of law school graduates]. *Vysshee obrazovanie v Rossii, 1,* 45–54.

Pridemore, W. A. (Ed.). (2005). *Ruling Russia: Law crime, and justice in a changing society.* Lanham, MD: Rowman & Littlefield Publishers.

Prozumentov, L. M., & Shesler, A. V. (2014). Otechestvennie nauchnie koncepcii prichin prestupnosti [Local scientific concepts of the causes of crime]. *Criminology Journal of Baikal National University of Economics and Law, 1,* 49–58.

Quinney, R. (1970). *The social reality of crime.* New Brunswick, NJ: Transaction publishers.

Quinney, R. (1977). *Class, state, and crime: On the theory and practice of criminal justice.* New York: D. McKay Company.

Radaev, V. V. (2000). Est li shans sozdat rossiiskuyu natsionalnuyu teoriyu v sotsialnykh naukakh [Is there a chance to create Russian national theory in social sciences]. *Pro et Contra, 5*(3), 202–214.

Radaev, V. V. (2008). Vozmozhna li pozitivnaja programma dlja rossijskoj sotsiologii [Is positive program possible for the Russian sociology]. *Sotsiologicheskie issledovanija, 7,* 24–33.

Radishev, A. N. (2005). O zakonopolozhenii [On the laws]. *Rossijskij Kriminologicheskij Vzglyad, 1,* 8–17 ((Original work published 1801)).

Radzinowicz, L. (1965). Ideology and crime: The deterministic position. *Columbia Law Review, 65*(6), 1047–1060. doi:10.2307/1120566

Reshetnikov, F. M. (1965). *Sovremennaja amerikanskaja kriminologija* [Contemporary American criminology]. Moscow: Juridicheskaja Literatura.

Russian Criminological Association. (2017). *Ob assotsiatsii* [About Association]. Retrieved from http://crimas.ru/?page_id=23

Saar, J. (2004). Crime, crime control and criminology in post-communist Estonia. *European Journal of Criminology, 1*(4), 505–531. doi:10.1177/1477370804045694

Sakharov, A. B. (1961). *O lichnosti prestupnika i prichinah prestupnosti v SSSR* [On the personality of the offender and causes of crime in the USSR]. Moscow: Gosjurizdat.

Sakharov, A. B. (1995). *Prichiny i uslovija individualnogo prestupnogo povedenija* [Causes and conditions of the individual criminal behavior]. Moscow: MVShM.

Samovichev, E. G. (2011). O nekotorih problemnih voprosah prepodavanija obshej chasti uchebnogo kursa "Kriminologija" [On some questions of teaching general part of the "Criminology" discipline]. *Rossijskij kriminologicheskij vzglyad, 2,* 174–185.

Savelsberg, J. J., King, R., & Cleveland, L. (2002). Politicized scholarship? Science on crime and the state. *Social Problems, 49*(3), 327–348. doi:10.1525/sp.2002.49.3.327

Sergeevskij, N. D. (1879). Prestuplenie i nakazanie kak predmet juridicheskoj nauki [Crime and punishment as subjects of legal science]. *Juridicheskij vestnik, 12,* 887–904.

Shearing, C. D., & Stenning, P. C. (1981). Modern private security: Its growth and implications. *Crime and Justice, 3,* 193–245. doi:10.1086/449080

Shelley, L. (1979a). Soviet Criminology after the Revolution. *The Journal of Criminal Law and Criminology, 70*(3). doi:10.2307/1142581

Shelley, L. (1979b). Soviet criminology: Its birth and demise, 1917-1936. *Slavic Review, 38*(4), 614–628. doi:10.2307/2496566

Sheptycki, J. (2008). Transnationalisation, orientalism and crime. *Asian Journal of Criminology, 3*(1), 13–35. doi:10.1007/s11417-008-9049-0

Shestakov, D. A. (2006). *Kriminologija* [Criminology]. St.Petersburg: Juridicheskij Center Press.

Shestakov, D. A. (2015). *Ot prestupnoj ljubvi do prestupnogo zakonodatelstva* [From the criminal love to the criminal legislation]. St. Petersburg: Alef-Press.

CRIMINOLOGY AND CRIMINAL JUSTICE IN RUSSIA

Shipunova, T. V. (2012). *Deviantologija: Sovremennie teoretiko-metodologicheskie problemi* [Deviantology: Contemporary theoretic and methodological problems]. St.Petersburg: St.Petersburg University Press.

Slade, G., & Light, M. (2015). Crime and criminal justice after communism: Why study the post-Soviet region? *Theoretical Criminology, 19*(2), 147–158. doi:10.1177/1362480615571724

Smorgunova, A. L. (2005). *Sovremennaja zarubezhnaja kriminologija: Kriticheskoe napravlenie* [Contemporary foreign criminology: Critical tradition]. St.Petersburg: Herzen University Press.

Sokolov, M. (2009). Rossijskaja sotsiologija posle 1991 goda: Intellektualnaja i institutsionalnaja dinamika "bednoj nauki" [Russian sociology after 1991: Intellectual and institutional dynamics othe 'poor science']. *Laboratorium, 1*, 20–57.

Sokolov, M. M. (2012). O protsesse akademicheskoj (de)tsivilizatsii [On the process of sociological (de)civilization]. *Sotsiologicheskie issledovanija, 8*, 21–30.

Solomon, P. H. (1974). Soviet criminology: Its demise and rebirth, 1928-1963. *The Soviet and Post-Soviet Review, 1*(1), 122–140. doi:10.1163/187633274X00090

Solomon, P. H. (1978). *Soviet criminologists and criminal policy. Specialists in policy-making.* NY: Columbia University Press.

Solovyov, A. I. (2015). Rossijskaja politologija v sovremennom kontekste: Subjektivnie zametki [Russian political science in the contemporary context: Subjective notes]. *Vestnik Povolzhskogo instituta upravlenija, 6*(51), 10–17.

Spiridonov, L., & Gilinskiy, Y. (Eds.). (1977). *Chelovek kak object sotsiologicheskih issledovanij* [Person as an object of sociological research]. Moscow: Nauka.

Suspitsyna, T. (2016). *Adaptation of Western economics by Russian Universities: Intercultural travel of an academic field.* Oxon: Routledge.

Tagantsev, N. S. (1902). *Russkoje ugolovnoe pravo: Lektsii* [Russian criminal law: Lectures]. St.Petersburg: Gos.Tip.

Taylor, I., Walton, P., & Young, J. (1973). *The new criminology: For a social theory of deviance.* London: Routledge and Kegan Paul.

Thornberry, T. P. (1990). Cultural literacy in criminology. *Journal of Criminal Justice Education, 1*(1), 33–49. doi:10.1080/10511259000082041

Tlostanova, M. (2008). The Janus-faced empire distorting orientalist discourses: Gender, race and religion in the Russian/(post)Soviet constructions of the "Orient" . *Worlds and Knowledges Otherwise, 2*(2), 1–11. Retrieved from www.jhfc.duke.edu/wko/dossiers/1.3/documents/TlostanovaWKO2.2.pdf

Tlostanova, M. (2015). Can the post-Soviet think? *Intersections. East European Journal of Society and Politics, 1*(2), 38–58.

Turk, A. T. (1977). Class, conflict, and criminalization. *Sociological Focus, 10*(3), 209–220. doi:10.1080/00380237.1977.10570288

Ugolovno-protsessualnij kodeks RSFSR [Criminal Procedure Code of RSFSR]. (1961). Retrieved from http://www.consultant.ru/document/cons_doc_LAW_3275/

Utevskij, B. S. (1964). Sotsiologicheskie issledovanija i kriminologija [Sociological studies and criminology]. *Voprosy Filosofii, 2.*

Volzhenkin, B. V. (1975). Neposredstvennaja prichina prestuplenija [Immediate cause of crime]. In A. B. Sakharov (Ed.), *Voprosy izuchenija prestupnosti i borby s nej* (pp. 159–165). Moscow: Izdateelstvo Vsesojuznogo instituta po izucheniju prichin i razrabotke mer preduprezhdenija prestupnosti.

Wallerstein, I. M. (2004). *World-systems analysis: An introduction.* Durham, NC: Duke University Press.

Weisburd, D., & Piquero, A. R. (2008). How well do criminologists explain crime? Statistical modeling in published studies. *Crime and Justice, 37*(1), 453–502. doi:10.1086/524284

Yakovlev, A. M. (1976). Determinism i "svoboda voli": Perspectivi izuchenija lichnosti prestupnika [Determinism and «free will»: Perspectives of studying personality of the ofender]. *Pravovedenie, 6*, 63–72.

Yakovlev, A. M. (1985). *Teorija kriminologii i sotsialnaja praktika* [Theory of criminology and social practice]. Moscow: Nauka.

Zedner, L. (2007). Pre-crime and post-criminology? *Theoretical Criminology, 11*(2), 261–281. doi:10.1177/1362480607075851

Zhalinskiy, A. E. (2007). Sovremennie problemy kriminologicheskogo diskursa [Contemporary problems of criminological discourse]. *Rossijskij kriminologicheskij vgljad, 4*, 91–98.

Zhalinskiy, A. E. (2011). Obnovlenie kriminologii [Renewal of Criminology]. *Rossijskij kriminologicheskij vgljad, 2*, 165–173.

Zhigarev, E. S. (2012). *Metodologija kriminologii: Problem, poiski, reshenija* [Methodology of criminology: Problems, searching for way out, solutions]. Moscow: Izdatelstvo "Scheet-M".

Zhigarev, E. S. (2013). Dogmy teoreticheskoj Kriminologii: Metodologicheskij Vopros [Dogmas of theoretical criminology: Question of methodology]. *Rossijskij Kriminologicheskij Vzglyad, 3*, 292–303.

Zhmurov, D. V. (2013). Sovremennaja kriminologija: Sostojanie i tendentsii razvitija [Contemporary criminology: Its state and tendencies of development]. *Prolog, 3*, 46–50.

Zvirbul, V. K., Klochkov, V. V., & Minkovskij, G. M. (Eds.). (1977). *Teoreticheskie osnovy preduprezhdenija prestupnosti* [Theoretical foundations of crime prevention]. Moscow: Juridicheskaja literatura.

Appendix 1. Distributions and descriptive statistics of respondents in the study of criminal law and criminology professors in Russia (*N* = 110)

Variable	Description	N (%)	Mean (SD)	Min	Max
Age (*n* = 91)[a]	0 = ≤35	28 (30.8)	43.2 (14.3)	21	82
	1 = 36–50	31 (34.1)			
	2 = >51	32 (35.2)			
Gender (*n* = 96)[a]	0 = Female	46 (47.9)			
	1 = Male	50 (52.1)			
Education (*n* = 97)[a]	0 = no graduate degree	28 (29.9)			
	1 = Candidate of Science	43 (43.0)			
	2 = Doctor of Science	26 (27.1)			
Position (*n* = 105)[a]	0 = student	23 (21.9)			
	1 = assistant professor or senior lecturer	17 (16.2)			
	2 = associate professor (docent)	32 (30.5)			
	3 = professor	33 (31.4)			
Region (*n* = 102)[a]	0 = Moscow and St. Petersburg	49 (48.0)			
	1 = other	53 (52.0)			
Criminology as primary area (*n* = 110)[a]	0 = no	73 (66.4)			
	1 = yes	37 (33.6)			
University (*n* = 107)[a]	0 = State University	49 (45.8)			
	1 = Professional Law-Enforcement University	34 (31.8)			
	2 = Private University	24 (22.4)			
Years of teaching experience (*n* = 58) [a]	0 = ≤ 4	20 (34.5)			
	1 = 5–10	18 (31.0)			
	2 = 11–20	15 (25.9)			
	3 = >21	5 (8.6)			
Teaching experience before 1991 (*n* = 110)[a]	0 = no	100 (90.9)			
	1 = yes	10 (9.1)			
Law-enforcement experience (*n* = 110)[a]	0 = no	38 (34.5)			
	1 = yes	72 (65.5)			
Textbook authorship (*n* = 110)[a]	0 = no	82 (74.5)			
	1 = yes	28 (25.5)			

[a]Missing cases were excluded from the analysis.

Appendix 2. Questions and distribution of responses in the study of criminal law and criminology professors in Russia (*N* = 110)

Questions[a]	Strongly disagree/disagree	Neutral	Strongly agree/agree	
	N (%)	*N* (%)	*N* (%)	Mean (SD)
Criminology as a discipline has significantly transformed during post-soviet times in terms of the topics covered	22 (21.6)	20 (19.6)	60 (58.8)	4.8 (1.6)
Criminology as a discipline has significantly transformed in terms of content in the last 25 years	18 (17.3)	20 (19.2)	66 (63.5)	5.0 (1.5)
Ideas of Russian criminologists are relevant for the world criminology	41 (39.4)	20 (19.2)	43 (41.3)	4.1 (1.7)
Ideas of Russian criminologists are requested by the practitioners	43 (42.2)	21 (20.6)	38 (37.3)	4.0 (1.8)
Legislators take into account the opinion of criminologists when amending criminal legislation	71 (68.9)	16 (15.5)	16 (15.5)	2.7 (1.6)
Narrow specialisation in the field of Criminology is on high demand in the job market in Russia	72 (69.2)	14 (13.5)	18 (17.3)	2.9 (1.6)
Without basic knowledge of Criminal Law it is not possible to master a course in Criminology	11 (10.5)	7 (6.7)	87 (82.9)	5.9 (1.7)
A good specialist in the area of Criminal Law must have an understanding of criminological issues	7 (6.7)	8 (7.7)	89 (85.6)	6.1 (1.5)
Russian Criminology has well integrated into the world academic community	45 (43.3)	20 (19.2)	39 (37.5)	3.9 (1.7)
Criminology is an interdisciplinary area and must be taught not just for lawyers	18 (17.1)	20 (19.0)	67 (63.8)	5.1 (1.8)
Foreign theories do not adequately explain causes of crime in Russia	44 (41.9)	16 (15.2)	45 (42.9)	3.9 (1.9)
Crime is caused by similar factors in all modern market economies	17 (16.2)	20 (19.0)	68 (64.8)	4.9 (1.5)

[a] Responses range from: 1 = strongly disagree; 2 = disagree; 3 = somewhat disagree; 4 = neutral; 5 = somewhat agree; 6 = agree; 7 = strongly agree.

Soviet and post-Soviet Russian criminology – an insider's reflections

Yakov Gilinskiy

ABSTRACT

This article provides a reflection on various stages in the development of criminology in Soviet and post-Soviet Russia. I begin with an outline of the key phases of the development of the field as a discipline followed by four critical areas of the developmental processes that include research and academia, as well as emerging areas that are critical for further growth of the field. More specifically, I touch upon the important topics that Russian criminologists pursued in empirical research; exposure to international scholarship and networking; and finally, criminology course offerings in Russian law schools.

Introduction

In May 2015, I organised the annual Baltic Criminology meeting in St. Petersburg kindly hosted by the Russian State Pedagogical University of Herzen. During this conference, my colleague, Dr. Anna Gurinskaya, and I had numerous conversations with the Editor-in-Chief of the *International Journal of Comparative and Applied Criminal Justice* who invited us to consider writing a special issue for his journal. We believed the opportunity was ripe for two reasons. First, Western exposure and access to English language scholarship of Russian Criminology was limited; and, secondly, English language scholarship from within Russia and by Russian scholars was (and continues to be) limited as well. Criminology, as all sciences, is international, but it is well known that for many decades, Russian criminology existed in conditions of isolation from the greater world of science and under rigorous political and ideological control. Consequently, Russian criminology and the works of Russian criminologists are not well known abroad. We believed this was a good occasion to communicate to the larger audiences of criminology through the official journal of the American Society of Criminology's International Division and accepted the invitation to produce a special issue on Crime and Criminal Justice in post-Soviet Russia.

My career in the field of criminology began in the late 1960s. To date (2017), I am still actively engaged in teaching and research publishing in Russian, English, and other languages. I am privileged to have had the opportunity to witness the changing landscapes of Soviet and post-Soviet Criminology spanning over almost 50 years – some of which are encouraging and inspiring and some not so. While this introduction is by no means meant to be a comprehensive chronological account and analysis of the nature, scope, and development of Soviet and post-Soviet Criminology, in this essay, I reflect on some of the key phases of the development of the field as a discipline of research and in academia, as well as emerging areas that are critical for further growth of the field.

Russian criminology: general review

Outlined below are the main stages of development of Russian criminology, more specifically the contemporary post-Soviet period. In the Soviet Union, criminology of Russia developed in connection with criminology of other Soviet republics – Estonia, Georgia, Latvia, Lithuania, Ukraine, and others, primarily through professional conferences, joint research projects, and publications in criminological journals. The Russian Criminological Association (from 1991), the Baltic Criminological Seminar (from 1986), and activities of the St. Petersburg's International Criminological Club (from 1999) have been the key players in facilitating these professional exchanges, among others.

Russian criminology has gone through various stages in its development (Gilinskiy, 2014; Gurinskaya, 2017). In its earliest stages, the *first* period, the sociological perspective, played a key role in shaping the nature of criminological inquiry. Later, Tarnovsky (1898) developed the economic model, analysing dynamics of theft and their relation to the price of bread, concluding the significance of national bread price average as a national economy indicator in an explanation of property crimes. Liberal Russian criminologists opposed the death penalty and insisted on the importance of crime prevention (see Gernet, 1913). The *second* period was from 1917 to the 1930s. Old "bourgeois" criminology continued to develop in the new socio-economic conditions. However, Marxist ideology has since gradually limited studies to "personality of the offender," clinical criminology, and penitentiary research. Orthodox Marxism suggested that the Revolution destroyed the capitalist mode of production and with it, the root causes of crime. Criminology became ideologically unnecessary.

Studies of the individual characteristics of criminals and the "personality of criminals" dominated in this period, as social causes could not possibly influence crime in a socialist society. In 1918, *The department of moral statistics* was established to collect and analyse statistics on crime, suicide, and alcoholism. Penitentiary Criminology (criminology with the focus on punishment) developed. Additionally, many "bourgeois" criminologists were repressed towards the end of this period.

The *third* stage was "Stalin's epoch": criminology was prohibited *de facto*, and criminological studies were absent. But there was rudimentary criminological knowledge in penal law and criticism of "bourgeois" criminology. *The fourth* was a "stage of revival" from Khrushchev's "Thaw" in the 1960s to Gorbachev's "Perestroika" beginning in the late 1980s and onwards. The *Institute for Research of Crime Causes and Crime Prevention* was founded in Moscow in 1963 and a course named "Criminology" was included in the curriculum in law schools in 1964. During the early 1970s, there was impetus for empirical work. Many empirical criminological studies were organised in two Russian regions under the leadership of Sakharov (1979). Empirical studies in other regions of Russia under the leadership of Spiridonov and Gilinskiy (1977) were also undertaken during this period. More details on this are provided later in this narrative.

During this period, the significance of methodology in the criminological enterprise was recognised. Similarly, various typologies of criminology also were coined. Among them were Family Criminology, Penitentiary Criminology, Geography of Crime, Victimology, Criminology of Economic Crime, Criminology of Crime of Teenagers and Youth, and Criminology of Violence Crime, among others.

During this late-Soviet stage of the development of criminology, two competing approaches emerged. The first one was in line with the communist ideology: crime was portrayed as the result of the vestiges of "bourgeoisie consciousness" and "the capitalist environment." A competing approach viewed crime as a social phenomenon caused by economic, political, and social factors, and socio-economic inequality. Labeling Theory, the concepts of Durkheim, Merton, and Sutherland of the Chicago School, commonly used in Western Criminology, may have well applied to Soviet conditions. Only a few scholars have gradually weakened and eroded the stereotypes of official ideology through their work and helped create a national criminology. Chief among them are Avanesov, Bluvstein, Gilinskiy, Karpets, Khochrjakov, Kogan, Kudryavtsev, Nikiforov, Sakharov, Spiridonov, Vitsin, Yakovlev, and Zabrjansky.

Joint conferences and networking with foreign criminologists began towards the end of the Soviet period. For example, in 1980, a colloquium of the *International Society of Social Protection* was held in Moscow, resulting in numerous conference proceedings and articles produced by scholars hailing from Russia and from around Europe and North America. In 1983, the Soviet–Scandinavian symposium took place in Moscow with representatives from Finland, Denmark, Norway, and Sweden, along with Russian scholars. These meetings resulted in many published documents.

In the mid-1980s, criminologists, who understood the insignificance of official ideology as it related to criminology, decided to unite and meet annually to engage in discourses of criminology and crime in the USSR. During this time, I helped bring together a group of criminologists from Leningrad, Moscow, Latvia, Lithuania, and Estonia with the main objective of holding conferences on a regular basis in Leningrad (formerly St. Petersburg) and the Baltic Republics. These locations offered greater freedom for discussions and publications than other regions of the Soviet Union. In 1987, the First Baltic criminological seminar took place in Estonia followed by Riga (1988), Vilnius (1989), and Leningrad (1990). These meetings continue to be organised with the most recent seminar (30th) was held in Riga in 2017.

The political situation changed. The republics of Baltic achieved independence, and the Seminar continued to exist and develop, involving an increasing number of participants from the countries of Europe and North America. Proceedings from the majority of these seminars were published. Since 1991, the Baltic criminological conference has become international, not only due to the independence achieved by Latvia, Lithuania, Estonia, but also because of access to participants from the countries of the Baltic region (e.g., Germany, Denmark, Norway, Poland, Finland, Sweden), and eventually becoming more visible to other countries. This annual event continued without disruption and the last conference was held in Tallinn in 2016.

The *fifth* stage of the development of Russian criminology corresponds to contemporary times (beginning in the late 1980s). The freedom to teach and carry out research, to foster professional contacts with foreign colleagues, appeared only at the end of the 1980s and in the beginning of the 1990s, due to the Gorbachev's Perestroika.

Main characteristics of post-Soviet criminology

Some of the key developments of post-Soviet criminology are as follows:

(1) Development of *criminological theory* without censorship and an ideological ban, requirements, and restrictions.
(2) Carrying out *empirical criminological researches*, the analysis of statistics, which became available, and the use of mathematical methods of the analysis of criminological information.
(3) Gradual, step-by-step, *entry into the world criminology* (participation in the international conferences, in joint projects, free trips abroad and reception foreign colleagues in Russia).
(4) *Criminology teaching* as a subject at all juridical universities, schools, and colleges.

Let's consider these directions of development of criminology in more detail.

Development of criminological theory

The most important theoretical ideas of post-Soviet criminology were the understanding of crime as a social construct (Gilinskiy, 2009, 2014); understanding of the role of a political regime in criminalisation/decriminalisation of actions (Burlakov, Volkov, & Salnikov, 2001); refusal of search of the unique reason of "crime" and identification of a social and economic inequality as one of the main criminogenic factors (Olkov, 2007; Skifskiy, 2007); the understanding of "punishment crisis," and discovering ways of minimisation of negative consequences of punishment, especially of prisons, and unconditional ban of the death penalty.

In reality, there is nothing which could be considered criminal *sui generis*, per se; crime and criminality are relative terms, conventional and contractual (a legislative agreement). In reality, they are *social constructs*, reflecting certain social realities: some people murder others, some steal from others, cheat others, etc. But actions with the same characteristics in other contexts are not criminal: killing an enemy in a war, capital punishment, court seizures of people's property, etc.

Although such a criminological consciousness (applicable to our subject) was already present in Ancient Rome (*ex senatusconsultis et plebiscitis crimina exercentur*, criminal acts arise from the decisions of both senators and the public), in contemporary criminology, the recognition that crime was a social construct came comparatively late. Today, many Western criminologists share such a viewpoint. Hess and Scheerer (1997) suggest that criminality is not so much an ontological phenomenon as a mental construct having an historical and protean character. On the contrary, they suggest that criminality is constructed almost completely by the controlling institutions, which establish norms and attribute determinate meanings to certain acts; criminality is in this sense a social and linguistic construct. A detailed analysis of the social construction of crime and social control is presented in "The Oxford Handbook of Criminology" (Maguire, Morgan, & Reiner, 2007, pp. 179–337).

Public opinion, mass media, and politicians take part in designing crime. Formally, "the last word" belongs to the legislature. The legislative body adopts the criminal law defining acts that are harmful to the society. But in fact, the chief "designer" of crime is the political regime. It defines both the decision of the legislator and law-enforcement activity. The role of a political regime in crime designing, criminal policy, law-enforcement activity, and penitentiary policy is well established in the *Political Regime and Criminality* (Burlakov et al., 2001).

More recently, Russian criminologists have been referring to "cultural criminology" (Gilinskiy, 2014), understanding crime and social control as manifestations (product) of culture and society as its generations are close to our understanding. I believe that each culture has such crime and punishment, which it deserves.

I think the new topic "crime and social control in the post-modern world" is very important in contemporary criminology (Gilinskiy, 2015). There are some characteristics of a postmodern society, which are important for understanding contemporary forms of crime, social control over crime, and the development of criminology. Among them are *Globalization* of economy, transport, finances, technologies, and crime (especially organised crime: drug trafficking, human trafficking, arms trafficking, etc.); heightened migration of people across the porous international boundaries results in the escalating "conflict of cultures" (Sellin, 1938); and "hate crimes" as result of mass migration and policy of the authorities "Divide et impera!" ("Divide and dominate!") that enhances conflict and crime. "Virtualisation" of life and activity includes cybercrime; society is a "consumer society" (Bauman, 2001, 2007) and the idea "all on sale" results in numerous crimes: street crimes (e.g., thefts, robberies, and fraud) and white-collar crime, including corruption and different deviance. The consequent growth in economic and social inequality and a share of the "excluded" is the main social base and factor of crime and others deviance.

Many criminologists gave up trying to find the causes of crime a long time ago and turned to the study of correlation dependence: "correlation versus causality" (Winfree & Abadinsky, 1996, p. 9). It is impossible to find a specific cause for a construct, which capriciously changes its form in time and space at the whim of a legislator (or power); such a search leads to a truism: criminality is caused by the whole socio-economic system or criminality is the result of the penal code. Meanwhile, many Russian criminologists continue to search for the reasons for crime causation, considering "the reasons of the first level," "the reasons of the second level," "the circumstances promoting commit a crime," and so on.

As a result of correlation or factorial analyses, "structural criminology" has established the interdependency of criminality and factors such as "gender, age, class and race" (Hagan, 1989; Messerschmidt, 1997). It is important theoretically and practically to define the specific "weight," "power," value of each factor in genesis of criminality, and its separate types. An important integrative "criminogenic" (in general "delictogenic") factor is the fundamental contradiction between the relatively even distribution of human demands and the inequality in the existing opportunities to satisfy these demands, depending first of all on a person's position in the social structure.

Both conflict and mainstream criminologists have written about economic inequality and crime and studied the relationships empirically. The relationship between serious violent crimes and suicides and economic inequality were empirically confirmed by Olkov (2007) and Skifskiy (2007). Many factors influence violent crimes (homicide, grievous bodily harm, rape, assault with robbery) such as the presence of alcoholism, the demographic structure of the population, consumption of drugs, economic statues, with the last factor appearing to be the most considerable (Olkov, 2004). The catastrophic social and economic inequality in Russia was the main factor of crime and other deviant manifestations.

A new and very important "delictogenic" factor is the change in society from hierarchical relationships to one based on differentiation with the meta-code *inclusion/exclusion*. It is clear that the excluded constitute the social basis of criminality, drug-addiction, alcoholism, and other negative deviations (Finer & Nellis, 1998; Young, 1999).

The *social control* over criminality, *"crisis of punishment"* is one of the primary problems in the contemporary world (Mathiesen, 1974; Rothwax, 1996). Street crime, organised crime, violent crime, terrorism, and so on affect people, especially middle class, and give rise to "moral panic" (Cohen, 1973) and fear of crime. Legislators, politicians, police, and criminal justice officials try, often habitually, by repressive methods to gain control over criminality, drug abuse and drug traffic, prostitution, corruption, terrorism, etc. However, traditional measures have not obtained the desired results.

"Crisis of punishment" is a very real topic for Russia. Unfortunately, social control over criminality also remains very strict in contemporary Russia. The last Criminal Code (CC) of the Russian Federation (RF) from 1996 contains very stern punishments: death penalty (Art. 59 CC PF), life imprisonment (Art. 57), deprivation of freedom for 20 years, and by combined of crime – to 30 years, by combined of sentences – to 35 years (Art. 56). There are no such punishments (life imprisonment of up to 35 years) in any previous CCs of Russia, including during Stalin's period, which was considered a period of tyranny. There is moratorium of the death penalty from 1997.

Social control over crime is a very important topic in Russian criminology. Social and economic inequality, as a criminogenic factor, generates social conflict, dissatisfaction, envy, and crime (Gilinskiy, 2014). Unfortunately, repressive social control is used to marginalise Russian citizens and occurs through the biased selection process in the police and criminal justice system, further increasing crime rates.

Of course, not all contemporary Russian criminologists think alike. Some are opponents of constructivist understanding of crime, many support retribution and the application of the death penalty, and some continue to look for crime causation.

Russian empirical criminological research

Empirical criminological research began during the late Soviet period. In the 1970s, a group of criminologists from Moscow conducted a comparative research of crime in two regions of Russia: the Oryol and Kemerovo areas. The findings suggested that the crime rate is higher in the Kemerovo area where not only the level of income of the population was higher, but also the economic inequality was greater (Sakharov, 1979). Scientists in Leningrad in the Oryol region conducted similar research in the same year. Findings supported the interrelationship of crime with alcoholism and suicide in the population. The same group of researchers carried out the first studies on prisoners in four penitentiary institutions of the Oryol region (Spiridonov & Gilinskiy, 1977).

The post-Soviet period saw expanded criminological research conducted at St. Petersburg University, the universities of the Ministry of Internal Affairs, and the Prosecutors Office in the 1990s. For instance, criminologists at St. Petersburg's State University conducted empirical research of violent crimes in St. Petersburg and the surrounding areas in 1991. The sample included all the convicted offenders for serious violent crimes (e.g., homicide, assault grievous bodily harm, and rape) serving sentences in city and area prisons. The faculty in the department of psychology analysed the data and the results were published in various academic outlets.

Between 1994 and 1998, criminologists of the Sociological institute of the Russian Academy of Sciences under my leadership participated in an ambitious empirical research of crime, a drug abuse, alcoholism, and other types of deviant behaviour in countries in the Baltic Sea areas. Annually, research participants from Finland, Poland, Germany, Denmark, Estonia, Latvia, Lithuania, and Russia coordinated and conducted research on crime issues in the region.

From 1998 to 2000, criminologists of the Sociological institute of the Russian Academy of Sciences conducted the research "Population and Police," including the crime victims survey of the population in St. Petersburg, Volgograd, and Borovichi (a small city in the North-Western region). Results were published and discussed with the management of police of St. Petersburg (Davis, Ortiz, Gilinskiy, Ylesseva, & Briller, 2004). Similar findings were drawn from the research by Semukhina (2014).

In 2004 and 2005, research on torture in police custody in the following five regions of Russia was conducted: St. Petersburg, Pskov, Komi Republic, Nizhny Novgorod, and Chita. Results from this research were published in the monograph *Sociology of Violence* (Committee Against Torture, 2006) and articles also appeared in many other reputable outlets (Gilinskiy, 2011). What we have learned about torture mostly comes from the media, which describe different torture techniques used by police. These techniques include the "baby elephant" (the use of a gas mask to reduce or stop breathing, sometimes using a gas), "the swallow" (hanging with ropes), crucifixion (the name is self-explanatory), and "the envelope" (when the victim is folded like an envelope). New sexual tortures by police include the "baton spread," involving rape using a police baton. According to the media accounts, torture has become an everyday practice in Russia. The *Obshchaya Gazeta* ("Common Newspaper") introduced a regular column called "Torture as Everyday Routine in Russia" at the end of the 1990s, and the *Novaja Gazeta* ("New Newspaper") began a column "Public Verdict" devoted to the same issue.

Our research supported such media reports. Based on the results obtained from the survey of residents in the five regions, the following affirmative responses from suspects in custody were recorded: in St. Petersburg 3.3% of the respondents, in Pskov 4.6%, in Nizhny Novgorod 3.4%, in Komi 4.6%, in Chita 4.1% of the population were victims of police torture. In Komi, 39.0% of convicts claimed to have been subject to unlawful or unjustified cruel physical treatment or threat of such treatment, including 10.1% who said that mistreatment was "systematic." In Chita, the percentage of convicts who said they were subjected to unlawful or unjustified cruel physical treatment or threats of such a treatment was 61.3% (including 21.3% systematically). The torture practices continue despite the emphasis placed by the Ministry of the Internal Affairs on training (Morn & Sergevnin, 1994). In sum, the late 1990s through early 2000s saw many empirical works conducted on the topics of crime and punishment.

Entry into the world criminology

Permanent contacts of Russian and foreign criminologists began following post-"Perestroika" in the late 1980s. I have reflected on small but sporadic interactions with international criminologists in the earlier part of this essay. One of which is the Baltic criminological conference which has been international since 1991, not only due to the achievement of independence by the former Soviet Republics such as Latvia, Lithuania, and Estonia, but also due to access to participants from the countries of the Baltic region and the rest of Europe.

Opportunities for international exchange and collaborations have also emerged since perestroika. It began with the Russian–Scandinavian symposium with participation of well-known Russian and Swedish criminologists held in near Stockholm, Sweden in 1990. Subsequently, Russian criminologists participated in many international conferences including the World Congresses of Criminology in Seoul (1998), Rio de Janeiro (2003), Barcelona (2008), and Kobe (2011), annual conferences of the European

Society of Criminology (since 2001), annual symposiums in Stockholm, and other international meetings. In addition, many international scholars participated in conferences organised in Russia.

Criminology teaching

Criminology was an obligatory subject at all juridical Universities and colleges. As a subject, criminology was expected to be taken in a student's third or fourth year. There are many textbooks of criminology by various Russian authors. In addition, textbooks by German and Americans, G.J. Schneider, and J. Sheley were translated into Russian. Criminology and its components were taught at bachelor degree, magistracy, and postgraduate levels. Criminology became an elective subject for law school students in 2012.

The main topics of contemporary Russian criminology include organised crime, violent crime, corruption, hate crimes, economic crime, drug trafficking, human trafficking, and social control over crime (Gilinskiy, 2006, 2014; Luneev, 2005). Currently, main research methods are statistical analyses, surveys of the general population, victims, experts and prisoners, and interviews. Comparative studies are widespread (Gilinskiy, 2000; Paoli, 2001). Criminologists actively use mathematical methods (factor analysis, correlation analysis, and others) to analyse the results of research (Jusichanova, 2005; Olkov, 2007; Skifskiy, 2007).

Final thoughts on Russian criminology

Crime is a serious subject matter and requires considerable attention. Unfortunately, official police statistics are not complete and the dark figure of crime (latent) is very high. Therefore, the analysis of latency is an important part of research (Inshakov, 2011). Statistical data are published online on the site of the Ministry Internal Affairs (MVD) and in the corresponding annual publication "Crime and Delinquency, Statistical Review" of the MVD and the Ministry of Justice. The full data of the recorded crime and criminals published in the annual publications of the Russian Criminological Association under the editorship of Dolgova (2000, 2003) and in the "Criminological Journal of Baikal State University of Economic and Law."

The main research institutions are the Research Institute of the General Prosecutor's Office of the Russian Federation (Moscow), the Research Institute of the MVD (Moscow), Center of Deviantology (Sociology of Deviance) of the Sociological Institute of the Russian Academy of Sciences (St. Petersburg), Saratov's Center of Research of Organized Crime and Corruption (Saratov), and others.

Apart from the regularly recorded violent and property crimes, other forms of violent and property crimes increased during the decades of the establishment of RF. One of the more serious violent crimes was organised crime. Organised crime as a social problem began to take centre stage in Russian Criminology and generated considerable attention in the post-Soviet Russia (Dolgova, 2003; Gilinskiy, 2003; Gilinskiy & Kostjukovsky, 2004; Ovchinsky, 2001; Repetskaja, 2001). These developments came on the heels of its early genesis in small illegal business and legal co-operative societies of the early 1960s and 70s. The late 1980s and early 1990s, prior to the Soviet collapse, witnessed the emergence of mafia-type criminal organisations in St. Petersburg and other major cities around Russia. These organisations were primarily engaged in drug trafficking, "protection" (racket) small and middle business, market trade, sex trade, theft, and sale of cars, gambling, trade and marketing in counterfeit products and raw materials, and illegal arms, among others. Eventually, organised crime penetrated and infiltrated into the city politics and government (Zorkin, 2010).

Other related violent crimes of the decades following the 1990s are the prevalence and an increase in hate crimes. Fear of migrants and xenophobia led to the growth of homegrown fundamentalism and right-wing violence giving birth to protest slogans such as "Russia is for Russians!," "Migrants go home!," "Fight the blacks!." Hate crimes are most often recorded in large cities such as Moscow, St. Petersburg, Voronezh, and the Krasnodar region (i.e., a region in the southern part of the

European part of Russia) (Laryš & Mareš, 2011). Hate crime, though sporadic, saw a sharp increase between 2001 and 2008 (Arnold, 2010).

Perhaps, a more insidious but less visible for violence experience in the post-Soviet Russia is human trafficking. Trafficking in the form of forced prostitution of minors occurs in various Russian cities (Gurvich, Rusakova, Pyshkina, & Yakovleva, 2002). Chief among the victims are children trafficked for pornography and illegal adoption with primary consumers being "new Russians," city "authorities" and foreign visitors, particularly not only from Finland but also from Sweden, Germany, Norway, and England (Gurvich et al., 2002).

Criminology is generally an "unpleasant" science for those in power. The economic, social, and political situation in Russia is very adverse (a catastrophic economic inequality, total corruption, repressive policy, international conflicts, mass discontent, etc.). Moreover, in general, all science appeared out of priority interests of those in positions of political power.

It is not surprising, therefore, that discipline of "criminology" was eliminated as obligatory subjects of law departments and schools. Almost completely, there is no financing of empirical criminological researches. There is no financing for participation of criminologists in the foreign congresses, conferences, and seminars. Translation of foreign criminological literature is carried out seldom (much less than in the 1970s–1980s). Official statistical data on crime are incomplete and don't correspond to the accepted volume in the developed countries (e.g., "Polizeiliche Kriminalstatistik Bundesrepublik Deutschland" in Germany, "Summary of the White Paper on Crime" of Government of Japan, etc.). Contemporary Russian criminology exists and develops only thanks to the diligence and initiatives of criminologists without necessary provision of finances, technology, and skilled workers. Certainly, criminology will not be "forbidden" as it was under Stalin, but its development in the next years (from 2000) is very complicated and uncertain.

References

Arnold, R. (2010). Visions of hate: Explaining neo-nazi violence in the Russian Federation. *Problems of Post-Communism, 57*(2), 37–49. doi:10.2753/PPC1075-8216570203

Bauman, Z. (2001). *Work, consumerism and the new poor*. Buckingham: Open University press.

Bauman, Z. (2007). *Consuming life*. Cambridge: Polity.

Burlakov, V., Volkov, Y., & Salnikov, V. (Eds.). (2001). *Politicheskij regim i prestupnost. Problemi politicheskoj kriminologii* [Political regime and criminality. The problems of political criminology]. St. Petersburg: Juridechskij tsentr press.

Cohen, S. (1973). *Folk devils and moral panics*. London: Paladin.

Committee Against Torture. (2006). *Sociology of violence. Arbitrariness of law enforcement bodies by the eyes of people*. Nizhny Novgorod: Committee Against Torture.

Davis, R. C., Ortiz, C. W., Gilinskiy, Y., Ylesseva, I., & Briller, V. (2004). A cross-national comparison of citizen perceptions of the police in New York City and St Petersburg, Russia. *Policing: an International Journal of Police Strategies & Management, 27*(1), 22–36. doi:10.1108/13639510410519895

Dolgova, A. (Ed.). (2000). *Korruptsija I borba s nej* [Corruption and the fight with corruption]. Moscow: Russian Criminological Association.

Dolgova, A. (2003). *Prestupnost, ee organizovannost' i kriminalnoe obshestvo* [Criminality, its organization and criminal society]. Moscow: Russian Criminological Association.

Finer, C., & Nellis, M. (Eds.). (1998). *Crime and social exclusion*. Oxford: Blackwell Publishers.

Gernet, M. (1913). *Smertnaja kazn* [Death penalty]. Moscow: Tip. Y.Dankin &Y.Homutov.

CRIMINOLOGY AND CRIMINAL JUSTICE IN RUSSIA

Gilinskiy, Y. (2006). Crime in contemporary Russia. *European Journal of Criminology, 3*(3), 259–292. doi:10.1177/1477370806065583

Gilinskiy, Y. (2009). Konstruktivizm v sovremennoj kriminologii [Constructivism in contemporary criminology]. *Criminalist, 1,* 94–98.

Gilinskiy, Y. (2011). Torture by the Russian police: An empirical study. *Police Practice and Research: An International Journal, 12*(2), 163–171. doi:10.1080/15614263.2010.512138

Gilinskiy, Y. (2014). *Kriminologija: Teorija, istorija, empiricheskaja osnova, sotsialnij kontrol* [Criminology: Theory, history, empirical basis, social control]. St. Petersburg: Alef-Press.

Gilinskiy, Y. (2000). Analysis of statistics on some forms of social deviation in St. Petersburg from 1980 to 1985. In H. Leifman & N. Henrichson (Eds.), *Statistics on alcohol, drugs and crime in the Baltic sea region* (pp. 175–198). Helsinki: NAD Publication. N37.

Gilinskiy, Y. (2003). Organized crime: A perspective from Russia. In J. Albanese, D. Das, & A. Verma (Eds.), *Organized crime. World perspectives* (Ch. 6, pp. 146–164). Upper Saddle River, NJ: Pearson Education.

Gilinskiy, Y., & Kostjukovsky, Y. (2004). From thievish *Artel* to criminal corporation: The history of organised crime in Russia. In C. Fijnaut & L. Paoli (Eds.), *Organised crime in Europe. Concepts, patterns and control policies in the European Union and beyond* (Vol. 4, pp. 181–202). Dordrecht, Norwell: Springer

Gilinskiy, Y. (2015). Prestupnost, sotsialnij kontrol I kriminologija v obshestve postmoderna [Crime, social control and criminology in the society of a postmodern]. In Y. Gilinskiy (Ed.), *Prestupnost i sotsialnij kontrol v obshestve postmoderna* [Crime and social control in the society of postmodern] (Vol. I, pp. 89–95). St. Petersburg: Alef-Press.

Gurinskaya, A. (2017). Russian criminology as "terra incognita": Legacies of the past and challenges of the present. *International Journal of Comparative and Applied Criminal Justice, 41*(3), 123–143.

Gurvich, I., Rusakova, M., Pyshkina, T., & Yakovleva, A. (2002). *The commercial sexual exploitation of children in St. Petersburg and Northwest Russia.* Stockholm: Save the Children.

Hagan, J. (1989). *Structural criminology.* New Brunswick, NJ: Rutgers, the State University.

Hess, H., & Scheerer, S. (1997). Was ist Kriminalität? Skizze einer konstruktivistischen Kriminalitätstheorie. *Kriminologisches Journal, 29*(2), 83–155.

Inshakov, S. (Ed.). (2011). *Teoreticheskie osnovy issledovanija i analisa letentnoj prestupnosti* [Theoretical bases of research and analysis of latent crime]. Moscow: UNITY.

Jusichanova, E. (2005). *Modelirovanie kriminogennih protsessov v subjektah Rossijskoj Federatsii* [Modelling of criminogenic processes in the subjects of the Russian federation]. Tjumen: Vector Book.

Laryš, M., & Mareš, M. (2011). Right-wing extremist violence in the Russian Federation. *Europe-Asia Studies, 63*(1), 129–154. doi:10.1080/09668136.2011.534308

Luneev, V. (2005). *Prestupnost XX veka: Mirovie, regionalnie i Rossijskie tendentsii* [Criminality XX century. The world, regions and Russian tendencies.] (2nd ed.). Moskow: Wolters Kluwer.

Maguire, M., Morgan, R., & Reiner, R. (Eds.). (2007). *The oxford handbook of criminology* (4th ed.). Oxford: Oxford University Press.

Mathiesen, T. (1974). *The politics of abolition. Essays in political action theory.* Oslo: Universitetsforlaget.

Messerschmidt, J. (1997). *Crime as structured action: gender, race, class, and crime in the making.* London: SAGE.

Morn, F, & Sergevnin, V. (1994). Police training in modern Russia. *International Journal of Comparative and Applied Criminal Justice, 18*(1–2), 119–128. doi:10.1080/10439463.1990.9964604

Olkov, S. (2004). O polze i vrede neravenstva (kriminologicheskoe issledovanie) [The benefits and harms of inequality (criminological research)]. *Gosudarstvo I Pravo, 8,* 73–78.

Olkov, S. (2007). *Analiticheskaja kriminologija* [Analytical criminology]. Kazan: Poznanie.

Ovchinsky, V. (2001). *XXI vek protiv mafii* [XXI century against mafia]. Moscow: INFRA-M.

Paoli, L. (2001). *Illegal drug trade in Russia.* Freiburg i. Br.: Iuscrim.

Repetskaja, A. (2001). *Transnatsionalnaja organizovannaja prestupnost: Harakteristiki, prichini, strategii kontrolja* [Transnational organized crime: Characteristics, causes, strategy of control]. Irkutsk: IGEA.

Rothwax, H. (1996). *Guilty. The collapse of criminal justice.* New York, NY: Random House.

Sakharov, A. (Ed.). (1979). *Metodologicheskie i metodicheskie voprosi izuchenija I preduprezhdenija prestupnosti v bolshom gorode* [Methodological and methods questions of the study and prevention of criminality in a large city]. Moscow: Institute of General Prosecutor's Office.

Sellin, T. (1938). Culture conflict and crime. *American Journal of Sociology, 44*(1), 97–103. doi:10.1086/217919

Semukhina, O. (2014). Unreported crimes, public dissatisfaction of police, and observed police misconduct in the volgograd region, Russia: A research note. *International Journal of Comparative and Applied Criminal Justice, 38* (4), 305-325. doi:10.1080/07418820600985339

Skifskiy, I. (2007). *Nasilstvennaja prestupnost v sovremennoj Rossii: Objasnenie I prognozirovanie* [Violent crime in contemporary Russia: Explanation and forecasting]. Tumen: Vector Books.

Spiridonov, L., & Gilinskiy, Y. (Eds.). (1977). *Chelovek kak object sotsiologicheskih issledovanij* [Person as object of sociological research]. Moscow: Nauka.

Tarnovsky, E. (1898). Vlijanie hlebnih tsen I urozhaev na dvizhenie prestuplenij protiv sobstvennosti v Rossii [Influence of grain prices and yields on the movement of crimes against property in Russia]. *Jurnal Ministerstva Justitsii, 8*, 73–107.

Winfree, L., & Abadinsky, H. (1996). *Understanding crime. Theory and practice.* Chicago: Wadsworth Publishing Company.

Young, J. (1999). *The exclusive society: Social exclusion, crime and difference in late modernity.* London: SAGE Publications.

Zorkin, V. (2010, December 10) Konstitutsija protiv kriminala [Constitution against crime]. *Rossijskaja gazeta,* N5359 (280). Retrieved April 5, 2017, from https://rg.ru/2010/12/10/zorkin.html

Social values and delinquency of Russian youth

Olga Siegmunt and Peter Wetzels

ABSTRACT

This article analysed youth attitudes towards social values, youth's delinquent behaviour, and the relationship between the two were analysed. A sample of ninth-grade school students ($n = 1747$) was surveyed in a Russian city (Volgograd) in 2000. A latent class analysis was conducted to identify different groups of youth based on their attitudes towards social values. Three latent groups were identified: indifferent, competitor-centred, and traditional youth. More specifically, the study examined if youth perceptions of societal values determine their participation in violent offenses. All crimes were grouped as either instrumental violence (e.g., robbery or extortion) or non-instrumental violence (e.g., assault or threat with weapon). The results show that the competitor-centred youths are proportionally more criminal (35% of instrumental and 34.6% non-instrumental violent crimes) than the other groups. The traditional youths are least criminal of all.

1. Introduction

The present study is part of a large, empirical project about juvenile delinquency among others in Russia that was conducted in the Russian city of Volgograd in 2000. The main research question of this project was to explain youth delinquency with traditional predictors like family socio-economic situation, attitudes towards violence, or self-control (Siegmunt, 2013a). The results of the factor analysis from a previous study suggested that attitudes towards violence in Russia have two dimensions: instrumental and non-instrumental violence. Instrumental violence refers to behaviours against another person in which it will primarily be used as an attribute of power. Violence is utilised in these instances as an instrument to reach the perpetrator's goals: "If I want to show what I can I would use violence." The non-instrumental violence is based on use of force only. In this case, the goal is the satisfaction of the using of force. Survey questions used to capture attitudes towards non-instrumental violence included: "Sometimes violence is necessary to have fun".

The classification of attitudes towards violence into instrumental and non-instrumental gave a reason to classify the juvenile's violent delinquency into the two similar groups. As such, we extracted two dimensions: juveniles who engaged in both instrumental and non-instrumental violence. Instrumental violent delinquency refers to many behaviours against another person with a goal of appropriating their property. This type of delinquency is also economically motivated (such as in the case of robbery and extortion). In contrast, non-instrumental violent delinquency refers to behaviours against another person with the goal of having fun using force. In this case, victims will be injured, or they will be threatened with injury. Examples of non-instrumental delinquency include assault and threat with weapon.

The present article expands on our earlier analytic strategy. We analyse not only the various dimensions of violent behaviour, but also the structure of attitudes towards society as a whole, and the relationship between these attitudes and youth's violent behaviour. In doing so, we are examining that the questions prior research (2013a) did not address. To do this, we used the unique data which reflect human attitudes and human behaviour in a specific social and historical context. Looking at the background of the development of Russian society will help to inform this specific context.

In 1991, the political system in Russia changed from a socialistic to a capitalistic structure. Because of this, the rights and duties were changed. Russian society became a multi-party system rather than a one-party system, and its citizens obtained ownership of real estate for the first time. At the same time, much of the national industry crashed and many people lost their jobs.

In a short period of time, Russia also moved from being a socialistic society with traditional values like need of hierarchy and authority to a free market society with modern individualistic values like acceptance of competition and autonomy of the individual. The free market is rule-based, though it is not as stringent as in a traditional society. The rational action associated with a free market society requires creativity and flexibility.

The present article's research is driven by two main hypotheses. First, *attitudes towards society are heterogeneous.* This study occurs during the transition period from socialistic to modern individualistic society. This process causes a weakening of collectivistic values and a strengthening of individualistic values. Collectivistic values are based on tradition and action to rule. In contrast, individualistic values include the pursuit of free action, personal responsibility, and creativity. To capture these values, a scale was developed with 14 questions that examine juvenile's attitudes and asked whether respondents recognise future perspectives, are competitive oriented, or prefer earlier communistic system. Three groups of attitudes were identified by a principal component factor analysis: egoism/orientation to competition, future prospects, and pro-communistic attitudes.

Results of the study suggest that juveniles have different attitudes towards society: some prefer modern societal structure with new perspectives and the belief in opportunity to achieve one's goals independently, without the help of others. In contrast, other juveniles preferred the old system (indicated in the study by items like "Communism is a good political and social idea"). A latent class analysis (a method of statistical classification used to relate observed discrete variables to latent variables) was conducted to test this hypothesis. In this way, groups of cases in the multivariate categorical data were found. This method determines the number of groups which are called "latent classes." As a result, three latent groups of juveniles were identified. Based on the profiles, we named them "indifferent," "competitor-centred," and "traditional" youth.

The second hypothesis of this study was that *type of attitudes towards society predicts a juvenile's delinquent behaviour.* The study hypothesised that juveniles with strong individualistic attitudes commit more violent crime, specifically more instrumental crime than other juveniles. This hypothesis is based on the observation that crime rates are higher in Western societies with free market structures than in Eastern societies (e.g., Horsley, 2010; Komiya, 1999). While the present study does not test an existing criminological theory, this study is important because of its unique database.

This second hypothesis will be tested in two steps. First, the percentage of instrumental and non-instrumental violent delinquency will be estimated for every type of attitude towards society. Second, the effects of the different types of attitudes towards the society will be tested in two multivariate models for instrumental and non-instrumental violence.

2. Literature review

2.1. *Youth studies and attitudes towards social values in Russia*

A large number of researchers have studied social problems, attitudes, morals, and behaviours of young people in the 1990s to 2000s in Russia. The two biggest representative surveys were conducted by the Levada-Centre and the All-Russian Centre for Public Opinion Research (VCIOM). The data for these studies were drawn from youth samples with a minimum age of 16 to 18 years old.

The most comprehensive repeated youth studies were conducted by the Russian Academy of Sciences. The first wave of the study "Youth of the New Russia" was completed in 1997 by a research group from the Independent Russian Institute for Social and National Problems; the second wave of this study was conducted in 2007 by researchers from the Institute of Sociology of the Russian Academy of Sciences.[1] Both waves were completed in cooperation with the Fridrich-Ebert-Foundation. Overall, the findings suggest: young people who aspired to accomplish more in their lives than their parents (1997: 50% and 2007: 53%) want to "be different than others" and to "live unlike others" (2007: 67%); they believe that "their financial situation depends on themselves only" (77%; Institute of Sociology of the Russian Academy of Sciences, 2007, p. 36). In addition, more than half of the respondents felt that it is fair that some people are less wealthy than others because people are responsible for their financial success by themselves. Researchers did not interpret this result in terms of hardness or egoism, but in terms of the break-down of collectivistic awareness. In their opinion, the beginning of collectivistic values took place in the community, which cared for their poorest members. Instead, the utility awareness was established without a commitment to the community. The principal point of this view is that a person is self-made: each individual has to create their own self and is responsible for the results of their own actions (Independent Russian Institute for Social and National Problems, 1998, pp. 20–21).

In these studies, Russian youth did not definitely prefer one of the societal forms like socialism, capitalism, or liberalism in the 1990s: 26.2% of respondents supported a combination of all these forms; 41.0% don't prefer one of them over the others; 13.1% of respondents preferred liberalism (a modern society with radical market reforms orientation), 4.5% favoured socialism, and 15.2% supported capitalism with "Russian character." The fewest number of respondents favoured socialism, perhaps recognising a comeback of socialism, is unlikely. Moreover, young people may not consider the potentially positive sides of socialistic lifestyle as they experienced more often the problems and negative consequences of socialism. Interestingly, most respondents who preferred societal forms also preferred liberalism. For young people, liberalism was not a list of abstract terms like democracy, human rights, or free market. It was instead the economical and political reality. The majority of respondents preferred capitalistic societal structure. Indeed, the capitalistic philosophy is based on a national patriotic vision that Russia has its own way of development. (Independent Russian Institute for Social and National Problems, 1998, p. 30).

Young people from families with a high socio-economic status and an optimistic perspective about success of own professional career indicated a preference of liberalistic market values. Those with a middle class socio-economic status and less optimistic attitudes towards their own future preferred patriotic national values. Those who supported socialism were primarily young people with the poorest socio-economic relations and rather pessimistic attitudes towards career opportunity (Independent Russian Institute for Social and National Problems, 1998, pp. 30–31).

The youths of the 2000s are modern and single minded in general. They want to be different from most people and feel empowered to reach their desired financial status without the help of others. The attitudes of young people towards society are heterogeneous and depend on the family's socio-economic status and optimistic attitudes towards their own chances. However, more young people are also competition-oriented and prefer liberalism as an economic and political basis of the society.

2.2. *Juvenile's social values and delinquency*

Studies about the relationship between social values and delinquency have a long history in Western countries (Cernkovich, 1978; Matza & Sykes, 1961; Rainwater, 1970). Matza and Sykes (1961) discussed the connection between a juvenile's delinquency and underlying values. They asked "Why some adolescents convert subterranean values into seriously deviant behaviour while others do not?" (Matza & Sykes, 1961, p. 719).

Cernkovich's (1978) conceptual model points to "a commonality of value orientations at various socio-economic locations in the society". Cernkovich (1978) surveyed 14–18 year-old male students and differentiated between conventional and subterranean value orientations. Conventional value orientations are defined as "adherence and commitment to such overt, formal, and official values as deferred gratification, hard work, practicality, the worth of formal education, progress, and secular rationality" (Cernkovich, 1978, p. 449). The subterranean value orientations are defined as "adherence and commitment to such covert, informal, and unofficial values as short-run hedonism, thrills, excitement, trouble, toughness, the ability to make a "fast buck," the ability to con or dupe others, and so on (Cernkovich, 1978, p. 450).

Each of these – conventional and subterranean value orientations – permeates all levels of the stratification system. Indeed, he summed up that previous studies investigated lower- and middle-class delinquency; upper-class delinquency did not exist. Cernkovich supposed (1978, p. 448): "(1) the greater the degree of commitment to the overt, official, and conventional value standards of American society, the lesser the seriousness and frequency of involvement in delinquent activities, (2) the greater the degree of commitment to the covert, unofficial, and subterranean value standards of American society, the greater the seriousness and frequency of involvement in delinquent activities." These assumptions were confirmed.

Indeed, none of the existent studies analysed the importance of the relationship of social values and youth's delinquent behaviour in Russia. The presented study fills this academic void.

3. Present study: excursus about change of social values

The social situation in Russia from the end of 1980s into the end of 1990s was a field for a "natural experiment of the collapse of the Soviet Union" (Pridemore & Kim, 2006, p. 82). Many researchers analysed the change of values from Soviet ideology to market economy (Coulloudon, 2000; Gerber, 2002; Petukhov & Federov, 2006). Social values were also transformed in this time from traditional to modern. Moreover, old social values and norms did not work any more, and the new ones were still not fully formed. For this reason, all data from this time period are useful to test hypotheses inferred from anomie theories. Some researchers describe this time as a "transitional period" (Pridmore, Chamlin, & Cochran, 2007). Russian sociologists Lapin and Beljaeva (Lapin & Beljaeva, 1994; Lapin, Beljaeva, Naumova, & Zdravomyslov, 1996; Lapin, 1993; 1994; 1996, 2007) analysed social values in the transitional period within three representative surveys in 12 federal states and three crisis areas in 1990, 1994, and 1998. The researchers identified three phases of the social crisis in Russia: 1) destabilisation of the social order (until the middle of the 1990s); 2) acute conflict; and 3) crisis resolution (Lapin & Beljaeva, 1994, p. 75). Certainly, they examined both initial phases only because of time limitations of their project; the last survey took place during the second phase.

We also defined three phases of social development between the end of 1980s and the end of 1990s. The first phase corresponds to the *downstream period*. Feeling of anomie, doubt about the validity of existing values, and norms and general mistrust are typical for this period. The second phase can be described as a *deepness period*. Both the active embodiment of modern values and the return to traditional values gave distinction to this period. The third phase is connected to the *mobilisation period*. A high individualism of human life was typical for this period.

The *downstream period* held up between the beginning and the middle of the 1990s. The planned economy and Soviet ideological system did not work before the collapse. After the collapse, all social systems broke down: neither economic nor political system nor civil institutions were functional. The norms and values lost their importance and the anomie ruled. Some researchers saw a national characteristic of Russian culture as an "openness for changes" (e.g., Oslon, Melikov, Tscheschkov, & Gudimenko, 1994) whose causes are in the "catch-up development" that was determined by economic leeway. This openness for changes is caused by the permanent derecognition of existing reality, and it corresponds with an unsatisfactory feeling.

Traditional values dominated during the first few years after perestroika (Rassadina, 2006, p. 97). They differed little from the values before perestroika: 45% of the population before perestroika (1989), and 54% after perestroika (1994) attached importance to a small but stable income and guaranteed future instead of excessive working for a higher income. An activity of an independent character was not seen as a real opportunity: 9% in 1989 and 6% in 1994 wanted first to get their own business (Levada, 1995). In this time, there was a strong nostalgic feeling about the time before perestroika besides the criticism on national originality. In fact, it was a desire for economic stability and personal security.

The *deepness period* began after the downstream period. It was spurred by the Russian financial crisis on 17 August 1998 when the ruble was devaluated and the national debt defaulted. At the same time, this period indicated a turn in the social crisis. Economically motivated, pragmatic, and individualistic values developed intensively in this period. Most people kept themselves busy with the problem of individual survival. Russian citizens were introduced to the free market and its rules during this time as well.

The *mobilisation period* began at the end of the 1990s. Russian society mobilised power gradually in this period. The modernisation of the socio-cultural field connected to economic processes. Amazingly, the annual subjective assessment of citizens about the efficiency of the economic system correlated with the objective development of the gross domestic product (GDP; e.g., Rose, Mishler, & Munro, 2006, pp. 152, 173). The GDP decreased continuously until 1997, and it increased ever since 1998. Independent of that, respondents assessed the economic development as follows: the situation was constant until 1998; it improved from 1998 to 2005 at least.

Russian society recovered after the default in 1998. People had ever stronger individualistic values besides the distinctive traditional attitudes. This trend was visible as an example in the city of Ulyanovsk and in the Ulyanovsk region in 1999, 2001, and 2003 (Rassadina, 2004). The role of traditional values in the modernisation process was to develop new integration mechanisms. The meaning of old traditional values was changed, but they certainly still exist.

One study analysed the value concept of Rokeach (1973) for a few years (e.g., Lapin, 2007; Lapin & Beljaeva, 1994) and obtained the following results. First, liberal values increased across the population continuously between 1990 and 2002. Second, this increase was not constant. Most respondents preferred terminal traditional values (goals) such as tradition and family, whereas instrumental traditional values (means) such as willingness to make sacrifices and highhandedness were the lowermost and slightly decreased during the work time. Terminal liberal values (goals) such as life and freedom were lower than terminal traditional values in this study. Terminal liberal values increased between 1990 and 1994, decreased over the next four years, and increased again between 1998 and 2002. Instrumental liberal values (means) such as independence and initiative developed in the same way, with the exception that both increased between 1990 and 1994 and that 1998 and 2002 showed a sharper increase.

During this time, the Soviet system had a strong political and governmental power. It controlled all social institutions, including the economy and civil institutions. The connections between social institutions were eliminated after the collapse in the 1990s. Single institutions developed in a so-called free run and the economy grew faster than others. It was a time of a "wild market" that lasted from the beginning to middle of the 1990s. In this time, all social institutions were misbalanced. A trend to an institutional stabilisation was on the horizon only in 1998. Civil institutions such as the educational system and religion recovered and advanced in the meantime. The free market was established. It was controlled by political power and governance for the most part. Additionally, a new formation of the economy and market was developed.

The excursus about the phases of the social crisis in Russia in the 1990s should help to understand the structure of the social values and the research questions of this study.

4. Method: sample and questionnaire

The data for this study were collected by the Criminological Research Institute of Lower Saxony (Germany) in cooperation with the Volgograd State Educational University (Russia). Ninth grade school students were surveyed in the Russian city of Volgograd in April 2000.

The Russian school system is divided into three levels: primary general education (first three or four years), lower secondary education (subsequent five years), and upper secondary education (final two years). After primary school, the system differentiates among three main types of school: "general schools" (including "general schools with intensive learning programs"; for example, languages, sports, or music), which normally offer general education programs; "gymnasiums," which offer humanities knowledge besides the general education programs; and "lyceums," which offer other knowledge areas, in this case, out of natural science and technology besides the general education programs that the gymnasiums also offer (ConsultatPlus, 2012). Both gymnasiums and lyceums are nearly identical in their structure and programs. As such, they were joined in one group for the purposes of this study; this school type is called gymnasium (Siegmunt, 2012, 2013a, 2016a).

The reference period was also 1999. Data were based on a representative class sample of ninth-grade students. The school authority provided the research team a list with all ninth-grade classes in the city. The researchers then randomised the sample and extracted 110 school classes with 2765 school students. The final sample was $n = 1747$. The response rate was 75.7% based on the school enrolment in the participating classes. It was 93.4% based on the number of students present on the day of the questioning (Siegmunt, 2013a, p. 26).

Students were asked via a standardised paper and pencil questionnaire method of data collection. Standardised interviews were also conducted with a maximum duration of 60 minutes per interview that took place during school lessons in classrooms. The interviewers emphasised that participation in this study was by choice and that the data would be used anonymously.

The age of the participants ranged from 13 to 16 years; the average age was 14.6 years ($SD = 0.53$); 45.3% of the students were male. The majority of students (67%) attended general secondary schools (Table 1).

Table 1. Descriptive statistics ($n = 1747$).

Variables	M (SD)	%	n
age (min = 13, max = 16)	14.56 (.53)		1745
gender (0 = female, 1 = male)	.45 (.50)		1746
type of school (0 = gymnasium; 1 = non gymnasium)	.67 (.47)		1747
Socio-economic status (SES) (min = 27.67, max = 69.84)	47.10 (15.30)		1711
Socio-economic status (SES)			1711
1 = low		33.6	575
2 = middle		32.1	550
3 = high		34.3	586
attitudes towards the society			1495
1 = indifferent		65.8	984
2 = competitor-centred		17.6	263
3 = traditional		16.6	248
robbery, 12-month prevalence (min = 0, max = 1)	.04 (.19)		1546
extortion, 12-month prevalence (min = 0, max = 1)	.02 (.14)		1552
threat with weapon, 12-month prevalence (min = 0, max = 1)	.02 (.15)		1551
assault, 12-month prevalence (min = 0, max = 1)	.09 (.29)		1547
robbery, incidence (min = 0, max = 24)	.12 (0.95)		1546
extortion, incidence (min = 0, max = 16)	.06 (.61)		1552
threat with weapon, incidence (min = 0, max = 17)	.06 (.60)		1550
assault, incidence (min = 0, max = 31)	0.29 (1.57)		1544
instrumental violence, incidence (min = 0, max = 100)	46.45 (20.40)		1744
non-instrumental violence, incidence (min = 0, max = 100)	11.99 (18.05)		1736

5. Measures

5.1. *Dependent variables*

Delinquency was measured by four self-reported actions: assault,[2] threat with weapon,[3] robbery,[4] and extortion.[5] They were measured as 12-month prevalence and incidence. These four crimes are used singly or grouped in this study. Two kinds of violent delinquency were defined here: *instrumental violence* and *non-instrumental violence*. Similar definitions were used already in other studies.

Feshbach (1964) analyses violent behaviour and defined two kinds of aggression as the basic component of violent behaviour: hostile (or expressive) and instrumental aggression. The difference between the both kinds lies in the behavioural goals: instrumental aggression "is directed towards the achievement of nonaggressive goals" and hostile (expressive) aggression pursues the goal to cause "injury to some object" (Feshbach, 1964, p. 258).

The definition of "instrumental violence" is used in a large scope of empirical studies as the opposite of "expressive violence", to investigate the aggressive behaviour of homicide perpetrators (e.g., Salfati, 2000; Salfati & Canter, 1999; Salfati & Dupont, 2006; Salfati & Haratsis, 2001; Santtila, Canter, Elfgren, & Häkkänen, 2001; Thijssen & Ruiter, 2011). Salfati and Canter (1999) analysed the role of aggression in the offense and described the difference between both dimensions as follows: "these distinctions would be clearest for those crime scene indicators that reflect the instrument (cognitive) actions that shape the offense rather than the more expressive (impulsive and emotional) components." There are also differences between cognitive and emotional actions.

For theoretical reasons (Siegmunt, 2013a), the crimes were also grouped in this study as *instrumental violence* (e.g., robbery and extortion) and *non-instrumental violence* (e.g., assault and threat with weapon). In the case of robbery and extortion, violence was used as an instrument to appropriate foreign property. As a result, these crimes were named instrumental. In the case of assault and threat with weapon, violence was used just for fun. The purpose was to get satisfaction through the use of force. For this reason, assault and threat with weapon built a group of non-instrumental violence.

The results of the previous studies cannot be compared with the results of our study because of methodological differences. The homicide-studies used prison archives and analysed the co-occurrence of different variables with the statistical procedure Smallest Space Analysis (SSA) or with Proxscale (a non-metric multidimensional scaling analysis). Adult offenders and victims were surveyed only.

In the present study, the prevalence variables ranged from 0 to 1. The values for the incidences were controlled for outliers by a negative binomial regression. Robbery and extortion had no outliers. Assault had three outliers whose values were greater than 31. These three cases (0.11% of the valid cases) were deleted from the sample. Threat with weapon had one outlier whose value was greater than 17. This case (0.06% of the valid cases) was deleted from the sample. Instrumental and non-instrumental violence had incidence scores and were recoded into the scale from 0 to 100.

5.2. *Independent variables*

5.2.1. *Age and gender*

Age and gender are traditional predictors in the youth studies. In this study, age is a continuous variable with values between 13 and 16. Gender is a dichotomous variable with two values: 0 = female and 1 = male.

5.2.2. *School type*

The Russian secondary school system has three main school classifications: "general schools," "gymnasiums," and "lyceums." The last types of school, gymnasiums and lyceums, are nearly identical in their structure and programs and were joined in one group–named "gymnasium" for the purpose of this study. For this reason, two different *types of school* were analysed in this study. This was also a dichotomous variable with the following values: 0 = gymnasium and 1 = non-gymnasium (general secondary schools). Such dichotomy was very important for a comparison of Russian youth with German youth within our previous studies (e.g., Siegmunt, 2013a, 2013b, 2013c, 2016b). Because of successful prior usage, we retain this classification for the current study.

5.2.3. *Socio-Economic Status*

Some studies showed that *socio-economic status* (SES) had a strong relationship to social values of young people (e.g., Russian Independent Institute for Social and Public Problems, 1998). We used SES as predictor for juvenile delinquency in previous studies (e.g., Siegmunt, 2012, 2013a; Wetzels, Enzmann, Mecklenburg, & Pfeiffer, 2001). For this reason, the SES of the students' families was used in this study. The measure of the family's SES was conducted by asking the students about their parents' (separate for the mother and father) school education, professional education, occupational status, and current or most recent job. This information was classified according to the ISCO88 (International Standard Classification of Occupations). Empirical values,[6] those available for every ISCO occupational class, were appropriated to the parents as a measure of SES (Ganzeboom, De Graaf, & Treiman, 1992; Wolf, 1995). The quasi-continuous values were obtained for the SES, theoretically ranging from 16 to 90. Finally, the distribution of SES values was parted in three groups by quartiles. Group 1 means low SES, 2 means middle SES, and 3 means high SES.

5.2.4. *Attitudes towards society*

The present study occurs during the transition period from socialistic to modern individualistic society. This processes caused a weakening of collectivistic values and a strengthening of individualistic values. Many theoretical concepts exist to examine social values (Siegmunt, accepted): for example, the concept of value's system by Milton Rokeach (Rokeach, 1973), the concept of the change of values by Roland Ingelhart (Ingelhart, 1979), the concept of individualism-collectivism-syndrome by Harry Triandis (Triandis, 1995), the concept of basic human values by Shalom Schwartz (Schwartz, 1992; Schwartz & Bilsky, 1987), and the concept of the synthesis of the values by Helmut Klages (Klages, 1985).

Unfortunately, neither of these concepts can be used for our study because of special features of the Russian society at the end of the 1990s. For this reason, we developed a scale with 14 questions to examine juvenile's attitudes and asked whether the respondents recognise future perspectives, are competitive oriented, or prefer earlier communistic system.

The questionnaire also includes 14 ordinal scaled items to measure the *attitudes towards society*. The response scale has four values and ranges from "absolutely wrong" to "absolutely correct." A principal component factor analysis was conducted with these items. As a result of this analysis, three factors were extracted. They were labelled egoism and orientation to competition, future prospects, and pro-communistic attitudes (cf. Table 2).

In addition, a latent class model was conducted with the 14 items about attitudes (Enzmann & Siegmunt, 2005; Vermunt & Magidson, 2000). As a result, three groups – so called "latent groups" or "latent classes" – were founded.[7] As mentioned, based on the profiles, we named them "indifferent," "competitor-centred," and "traditional" youth (Figure 1).

The first latent group also includes "indifferent" youth. They are critical of modern values and favour traditional values such as solidarity and helpfulness. Simultaneously, they see a little bit of perspective for the future and do not miss the communist system. The second latent group includes "competitor-centred" youth. They prefer modern values more than traditional values such as solidarity and helpfulness. They see a clear perspective for the future and refuse the communistic idea. The third latent group includes youth with "traditional" attitudes. They do not see perspective for the future and adhere to the communistic system and communistic ideology. All following analysis will be realised by the use of these three latent groups.

Table 2. Factor loadings and item-total correlations of attitudes toward Russian society.

	F1 (FL) egoism & competition orientated	F2 (FL) future prospects	F3 (FL) pro communistic attitudes	r_{it}
03 Today it is true: the strong people win, the weak people lose	.67	.06	.05	.44
02 Today an unhuman fight dominates: all toward all	.62	−.12	.14	.32
07 Today week people will be considerate too less	.61	.01	−.09	.38
04 Our politician are only egoists, they think of himself and not of the country's well	.60	−.14	.10	.28
14 There are too little solidarity and helpfulness today	.57	−.16	−.24	.31
08 The clever one can get quickly rich in Russia today	.55	.32	.03	.45
09 A few people enrich himself at the expense of the majority of the population in the new Russia	.50	.13	−.03	.33
12 Values like solidarity and helpfulness are out of date, you've got to be clever and heedless today	.43	.03	.01	.26
06 The youth have good future prospects in the modern Russia	−.15	.73	.02	.13
05 You've get success in the new Russia when you've make enough effort	.08	.71	.06	.26
01 The new society offer plenty of chances	.04	.61	−.06	.21
11 It is good, that the best and the strongest assert oneself today	.02	.54	−.08	.20
13 The communistic system kept people down (*recoded*)	−.09	−.07	.82	.10
10 The communism is a good political and social idea	.12	−.00	.81	.08

Notes: FL: factor loadings; rit: item-total correlations; n = 1,495; principal component analysis; factor's correlation: r (F1, F2) = .08, r (F1, F3) = −.02, r (F2, F3) = −.16.

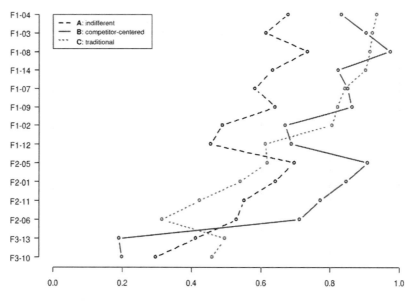

Figure 1. Profiles of attitudes against Russian society in the latent groups (means of the items) (source for the figure: Siegmunt, 2006).

6. Results

6.1. *Descriptive statistics and correlations*

The theoretical values of the SES range between 16 and 90. In our case, the smallest value was 27.67 and the highest value 69.84. The average of the SES is 47.1 (SD = .47); 33.6% of the juveniles' families have a low SES, 32.1% have middle SES, and 34.3% have high SES. The juveniles were also

Table 3. Correlations.

		1	2	3	4	5	6	7
1	Age	1.00						
2	Gender	.03	1.00					
3	type of school	−.03	.03	1.00				
4	SES (continuous)	−.03	.06*	−.14***	1.00			
5	SES (3 groups)	−.03	.05	−.12***	.95***	1.00		
6	attitudes towards the society	.03	−.01	.02	−.06*	−.06*	1.00	
7	instrumental violence (incidence)	.05	.19***	−.00	.03	.02	.06*	1.00
8	non-instrumental violence (incidence)	.02	.14***	.01	.01	−.00	.02	.34***

Level of significance: *: $p < .05$, ***: $p < .001$; numbers in the heading: 1 (age), 2 (gender), 3 (type of school), 4 (SES (continuous)), 5 (SES (3 groups)), 6 (attitudes towards the society), 7 (instrumental violence (incidence))

clustered into three groups: the first latent group (group A) includes "indifferent" youth; the second latent group (group B) includes "competitor-centred" youth; and the third latent group (group C) includes youth with "traditional" attitudes. Group A was the largest group ($n = 984$) and represented 65.8% of the sample. Group B was smaller ($n = 263$) and comprised only 17.6%. Group C was the smallest ($n = 248$), and it represented 16.6% of the sample.

The prevalence rates were different for measured offenses. The prevalence rates reported were as follows: one in 11 school students (9.31%) committed assault without weapon and one in 25 committed robbery (3.95%); one in 15 threatened someone with weapon (2.26%) or extorted someone (2.13%). The trend for the incidence rates was the same: the most frequent offense was assault without weapon followed by robbery; threat with weapon and extortion were seldom committed. The juveniles committed assault without weapon up to 31 times in the last 12 months. There were 24 robberies, 17 threats with weapon, and 16 extortions. Finally, instrumental and non-instrumental violence ranged between 0 and 100 crimes in the last 12 months.

The bivariate relationships all variables are analysed. Therefore, the correlations of these variables were expected (Table 3). Only the variable "gender" correlates with both kinds of violence – instrumental and non-instrumental violence: male students committed more violence than female. The correlation between attitudes towards the society and instrumental violence is too small, and the level of significance is too low. Therefore, this correlation may not be over-interpreted.

6.2. *Bivariate analyses: meaning of the attitudes towards the society*

The *first assumption* of this study is that attitudes towards society are heterogeneous. This study did not find differences in attitudes between the age groups[8] and types of school.[9] At the same time, the attitudes did differ by gender.[10] About 55.5% female of the sample was female. Significantly, more females than males belong to the group of indifferent youth: 56.9% females and 43.1% males. Females comprise still a larger part in the group of youth with traditional attitudes: 62.5% females and 37.5% males. Instead, males are more competitor-centred: 56.3% of males and 43.7% of females.

The SES[11] differs in general between youth with diverse attitudes. There were $n = 498$ juveniles with low SES, $n = 481$ with middle SES, and $n = 507$ with high SES. The differences between the "indifferent" youth were small: 31.3% with low SES, 35% with middle SES, and 33.7% with high SES. Most competitor-centred juveniles came from families with high SES (42.1%), the next largest group are juveniles with low SES (34.9%), and the smallest group were juveniles with middle SES (23.0%). One observed trend in the group of youth with traditional attitudes: the higher the SES, the smaller the number of juveniles. There were 40.7% with low SES, 31.9% with middle SES, and 27.4% with high SES.

Competitor-centred juveniles had the highest mean of SES (mean = 51.10). This was significantly higher than the SES of youth with traditional attitudes (mean = 47.75).[12] Indeed, it did not differ from the SES of "indifferent" youth (mean = 50.15).[13] The SES of the "indifferent" youth is higher than the SES of the juveniles with traditional attitudes.[14]

6.3. *Bivariate and multivariate analyses: attitudes towards the society and delinquency*

The *second assumption* of this study is also that the kind of attitudes towards society predicts juvenile's delinquent behaviour. This research question was tested in two steps. First, the percentage of instrumental and non-instrumental violent delinquency was estimated for every type of attitude towards society. Second, the effects of the different types of attitudes towards society were tested in two multivariate models for instrumental and non-instrumental violence.

First step: The indifferent youth (group A) also comprised the largest. They represented 65.8% of the sample and committed 49.8% of instrumental violent crimes. The competition-centred youth from group B (17.6% of the sample) committed 35% of instrumental violent crimes. Youth with traditional attitudes from group C (16.6%) committed 15.2% of instrumental violent crimes (cf. Figure 2, left). The incidence rate for instrumental violent crimes was four times higher in group B than in group A and two times higher in group C than in group A.[15]

The difference was smaller for non-instrumental violence. Indifferent juveniles committed 38.4% of non-instrumental violent offenses, competitor-centred youth 34.6%, and the youth with traditional attitudes 27% (cf. Figure 2, right). The incidence rate was about three times higher in group B than in group A and two times higher in group C than in group A.[16] The results of the descriptive analysis confirmed our assumptions. Juveniles with different attitudes committed different types of violent offenses.

Second step: The effects of the latent groups on instrumental and non-instrumental violence were tested after controlling for age, gender, type of school, and SES. Five multivariate models were expected for instrumental (Table 4) and non-instrumental (Table 5) violence, respectively. The same research question was tested here: whether the competitor-centred juveniles commit more violent crime and especially more instrumental crime than other juveniles.

Both dependent variables included the incidence data. For this reason, the negative binomial regressions were calculated. The independent variables are age, gender, type of school, SES, and the latent classes. Age, gender, type of school, and SES were used in these models because there are the traditional predictors for youth violent delinquency. The methodological question is whether the latent classes effect violence, and if these effects persist after statistical control of other variables. In the first model, the effects of the latent classes only were tested. In the next models, the effects of the latent classes after statistical control of age (model 2), gender (model 3), type of school (model 4), and SES (model 5) were tested.

In both first models, the competitor-centred youth (group B) committed more instrumental and non-instrumental offenses as indifferent youth (group A). Juveniles with traditional attitudes (group C) did not differ from the both other groups. The statistical control of age, type of school, and SES did change the effects of the latent classes. Only gender affects the relationship of societal attitudes and violence (models 3). The results are as follows: (1) males commit more instrumental

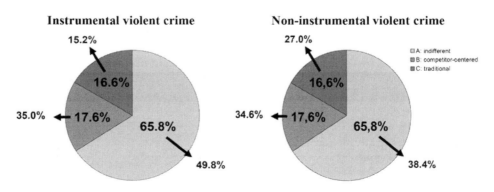

Figure 2. Instrumental and non-instrumental violent crime by different latent groups.

Table 4. Negative binomial regressions of instrumental violence.

	model 1			model 2			model 3			model 4			model 5		
	B	Exp(B)	p	B	Exp(B)	p	B	Exp(B)	p	B	Exp(B)	p	B	Exp(B)	p
Age				.25	1.29	.27									
gender							1.13	3.08	**<.001**						
(0 = female)															
type of school										.00	1.00	.987			
(0 = gymnasium)															
SES													.00	1.00	.899
latent classes															
(0 = A)															
(1 = B)	.56	1.75	**.050**	.55	1.74	**.053**	.41	1.51	.152	.56	1.75	**.050**	.56	1.75	**.050**
(2 = C)	.08	1.09	.818	.08	1.08	.831	.16	1.18	.645	.08	1.09	.818	.08	1.09	.818
intercept	−3.16		**<.001**	−6.83		**.042**	−3.78		**<.001**	−3.17		**<.001**	−3.23		**<.001**

n = 1360; bold: significant.

Table 5. Negative binomial regressions of non-instrumental violence.

	model 1			model 2			model 3			model 4			model 5		
	B	Exp(B)	p	B	Exp(B)	p	B	Exp(B)	p	B	Exp(B)	p	B	Exp(B)	p
Age				.27	1.31	.099									
gender (0 = female)							1.26	3.51	**<.001**						
type of school (0 = gymnasium)										−.06	1.06^{-1}	.735			
SES													.00	1.00	.596
latent classes (0 = A)															
(1 = B)	.57	1.77	**.006**	.57	1.76	**.007**	.41	1.51	**.050**	.58	1.78	**.006**	.54	1.72	**.010**
(2 = C)	.33	1.39	.164	.32	1.38	.173	.42	1.52	**.078**	.33	1.39	.163	.34	1.40	.157
intercept	−2.54		**<.001**	−6.49		**.007**	−3.42		**<.001**	−2.50		**<.001**	−2.73		**<.001**

n = 1362; bold: significant; ODDS-Ratios <1 = 1/Exp(B).

and non-instrumental violence than females. (2) After statistical control of gender, there are no differences between latent classes in respect of instrumental violence. (3) After statistical control of gender, the competitor-centred youth (group B) still committed more non-instrumental offenses as indifferent youth (group A). In this case, the traditional youths (group C) commit more violence as indifferent youth (group A), but this result cannot be overestimated because of a low significance level ($p = .078$). (4) The competitor-centred youth (group B) did not differ from the juveniles with traditional attitudes (group C).

The results of the multivariate models show that individual attitudes are an important predictor in explaining the level and structure of juveniles' delinquent behaviour. Gender is likewise a strong predictor, but not age, type of school, and SES.

7. Conclusions

This study helps to understand how youths' attitudes towards society predict their delinquency. The main research question of this study was generally confirmed. Juveniles with strong individualistic attitudes commit more violent crime and especially more instrumental crime than other juveniles. Individualistic attitudes were measured here by perception of a clear perspective for the future and refusing of solidarity and helpfulness.

The data of this study were collected in 2000 with a reference period of the year 1999. Unfortunately, the importance of social attitudes was not sufficiently analysed and described until now. These data are unique because it reflects human attitudes and human behaviour in a specific social context. A brief description of the development of Russian society will help to understand this specific social context. The country changed its political system in 1991 from a socialistic to a capitalistic structure. Because of this, the rights and duties of its citizens changed. Society obtained a multi-party system instead of a one-party system, and citizens received ownership of real estate. At the same time, most national industry crashed and many people lost their jobs. Some of them became self-employed and acted in the commerce branch.

After this transition, traditional values and norms of Soviet Russia did not work any more. Many families were broken because of financial problems and in general, the traditional image of the family and relationships between generations changed. A need for authority – the explicit hierarchy – was typical for the former Soviet Russia. This hierarchy was a part of socialisation in such a traditional country as USSR. Social values such as solidarity, conservativeness, and self-effacement are highly significant and transferred on every socialisation level.

The integrative power of a modern individualistic society is based on the free market. Personal identity is generated by rational action; it complies with an understanding between private interests and market dynamics in terms of demand and supply. The free market works with rules. Indeed, they are not so stringent as in a traditional society: rational action needs creativity and flexibility. Highly individualised societies have less traditional family combinations. This is not only due to a weakness of family bonding; it is also primarily a function of the changes of family structure. Decisions such as time for family planning or number of children depend strongly on personal working conditions and perspectives in a society with free market and strong competition.

The dependence on religion weakens in individualistic societies, too; people do not need religious or ideological orientations in its entirety. The modern societies are based on autonomy of individuals. This is a cause of disagreement as well in political matters. As a result, it is natural to expect an efficient multiparty system.

All developed industrialised societies involve both traditional pre-industrial and modern post-industrial values. Traditional values are often based on cultural conventions. The contemporary processes of Russian society comply with a stabilisation of religion and support of the relationship between the church and the state. It is rather an attempt to give people the possibility to fill the emptiness in the traditional values that arise in the 1990s.

A weakened sense of responsibility and double moral standards developed during the Soviet period outside of traditional attitudes. People did not learn to assume responsibility because they had no ownership and government property belonged to everyone, because the results of the production were held off of employers, and because they were held off of political decisions. The main target of the Soviet system was to transfer traditional collectivistic values by means of ideology. Modern values were increasingly appreciated after the collapse and changes in the economic and social systems.

Attitudes towards society were heterogeneous. Some people adapted fast to new social conditions. Some missed the old system and did not succeed in changing with the new system. Some did not have a plain view; they were neither for the old system nor for the new lifestyle, and they saw new processes with indifference. These processes regarded young people, too, because they know the old system and grew up in the new society.

The findings of this study can be important for crime prevention because they allow the use of specific prevention measures for different target groups. An efficient prevention measure could be a training program with a goal of transferring different values, such as readiness to help others or solidarity without ideological perspective. This study cannot show whether its results are replicable. For this purpose, additional studies are necessary.

The present study has some limitations. One limitation of the findings of this study is that only juveniles in Russia were asked about attitudes towards society. This lends to future research in Russia that can use the same scales and questions. But, these questions are very specific for Russia and cannot be used in other countries. Another limitation is that the theoretical framework was used only *post hoc* here. One suggestion for future research can be described as follow: (1) the universal questions about attitudes towards society must be developed. It is necessary for international studies. (2) The theoretical framework must be developed at the beginning of the studies. It can make possible the testing of theoretical assumptions. The benefit of this data, however, is that it was collected according to the most effective methodological requirements. Moreover, the same scales can be used in following studies and they allow the comparison of time.

Youths with individualistic values were among the "competitor-centred" group. This group is small with only 17.6% of the sample. There are significantly more males than females who prefer values such as cleverness and seeing good future prospects in the country. The juveniles of this group are from families of high or low SES. The SES in the group of competitor-centred juveniles is higher than in the other two groups. This small group of youth commits proportionally more violent offenses than the others. The percentage of instrumental violence is just the same as of non-instrumental violence. Looking at the results of the negative binomial regressions, the juveniles of this group commit significantly more violence than indifferent youth. However, this effect disappeared after statistical control of gender (only for instrumental violence).

The group of youth with "traditional" attitudes is the smallest one, making up 16.6% of the sample. More females than males share traditional attitudes towards society. The SES of the family has a definite trend: the higher the SES, the smaller the number of juveniles. This means that students with traditional attitudes are typically from socially disadvantaged families. These juveniles commit proportionally fewer violent offenses than the others. When these juveniles commit violent crimes, there are more non-instrumental offenses such as assault without weapon and threat with weapon. There are instead actions that are typical for this age. Looking at the results of negative binomial regressions here, juveniles with traditional attitudes did not commit more or less violence than other. There are no differences with other groups as well after statistical control of other variables.

The group of "indifferent" juveniles was the largest one in this sample. This shows that a large portion of juveniles existed between the old and the new world in this time, also between tradition and modernity. There are more females than males who cannot decide about their own views of society. These students are from families with different SES, though their SES is in general relatively high. This group has the smallest crime rates in the sample. The indifferent juveniles commit less violence as competitor-centred juveniles, when tested in a negative binomial regression. They also commit less non-instrumental violence as competitor-centred youth after statistical control of gender. However, the effect of instrumental violence disappeared after statistical control of gender, and they are delinquent just as other juveniles.

These data were collected in the period of modernisation of Russian society. The economy grew in this period, and it contained the pursuit of profit by any means. Students with high individualistic values such as cleverness and competitiveness committed more instrumental crimes than the other youth. Robbery and extortion were also more typically associated with this period than assault.

8. Outlook: criminological theories

Further studies showed that Russian youth (1) have strong attitudes towards instrumental violence and (2) their attitudes towards instrumental violence are stronger than attitudes towards non-instrumental violence (Siegmunt, 2013a). These results can be explained by the destruction of Soviet society following the socio-economic crisis. More than 100 years ago, Durkheim emphasised the importance of the "moral order" for the understanding of the deviant behaviour. He wrote about how rapid social changes and industrial society lead to anomie and change social norms. In the anomic situation, the new social norms cannot control goals and means anymore, and at the same time, they cannot control human moral behaviour.

This study identified three phases of social development between the end of 1980s and the end of 1990s: the *downstream period* (from the beginning into the middle of the 1990s), the *deepness period* (around 1998), and the *mobilisation period* (from the end of the 1990s). The development of social values and the relationship between values and delinquent behaviour can be explained for all three phases by different theoretical approaches which focused the explanation power on the anomic situation of the society. Some theoretical considerations will describe the possibilities for the future research.

The social processes during the *downstream period* can be explained by Emile Durkheim's (1992) anomie theory. The definition of anomy was first used by Durkheim at the end of nineteenth century to describe the consequences of the division of labour or rather of the social disintegration. The situation in Russia in the last years of the Soviet time was not exactly the same like in pre-industrial France at Durkheim's time. However, there are some analogies. For instance, there are horizontal social structures or weak differentiation between single members of the society. Such equality led to the relative independence of the society members from each other. The solidarity resulted mechanically in such societies through general moral attitudes. This is called *mechanical solidarity*. High division of labour and versatile dependence of the society members from each other led to the so-called *organic solidarity*. The anomic situation occurred in the case of a lack of organic solidarity: there were no longer any collective obligations, norms, and values to hold together the members of society.

High crime rates can be expected in a situation where there is a lack of organic solidarity. Moreover, high rates of economically motivated crime are supposable in the situation of the inefficacy of social norms and values. The anomy theory by Emile Durkheim does not differ between types of values. For this reason, we cannot assume a different frequency of delinquent behaviour in dependence to different attitudes. The knowledge about the first few years after social collapse and the theoretical background can help to interpret the results and to understand why the level of delinquency is high.

The processes of adaptation during the *deepness period* can be best explained by Robert Merton's (1938) anomy theory. The mechanism of this theory is that people choose institutionalisation to reach cultural goals. There are four main modes of adaptation: conformity (accepting both the societal goals and the legitimised means), innovation (accepting goals and rejecting means), ritualism (rejecting goals and accepting means), and retreatism (reject both the societal goals and the legitimised means).

Obviously, *innovation* as a mode of adaptation was most frequent in this time. These people originate from the social underclass (Merton, 1968, p. 205). The difference between poor and rich populations was increasingly bigger after the collapse. There was no middle class, and the majority of the people found themselves in an impoverished situation. Social pressure was high to reach cultural values such as economic success and affluence. Simultaneously, many people had no legitimate means for it. For this reason, people used often effective, but not legitimate means of reaching cultural values.

The middle class was established in this time. Certainly, the affiliation to the middle class involved not only the economic situation of the person but also the acceptance of relevant social values. There were few *ritualists*. They had low aspiration level and high moral standards. The *retreatists* built a larger mode of adaptation. There were people who retired from society altogether: they rejected cultural values as well as institutional means. According to Merton (1968, p. 207), "not sharing the common frame of values, they can be included as members of the society (in distinction from the population) only in a factional sense".

The innovators also pursued personal economical success. In this context, they are individualistic oriented. Because of their rejection of legitimate means, they were ready to commit economically motivated crimes.

The institutional anomie theory Messner and Rosenfeld (1994, 2001) is a modern anomy theory that was built on Durkheim's anomie theory and explains how the imbalance of the important social institutions affects crime (Siegmunt & Enzmann, 2006; Siegmunt & Wetzels, 2015). It is a good theoretical basis to explain the crime structure during the *mobilisation period*. The main idea of this theory is that different kinds of crime are dependent on different kinds of institutional misbalance. For example, the dominance of economy contains the pursuit of profit by any means. Individualistic values such as competitiveness are typical for this situation. This leads to a high level of crime with high instrumental motivation (e.g., property crime). The dominance of a political system produces distrust in political institutions, cynical attitudes towards personal responsibility, and accountability. It leads to corruption, black economy, and tax fraud. The dominance of civil institutions such as family, educational system, or religion contains hypermoralism. It leads to hate crimes, vigilantism, and violations of human rights (disproportionate victimisation of women). Thereby, the individual behaviour does not have to be influenced through the processes of the imbalance directly. It works indirectly through individual values and norms.

Because of the dominance of economy in Russia in the end of 1990s – 2000s, the high rate of economically motivated crime is expected. Unfortunately, it cannot be tested in this study. However, we can derive an assumption from the institutional anomy theory by Messner and Rosenfeld.

A great many of empirical studies have tested the theoretical assumptions of the Durkheim's anomy theory (Pridemore & Kim, 2006; Pridmore et al., 2007), the institutional anomy theory by Messner and Rosenfeld (Enzmann, Kammigan, Siegmunt, & Wetzels, 2016; Kim & Pridemore, 2005), and the general strain theory (Botchkovar & Broidy, 2013) in Russia.

Notes

1. The results of the first wave were published in Independent Russian Institute for Social and National Problems (1998); the results of the second wave were published in Institute of Sociology of the Russian Academy of Sciences (2007). The first group consisted of juveniles and young adults 17 to 26 years old (1997: $n = 1974$ and 2007: $n = 1796$), and the second group included adults 40 to 60 years old (1997: $n = 774$ and 2007: $n = 655$).
2. Did you already beat and hurt someone?
3. Did you already threaten another person with a weapon?
4. Did you already alone or with other people take something from someone mightily?
5. Did you already alone or with other people extort someone and thereby this person paid so not to be battered?

CRIMINOLOGY AND CRIMINAL JUSTICE IN RUSSIA

6. International Socio-Economic Index of Occupational Status (ISEI).
7. $L^2 = 24422.4$, $df = 26.8 \times 10^6$, bootstrap $p = .428$, entropie $R^2 = .745$, error of classification $= .090$.
8. $\chi^2 = 4.40$; $df = 6$; $p = .623$.
9. $\chi^2 = 1.35$; $df = 2$; $p = .509$.
10. $\chi^2 = 20.42$; $df = 2$; $p < .001$.
11. $\chi^2 = 22.86$; $df = 4$; $p < .001$.
12. $F = 16.213$; $df = 507$; $p = .003$.
13. $F = 18.793$; $df = 1236$; $p = .246$.
14. $F = 0.461$; $df = 1223$; $p = .005$.
15. $\chi^2(2) = 10.9$; $p = .004$.
16. $\chi^2(2) = 12.1$; $p = .002$.

References

Botchkovar, E., & Broidy, L. (2013). Accumulated strain, negative emotions, and crime a test of general strain theory in Russia. *Crime & Delinquency*, *59*(6), 837–860. doi:10.1177/0011128710382346

Cernkovich, S. A. (1978). Value orientations and delinquency involvement. *Criminology*, *15*(4), 443–458. doi:10.1111/crim.1978.15.issue-4

ConsultatPlus. (2012). Federal law about education system in Russian Federation Nr. 273-ФЗ from 29th of December 2012. Retrieved from http://www.consultant.ru/document/cons_doc_LAW_140174/.

Coulloudon, V. (2000). The divided Russian elite: How Russia's transition produced a counter-elite. In V. Sperling (Hrsg.), *Building the Russian state: Institutional crisis and the quest for democratic governance* (pp. S. 67-87). Boulder, Col. [u.a.]: Westview Press.

Durkheim, E. (1992). *Über soziale Arbeitsteilung: Studie über die Organisation höherer Gesellschaften*. Frankfurt am Mein: Surkamp.

Enzmann, D., Kammigan, I., Siegmunt, O., & Wetzels, P. (2016). *Was scheren mich die anderen? Marktmoral als kriminogener Faktor: Eine Studie zu Jugendkriminalität in Russland und Deutschland*. Wissenschaftlicher Verlag Berlin: Berlin.

Enzmann, D., & Siegmunt, O. (2005). Analyse der Jugendkriminalität in Russland und Deutschland: Ergebnisse einer Schülerbefragung in Wolgograd und Deutschland. *Standpunkt: Sozial*, *3*, 20–25.

Feshbach, S. (1964). The function of aggression and the regulation of aggressive drive. *Psychological Review*, *71*(4), 257–272. doi:10.1037/h0043041

Ganzeboom, H. B. G., De Graaf, P. M., & Treiman, D. J. (1992). A standard international socio-economic index of occupational status. *Social Science Research*, *21*, 1–56. doi:10.1016/0049-089X(92)90017-B

Gerber, T. P. (2002). Structural change and post-socialist stratification: Labor market transitions in contemporary Russia. *American Sociological Review*, *67*, 629–659. doi:10.2307/3088910

Horsley, M. (2010). Capitalism and crime: The criminogenic potential of the free market. *Internet Journal of Criminology*. http://www.internetjournalofcriminology.com/horsley_capitalism_and_crime_oct_2010.pdf

Independent Russian Institute for Social and National Problems. (1998). *Jugend des neuen Russland: Wie ist sie? Womit lebt sie? Wonach strebt sie? [Molodez novoy Rossii: Kakaja ona? Zem zivet? K zemu stremitsja?]*. Moskau: Russisches unabhängiges Institut für soziale und nationale Probleme.

Inglehart, R. (1979). Wertwandel in den westlichen Gesellschaften: Politische Konsequenzen von materialistischen und postmaterialistischen Prioritäten, S. 279-316. In H. Klages & P. Kmieciak (Hrsg.), *Wertewandel und gesellschaftlicher Wandel*. Frankfurt a. Main, New York, NY: Campus-Verlag.

Institute of Sociology of the Russian Academy of Sciences. (2007). *Jugend des neuen Russland: Lebensweise und Prioritäten von Werten [Molodez novoy Rossii: Obraz zizni i zennostnye prioritety]*. Moskau: Institut der Soziologie der RWA.

Kim, S. W., & Pridemore, W. A. (2005). Poverty, socioeconomic change, institutional anomie, and homicide. *Social Science Quarterly*, *86*(s1), 1377–1398. doi:10.1111/j.0038-4941.2005.00351.x

CRIMINOLOGY AND CRIMINAL JUSTICE IN RUSSIA

Klages, H. (1985). *Wertorientierungen im Wandel: Rückblick, Gegenwartsanalyse, Prognosen*. Frankfurt [u.a.]: Campus.

Komiya, N. (1999). A cultural study of the low crime rate in Japan. *British Journal of Criminology, 39*(3), 369–390. doi:10.1093/bjc/39.3.369

Lapin, N. I. (1993). Social values and reformations in the modern Russia [Sozial'nye zennosti i reformy v krisisnoy Rossii]. *Sotsiologicheskie Issledovaniia, 19*(9), 17–28.

Lapin, N. I. (1994). Values as a component of a social and cultural evolution in the modern Russia [Zennosti kak komponenty soziokulturnoy evoljuzii covremennoy Rossii]. *Sotsiologicheskie Issledovaniia, 20*(5), 3–8.

Lapin, N. I. (1996). Modernisation of the basic values of Russians [Modernizazija bazovyh zennostey rossijan]. *Sotsiologicheskie Issledovaniia, 22*(5), 3–23.

Lapin, N. I. (2007). Integrative function of the intelligentsia [Sozietalno-zennostnye funkzii intelligenzii]. *Knowledge.Understanding.Ability, 4*(1), 38–43.

Lapin, N. I., & Beljaeva, L. A. (1994). *Crisis society. Our society in three dimensions [Krizisnyi sozium. Nasche obzestvo v treh ismerenijah]*. Moscow: Russian Academy of Sciences.

Lapin, N. I., Beljaeva, L. A., Naumova, N. F., & Zdravomyslov, A. G. (1996). *The dynamic of the human values in the reformed Russia [Dinamika tsennostey naseleniya reformiruemoy Rossii]*. Moscow: Edumorial URSS.

Levada, Y. (1995). *"The Soviet person" five years later: 1989–1994 (Preliminary results of a comparative study).* ["Tschelowek sowjetskiy" pjat' let spustja: 1989–1994 (Predvaritelnye itogi sravnitelnogo issledovanija)]. Retrieved from www.levada.ru/levadabook/23.doc

Matza, D., & Sykes, G. M. (1961). Juvenile delinquency and subterranean values. *American Sociological Review, 26* (5), 712–719. doi:10.2307/2090200

Merton, R. K. (1938). Social structure and anomie. *American Sociological Review, 3*, 672–682. doi:10.2307/2084686

Merton, R. K. (1968). *Social Theory and Social Structure*. New York, NY: The Free Press.

Messner, S. F., & Rosenfeld, R. (1994). *Crime and the American dream*. Belmont: Wadsworth Publishing Company.

Messner, S. F., & Rosenfeld, R. (2001). An institutional anomie theory of crime. In R. Paternoster & R. Bachman (Eds.), *Explaining criminals and crime* (pp. 151–160). Los Angeles, CA: Roxbury.

Oslon, A. A., Melikov, V. V., Tscheschkov, M. A., & Gudimenko, D. V. (1994). Change of values of the Russian Society [Zennostnye izmenenija rossiyskogo obzestva]. *Sociological Journal [Soziologizeskiy Zurnal], 3*, 19–26.

Petukhov, V. V., & Federov, V. V. (2006). The transformation of the ideological values and political preferences of Russians. *Sociological Research, 45*(6), 68–92.

Pridemore, W. A., & Kim, S. W. (2006). Democratization and political change as threats to collective sentiments: Testing Durkheim in Russia. *The Annals of the American Academy of Political and Social Science, 605*(1), 82–103. doi:10.1177/0002716206286859

Pridmore, W. A., Chamlin, M. B., & Cochran, J. K. (2007). An interrupted time-series analysis of Durkheim's social deregulation thesis: The case of the Russian Federation. *Justice Quarterly, 24*(2), 271–290. doi:10.1080/07418820701294813

Rainwater, L. (1970). The problem of lower class culture. *Journal of Social Issues, 26*(2), 133–148. doi:10.1111/josi.1970.26.issue-2

Rassadina, T. A. (2004). Moral attitudes of the residentes in the Russian provinces [Nravstvennye orientazii ziteley rossiyskoy provinzii]. *Sotsiologicheskie Issledovaniia, 30*(7).

Rassadina, T. A. (2006). Transformations of the traditional values of the Russians after the perestroika [Transformazii tradizionnyh zennostey rossijan v postperestoeznyi period]. *Sotsiologicheskie Issledovaniia, 32* (9), 95–102.

Rokeach, M. (1973). *The nature of human values*. New York, NY: The Free Press.

Rose, R., Mishler, W., & Munro, N. (2006). *Russia transformed. Developing popular support for a new regime.* Cambridge: University Press.

Russian Independent Institute for Social and Public Problems [Russisches unabhängiges Institut für soziale und nationale Probleme]. (1998). *Jugend des neuen Russland: Wie ist sie? Womit lebt sie? Wonach strebt sie? [Molodez novoy Rossii: Kakaja ona? Zem zivet? K zemu stremitsja?]*. Moskau: Russisches unabhängiges Institut für soziale und nationale Probleme.

Salfati, C. G. (2000). The nature of expressiveness and instrumentally in homicide: Implications for offender profiling. *Homicide Studies, 4*(3), 265–293. doi:10.1177/1088767900004003004

Salfati, C. G., & Canter, D. V. (1999). Differentiating stranger murders: Profi ling offender characteristics from behavioral styles. *Behavioral Sciences and the Law, 17*(3), 391–406. doi:10.1002/(SICI)1099-0798(199907/09)17:3<391::AID-BSL352>3.0.CO;2-Z

Salfati, C. G., & Dupont, F. (2006). Canadian homicide: An investigation of crime-scene actions. *Homicide Studies, 10*(2), 118–139. doi:10.1177/1088767906288449

Salfati, C. G., & Haratsis, E. (2001). Greek homicide: A behavioral examination of offender crime scene actions. *Homicide Studies, 5*(4), 335–362. doi:10.1177/1088767901005004006

Santtila, P., Canter, D., Elfgren, T., & Häkkänen, H. (2001). The structure of crime-scene actions in Finnish homicides. *Homicide Studies, 5*(4), 363–387. doi:10.1177/1088767901005004007

Schwartz, S. H. (1992). Universals in the content and structure of values: Theoretical advances and empirical tests in 20 countries. *Advances in Experimental Social Psychology, 25,* 1–65.

Schwartz, S. H., & Bilsky, W. (1987). Toward an universal psychological structure of human values. *Journal of Personality and Social Psychology, 53*(3), 550–562. doi:10.1037/0022-3514.53.3.550

Siegmunt, O. (2012). *Selbstkontrolle: Einflüsse von Familie, Schule und Nachbarschaften. Eine kontrolltheoretische Studie in drei russischen Großstädten.* Berlin: Wissenschaftlicher Verlag Berlin.

Siegmunt, O. (2013a). *Kriminelle Russen, kriminelle Deutsche: Zur Jugendkriminalität im Hell- und Dunkelfeld.* Berlin: Wissenschaftlicher Verlag Berlin.

Siegmunt, O. (2013b). Offenders and victims of violent crime: Study to unreported crime of juveniles. *Legal Science and Law Enforcement Practice, 23*(1), 106–116.

Siegmunt, O. (2013c). Mit Vorsicht zu genießen! Zur Aussagekraft von Kriminalstatistiken und zum Anzeigeverhalten Jugendlicher in Deutschland und Russland. *Monatsschrift Für Kriminologie Und Strafrechtsreform, 96*(6), 461–476.

Siegmunt, O. (2016a). *Neighborhood disorganization and social control: Case studies from three Russian cities. Springer briefs in criminology.* Springer: Cham [u.a.].

Siegmunt, O. (2016b). Eine Gleichung mit mehreren Unbekannten oder was erklärt die Landesunterschiede in der Jugendgewalt? Eine Analyse mit deutschen und russischen Daten. *Neue Kriminalpolitik, 28*(4), 408–425. doi:10.5771/0934-9200-2016-4-408

Siegmunt, O. (2017). The social values in the sociological and criminological research: The considerations of definition and operationalization. *Juridica International.* Unpublished manuscript.

Siegmunt, O.(2006, August 26-29). Attitudes towards the society, normative orientations and delinquency in Russia and Germany. In *6th annual conference of the European society of criminology.* Tuebingen.

Siegmunt, O., & Enzmann, D. (2006). Differences and features of juvenile delinquency in Russia and Germany: Their importance for the anomy theory. *Criminology: Yesterday, Today, Tomorrow, 6*(1), 97–109.

Siegmunt, O., & Wetzels, P. (2015). Institutional anomie theory—Empirical testing [Instituzionalnajy teorija anomii —Empirizeskaja proverka]. *Sociological Studies, 42*(4), 78–87.

Thijssen, J., & Ruiter, C. D. (2011). Instrumental and expressive violence in belgian homicide perpetrators. *Journal of Investigative Psychology and Offender Profiling, 8*(1), 58–73. doi:10.1002/jip.v8.1

Triandis, H. C. (1995). *Individualism and Collectivism.* Boulder [u.a.]: Westview Press.

Vermunt, J. K., & Magidson, J. (2000). *Latent gold. User's guide.* Belmont, MA: Statistical Innovations.

Wetzels, P., Enzmann, D., Mecklenburg, E., & Pfeiffer, C. (2001). *Jugend und gewalt. Eine repräsentative Dunkelfeldanalyse in München und acht anderen deutschen Städten.* Baden-Baden: Nomos Verlagsgesellschaft.

Wolf, C. (1995). Sozioökonomischer Status und berufliches Prestige. Ein kleines Kompendium sozialwissenschaftlicher Skalen auf der Basis der beruflichen Stellung und Tätigkeit. *ZUMA-Nachrichten, 37,* 102–136.

State and the Multilateralization of Policing in Post-Soviet Russia

Gilles Favarel-Garrigues & Anne Le Huérou

This article deals with the evolution of policing in late- and post-Soviet Russia. It begins by showing that distinct auspices and providers of policing were to be found in the late-Soviet context, even if, from an institutional point of view, they almost always belonged to party-state agencies. Such a context emphasizes a process of informal multilateralization of policing prior to the Soviet break-up. The article then goes on to show what has changed with glasnost *and* perestroika, *exploring new demands for policing, new auspices and new providers. It argues that the market-oriented approach of policing finds blatant limits in such a context. Finally, the article attempts to assess the Russian state's recent willingness to take control of private protection companies, centralize criminal investigation departments and delegate public security missions to the municipalities. These trends are likely to give rise to opposing interpretations.*

In a recent report, David Bayley and Clifford Shearing (2001: 5) argued that policing, functionally defined as "providing security through physical constraint", is undergoing an "historic restructuring". They see worldwide a general process of "multilateralization" of policing that reflects two distinct tendencies: "the separation of those who authorise policing from those who do it and the transference of both functions away from government" (Bayley & Shearing, 2001: vii).

At first glance, the Russian case seems to illustrate this assertion particularly well, having rapidly moved from a Soviet past associated with an image of all-state policing to a period of transition where economic interests, residential communities, private security firms, security departments inside production units, organized crime groups and so on have entered the game and are now alleged to play a significant role in both authorizing and providing policing. This article attempts to study the multilateralization of both auspices and providers of policing in post-Soviet Russia, the reasons for it and the issues it raises for governmental agencies in the field of policing. It will begin by presenting the Soviet context of policing, reassessing its unilateral all-state nature. It will then go on to point out the diversity of security demands, showing that studying multilateralization of both auspices and providers should not be reduced to a market-oriented approach. Finally, the article will examine the recent move toward reinforcement of state control, thus questioning the new frontier to be found between public and private spheres.

Unilateralism in Soviet Policing

In their report, Bayley and Shearing consider that the protection of the regime constitutes the main goal of policing in authoritarian states, which the government attempts to monopolize. Assistance from the public is required "through mobilising groups ... but not by allowing them to participate in markets. This trajectory produces the pretence of multilateralization and a style of policing that is preoccupied with threats to governments rather than to individuals" (Bayley & Shearing, 2001: 27). The Soviet context to some degree reflected this assertion regarding policing in authoritarian states, as the protection of the state was seen as a primary objective,[1] and diverse social groups were mobilized through the ritual launching of anti-crime campaigns: law-enforcement agents, party and administration control bodies, media, *druzhiny*[2] and virtually any citizen was expected to play the role of an informer (Connor, 1972; Juviler, 1976; Shelley, 1996). Moreover, the Soviet militiamen—referred to as "social workers with sticks" (Shelley, 1996: 143)—played a key function of social control by keeping permanent watch on everyday life and policing the "deviant". In some respects, however, the unilateral nature of policing in authoritarian regimes may be discussed in the Soviet case.

One Auspice?

Who authorized policing in the Soviet context? Were citizens able to act as auspices of policing? Whistleblowing was indeed a social practice in the Soviet Union (Lampert, 1985), but it was not just an effect of mobilization. Many whistleblowers believed in the Soviet ideology and were truly scandalized by the illegitimate behaviour of officials. Soviet archives also show that congruent complaints from some citizens about the attitude of local policemen might lead to a governmental inspection (Favarel-Garrigues, 2000a: 198–211). This is also true in the case of public security or delinquency issues. Although less audible, the voice of the citizens could, in some cases, be discordant from the official one. As W. D. Connor (1972: Chapter 10) noticed, citizens' letters to newspapers expressed various reactions to deviant behaviour, some asked for a more tolerant attitude from the police, while others asked for more repression when experts sometimes seemed to underestimate the problem in order to preserve the system as a whole. If we admit this as a rise—albeit slight—in public awareness of crime issues, the all-state approach of policing should be reassessed. This means that in the Soviet context, citizens also acted as an auspice of policing, even if regional or federal authorities may not have chosen to take their complaints into consideration.

The role of regional political elites should also be discussed. It is well known that during the final decades of the Soviet Union, several scandals were linked to large-scale embezzlement networks implicating regional or Republican Party top officials in Uzbekistan, Georgia and in some southern regions of Soviet Russia (Vaksberg, 1992). Most of these scandals involved the active participation of high-ranking law enforcement agents. This means that regional political leaders had some autonomy in authorizing policing, primarily by substituting local goals for federal aims. There is evidence from everyday Soviet life to support this affirmation. Regional party leaders often interfered in local judicial matters, either to accelerate or stop investigations, as Boris Yeltsin has suggested in his memoirs (Yeltsin, 1990: 54). They also sometimes decided to implement, especially zealously, anti-crime campaigns to gain some legitimacy inside the party organization (Favarel-Garrigues, 2000a: Chapter 2; Pokhmelkin & Pokhmelkin, 1992).

These examples show that the party-state in the Soviet Union did not represent a homogeneous auspice of policing. They also underline how difficult it is to draw a line between public and private spheres in the Soviet context, where property rights formally used to belong to the state. In fact, power was gained or maintained by overlapping public and private interests, or more exactly by using one's function in the administration or the party organization in order to defend one's own interests, whether they were private, corporatist and/or local.

Finally, another auspice of policing can also be found in Soviet society. Illicit social practices, which were relevant to what Western scholars then called the "second economy", seem to have increased and changed during the 1970s (for pioneering works, see Grossman, 1977; Katsenelinboigen, 1977; for a comparative approach, see Los, 1990). Among them, the underground production of consumer goods started to spread in the Soviet Union. Consequently, underground entrepreneurs (called "*tsekhoviki*") quickly faced the need to protect their illicit activity from law enforcement agencies and the underworld, and therefore became auspices of policing.

One Provider?

Concerning the providers of policing in the Soviet Union, it is true that most of them were party-state agents and served the political regime's interests. The *druzhiny* have been presented as a paradoxical form of community policing from above, produced by the state's willingness to ask, and sometimes compel, society to protect a social order defined by the state itself. As Shelley (1996: 44) has noticed, "*druzhinniki* did not respond to law enforcement needs articulated by the community [but] they heeded the State's injunctions to police a society which itself had never been consulted about the means or manner of its control". The statute of *druzhiny* was, however, ambiguous because they not only defended the interests of the state, but sometimes also those of communities or individuals.

Despite little evidence from official Soviet literature or from archives (most of it coming from oral testimonies of *druzhinniki*), we may suggest the following hypothesis: Given the spread of petty offences during the 1960s and 1970s (often referred to as "hooliganism" in the Soviet Union), residential communities could search legal means (i.e., through institutional channels) to defend their neighbourhood, and by doing so defend their personal goods as well. In some cases, *druzhiny* were the institutional expression of the willingness of a group of citizens to provide policing in the name of their community—most of the time, their neighbourhood. Though this aim was not stated, it might have been the state's choice to delegate part of its policing functions to these units, both in response to public concern and as an attempt to rationalize costs while increasing efficiency.[3] Moreover, the *druzhiny*, though hierarchically linked to the militia, were often under the control of party instances. This situation could lead locally to divergent attitudes depending on the perception of each of these bodies of the need for emphasizing or hiding crime or deviant behaviour according to their own interests.

In the case of underground entrepreneurs, two providers of protection should be considered. The first option consisted in directly benefiting from privileged access to law enforcement agents, who were able to defend entrepreneurs from state interest through personal relationships (kinship, friendship, corruption, etc.). In the Soviet context, deciding to work in the police, especially in anti-economic crime units, was often motivated by opportunism (e.g., the desire to gain access to scarce goods; Favarel-Garrigues, 2002).[4] In these conditions, reaching informal agreements with local policemen as "private" providers was mutually advantageous.

The second option consisted in interacting with people from the underworld. In most cases, this option was not freely chosen by entrepreneurs, but was the result of pressure exerted by racketeers. However, the latter might also be considered providers of services such as protecting the client from other racketeers, arranging a relationship with law enforcement agencies or taking part in the marketing of illicitly produced goods. As we will see later, this embryonic demand for protection found a significant extension during *perestroika*.

Demands for policing seem to have changed and increased in Soviet society since the 1970s, which might possibly justify a comparison with West European contexts. There was a wide array of players involved in authorizing and providing policing in the late-Soviet era. Nevertheless, from an institutional point of view, all these players were acting within the framework of a single agency—the party-state. This is why, in our view, we should talk about a process of informal multilateralization of policing. Except in the case of mafia-type protection of underground entrepreneurs, this process reflected the instrumentalization of state functions of policing in order to satisfy a demand expressed by an individual, a group of individuals or a community. This is also why in our view, while the year of the Soviet break-up in 1991 undoubtedly represents a turning point, some historic trends must be taken into consideration in order to understand the evolution of policing in Russia. Some elements that seem to correspond to post-Soviet policing had been observed in Soviet society since the 1970s, while other crucial issues of post-Soviet policing appeared during *perestroika* and *glasnost* in the second part of the 1980s.

The Multilateralization of Policing since *Perestroika and Glasnost*

In our view, one of the most important changes in policing that occurred during *perestroika* and *glasnost* is that the processes that we have described gained in visibility and became widely publicized. Debates on the demands for policing appeared in the media, while answers to them found a more institutionalized expression than ever before. Briefly speaking, the competition in authorizing and providing policing has become open, and relies on both institutional and informal resources.

A Demand for Maintaining Order

Since the second half of the 1980s, at least two distinct aspects of what might be considered a demand for policing have been observed in Russian society. First, a high proportion of the Russian population has been facing a fear of crime. According to a widespread *cliché*, especially in the beginning of the 1990s, streets and public places were seen as unsafe, which was reputedly not the case during the Soviet era. This assumption is, of course, very difficult to prove as the usual methodological problems when dealing with police statistics are compounded in the Russian context by the prohibition of their publication until 1989. Some trends in crime, such as the increase in the number of homicides or armed robbery, are nevertheless undeniable (Kriminologicheskaya Assotsiatsiya, 1994). Several institutions that were involved in the Soviet way of policing suddenly declined in importance (e.g., *druzhiny*) or even disappeared (e.g., comrade courts and party control agencies inside plants or *kolkhoz*). Furthermore, the police bureaucracy has had to face a multifaceted crisis, in particular a formidable exodus of its agents to private security agencies, and a lack of means and know-how to contain the rise in crime (Favarel-Garrigues, 2000b; Galeotti, 1993; Trehub, 1989; Williams & Serrins, 1993). However, as the fear of crime is never a purely rational reaction to a set of objective social evolutions, it has also reflected the discovery of law-and-order issues in Soviet media during the *glasnost* era. Russian people went extremely quickly from a world where crime was partially hidden[5] to another world where it was over-publicized. Serial killers, contract killings, mafia business and clashes between mobs suddenly entered every-day Russian life, especially through the mass media (about the emergence of post-communist fear of crime, see Los, 2002: 166–169)

In the late 1980s, a few attempts were made to restore citizens' cooperation in maintaining law and order, especially in big factories. Workers' Detachments for Cooperation with the Police (ROSM or *Rabochii Otriad Sodeistviya Militsii*) were created after a first decision by Gorki (Nijnii-Novgorod) city soviet. Other cities soon followed suit (Galeotti, 1990; Tsypkin, 1989). In the VAZ car factory in Togliatti, the plant authorities themselves settled the brigade in conjunction with city police authorities. The Gorki experiment shows the rise of local administrative and political bodies as a potentially autonomous auspice of policing, whereas Togliatti brigades may be seen as the precursors of the private security services that have flourished in plants, firms, banks and companies since the end of the 1980s.

More than ten years later, we found a resurgence of such units in the Siberian city of Omsk. In one of the town districts, which is built around a huge tire plant that is its principal employer, the plant security manager is also chairman of the district local security council (Interview with the plant security manager, Omsk, 28 January 2002). By day, the plant security service acts as a fully equipped and licensed private security agency. Then, when work is finished at night, some of its agents, as members of the local security council, patrol on a voluntary basis the district streets where most of the factory workers live.[6] The manager (a former *druzhinnik*) regrets the late 1980s, when it was clear that the workers' detachments held a dominant position in providing policing. Party membership (or at least a recommendation from a party member) was the main source of authorization to take part in these brigades and secure the right to provide extensive policing, both in the factory and in the neighbourhood. Indeed, the party as an overall auspice, which was legitimized by ideological beliefs and opportunistic motivations, has disappeared to be replaced by multifaceted ones.

This case actually shows how different auspices (plant managers, residential community and local administrative bodies through the security council) may interact today. These potentially divergent sources of policing and interests merge to form at this micro-local level a dominant corporate source of policing, if we take into account the fact that the local district deputy is one of the tire plant managers. This case is only one example of the variety of local security initiatives that can be found in Russia today. Sometimes competing with one another, sometimes cooperating to provide public security, they often combine private and public, individual and collective elements to present a hybrid picture of local public security policies (Le Huérou, 2002),[7] as the following examples will show.

Reappearing in some places by the mid-1990s, *druzhiny* were revived in the emergency context of the Moscow apartment house bombings in the summer of 1999. Inhabitants were suddenly asked to form *druzhiny* to check basements and garrets, and also to control people, especially those coming from the Caucasus. In Moscow and Saint Petersburg, *druzhiny* brigades have been formally re-established and, in the case of Moscow, a relevant local law came into force in 2002 (Moscow City Council, Law No. 36, 20 June 2002). The inhabitants concerns could be compared in some respects to those of the "traditional societies" in which people may "organise to take responsibility for security, supplementing what is regarded as inadequate protection by the public police" (Bayley & Shearing, 2001: 8). Indeed, the feeling of a general failure of the state police to comply with its obligation for public security is the grounds for many grassroots resident mobilizations.

However, despite convincing self-promotion from its members (Interviews, Moscow and St Petersburg, June and November 2001)—in most cases retired army officers or police agents—these new *druzhiny* seem to show little ability in playing a significant role in local policing. As a kind of provider, even more as a low-cost auxiliary body, under the auspices of the state police (which thus tries to compensate for scarce resources and staff), they mainly fail to be a genuine auspice of policing, which residential communities are reputed to be in other contexts. In this respect, to use Bayley and Shearing's (2001: 7) term, *druzhiny* do not seem to be considered part of the "informalisation of policing" that can be noticed in many residential communities in developed countries. The activity of *druzhini* members is clearly under the control of the local police staff. They refer to them before patrolling the streets and work under their supervision when they are needed during mass meetings (sports and cultural events). They also play a useful role of "sworn witness" (*ponyatoi*) to help the police charge and convict offenders in court.

Since the beginning of the 1990s, Russia has also faced the revival of Cossack communities. Seeking to affirm a new identity after being repressed during the Soviet era, they re-settled in some places to act as auxiliary frontier guards (their main function in Tsarist Russia) and to participate in various ways in security tasks (e.g., guarding church property, creating private security agencies or making special arrangements with schools or garden plot owners to provide low cost security— without arms and without license). They also seek to attract young unemployed people to join them (Interviews and personal observation, Omsk, November 2001; St Petersburg, June and November 2001). In such trouble zones as North Caucasus, where Cossacks often emigrated from Chechnya to neighbouring regions after 1991, their auxiliary detachments to the local police have been known for their violent harassment of ethnic minorities.[8] Is this an instance of a cultural community serving as an auspice for policing by means of shared political and cultural beliefs (Bayley & Shearing, 2001, p. 8) in a way that contravenes Russian law as well as international legal norms? Or, since Cossacks are a legally registered auxiliary of the public police in those areas, do they perform an implicit discriminatory or racist public policy welcomed by regional authorities and left unpunished by the federal ones?

The case of one private security agency in the city of Omsk—the "Law Enforcement Centre" (*pravookhranitel'nyi tsentr*)—can provide another illustration of hybrid policing at the local level. Created by former *druzhinniki* as soon as the registration of private security agencies was allowed, this agency is not only the most powerful and well-equipped one in the city, but it has also concluded agreements with local police stations. Law Enforcement Centre members patrol the city streets in state police cars in order to provide security for their private clients, but also to help maintain public security. In the event of street disorder, they have the right to intervene, detain offenders and drive them to the nearest police station, or to call a state police patrol, since they share common radio frequencies. Moreover, its director, a typically enthusiastic former "*obshchestvennik*" (social activist), leads many operations for crime prevention with young people, and claims a much more substantial and proactive vision of public order and security than many state police agents or social departments in the city (Interviews and personal observation, Omsk, November 2001). This example shows an original hybrid case of authorizing policing. The main point is not so much that a private provider is fulfilling public commitments, but that it tends sometimes to replace the local state police agencies in the very definition of what is to be secured and protected in terms of public security.

A Demand for Protecting Property Rights

The second aspect of the demand for policing is the desire to protect private property. Two dimensions must be kept in mind here. First, a general need for protection of private goods has appeared in Russian society, as shown, for instance, in the growth of armoured doors in homes. The Extra-Departmental Protection Directorate of the Ministry of Internal Affairs (UVVO), in existence since 1952, is currently acting as the main player in the field of private security for individuals, groups of residents and companies. Seeming to benefit from a quite positive image,[9] UVVO is a state body that enters into contracts with individuals and firms to protect private goods and property. While doing this, they must also comply with state police requirements. If, for example, a patrol car is watching a group of private homes on the basis of private contracts with their owners, they must react in the event of any trouble occurring in the area. On the other hand, they act as competitors to private security firms, often winning the battle due to the resources they possess as a state institution, as will be shown later. One of this directorate's heads in the city of Omsk sums up the peculiar position of UVVO:

> [We are] *byudzhetniki* [civil servants], but we have to earn our living. ...We fulfil public missions, though we provide security for private buildings or individuals. In this respect, private security agencies are our competitors. ... But on the public highway, we have to intervene whatever happens. There is no difference with any other MOB [public security state police] department. (Interview, Omsk, 16 November 2001)

Second, *perestroika*, and later the economic reforms that were launched in the beginning of the 1990s, led to the development of private business and a strong demand for property rights protection. It should be remembered that the privatization process was seen not only as the touchstone of economic reform but also, simultaneously, as a crucial political measure as it was supposed to ensure an irreversible exit from the communist past (Nelson & Kuzes, 1995). This explains why the pace of property transfer was considered to be the main indicator of the reform's success, to the detriment of other issues. Among them, the low level of protection of newly acquired property rights was a source of concern for entrepreneurs. First, there were numerous loopholes in the legal framework that was supposed to surround the privatization process. For example, legislation on bankruptcy was really completed more than ten years after the beginning of this reform. Second, the relationships between entrepreneurs and law enforcement agencies as public, formal and impersonal providers of protection were hardly trustworthy, because, among other things, policemen were reputed to be hostile to private managers and entrepreneurs had to cope with an incomplete or inappropriate legislative framework and were therefore often obliged to resort to illicit behaviour. As a well-known example, tax pressure on private enterprises was so high that entrepreneurs were often obliged to find ways to escape. As a result, each entrepreneur had to worry about the protection of his own business. According to Radaev (2001), 57 per cent of Russian entrepreneurs considered at the end of the 1990s that, in the event of troubles, they would manage to find their own solutions, while only 13 per cent would ask the police (see also Hendley et al., 2000; about the "demand for law", see Hendley, 1999).

Protection needs may be satisfied by different kinds of partners on the basis of more or less formal agreements. Russian mafia agents are key actors in this business as, according to some scholars, providing private protection represents their main social function (Varese, 2001). Yet entrepreneurs may also build personal relationships with law enforcement agents, either by signing an agreement with the Extra-Departmental Protection Directorate of the Ministry of Internal Affairs, or more informally by gaining privileged access to some agents, active or not. Funding local police agencies is a current practice, especially among large plant managers. According to Vadim Volkov (2002: 169), "a study of charitable donations by Petersburg private businesses ... uncovered that the regional MVD organs are, after the disabled, the second largest receiver of charity from local business companies". All these key actors in protection provision may work in private structures such as internal security departments, which often exist in large plants or companies, or as private protection companies that have flourished in Russia since the end of the 1980s. In 1999, there were more than 11,000 private security agencies, including 6,775 private protection companies, and almost 200,000 licensed security agents entitled to possess and carry firearms (Volkov, 2002: 137).

The Limits of a Market-oriented Approach to Policing

In our view, these remarks should allow us to criticize a market-oriented approach, seeing protection and, in a wider sense, policing as a service which is asked for and supplied. Two reasons might be mentioned. The first is in fact a classical piece of criticism that has been directed at scholars that emphasized the social function of organized crime groups as private protection suppliers, as did Gambetta (1993) about *La Cosa Nostra* in Sicily or Varese (2001) about the Russian mafia. It raises the problem of finding a frontier between racket and protection, and therefore assessing whether protection suppliers are also those who threaten businessmen and then create the demand.[10]

We also consider that the market approach tends to occult a crucial feature of policing as a service to be exchanged. As Volkov (2002) has shown, several "violence-managing agencies," which include state agencies, private security agencies and criminal groups, have competed since the end of the 1980s in order to offer private protection (see also Oleinik, 2001). For managers, politicians and higher officials, having privileged access to any competitive "violence-managing agency" may represent an essential resource in order to maintain or gain power and/or legitimacy. In fact, violence-managing agencies may not only provide protection, but also other services such as debt recovery or contract enforcement. They are occasionally used not only for defensive matters, but also for offensive purposes.

Some official data might help to support this assertion. The level of murders officially registered as committed by hired killers remains high in post-Soviet Russia: 288 in 1993, 580 in 1996, and 326 in 2001. From 1998 to 2002, 46 per cent of the victims were businessmen (*Kommersant*, 18 April 2003). Furthermore, in 2002, Mr Ustinov (the Russian Federation's General *Prokuror*) expressed some concern about information proving that investigators from MVD were exploiting the content of some criminal cases outside of their work (Ustinov, 2002). He stated that there was a direct link between these practices and the development of *kompromaty*, which means compromising files against members of the political or economic elite. The use of *kompromaty* in economic and political battles has been widespread in Russia since the beginning of the 1990s. Privileged access to providers of policing represents an indispensable resource for gaining and maintaining power, in a relational sense, in post-Soviet Russia.

Given the widespread fear of crime in Russian society, providing policing for public security is also a source of legitimacy. Any candidate to local, regional or federal elections has to undertake to maintain order and, if elected, to show concrete signs of implementation. In 1994, in his bid for election as a deputy of the regional legislative body and strongly opposing the local governor, one of the most prominent entrepreneurs of the Omsk region (Western Siberia) based his programme on a project called "safeties" (this is the exact translation of the Russian term "*bezopasnosti*"; see Le Huérou, 1997). He contributed both funding and equipment to the local police station, and posted his own security service agents outside schools to reassure parents who were afraid of drug dealing and racketeering in the area. He also created a neighbourhood community centre to compensate the social care and cultural activity deficit, and to restore an overall sense of security. Once elected, he changed his mind and decided to cooperate with the governor. As he eventually became the vice-governor, he discretely abandoned the community centre and the "safeties" programme.

The Russian case also shows that if privileged access to providers of policing is considered a resource for power, then all functions of government law enforcement agencies are likely to be privatized. Bayley and Shearing notice that, in Europe and America, some signs underline a process of "division of labour where the public police increasingly specialise in investigations and counterforce operations while private police become decentralised, full-service providers of visible crime prevention" (Bayley & Shearing, 2001: 19). We will show later that the decentralization of crime prevention is an ongoing process in today's Russia. However, in this context, police judiciary and intelligence functions may also be privatized, or more exactly used for private purposes. In his memoirs, A. Korzhakov, who started his political career as Yeltsin's personal bodyguard before heading the Presidential Security Service, does not hide the fact that his activities included the collection of compromising information on a large number of higher officials, managers and politicians (Korzhakov, 1997).

Towards State Control of Providers?

Two recent trends may be observed in post-Soviet Russia. First, state agencies are trying to control the private protection sector. Second, there are several attempts from the government to gain control over local law enforcement agencies and define the framework of policing in Russia. These trends are likely to give rise to opposing interpretations.

Winning the Battle over Private Protection Companies

Russian entrepreneurs have been seeking more and more to benefit from state protection since the end of the 1990s. According to Radaev (2001), most entrepreneurs would like to be protected (formally or not) by the police—or better by the FSB—but are not always able to lay claim to such protection. Only big public or private firms are likely to possess the resources (financial assets and personal connections) that are necessary to get police protection from UVVO or other departments. According to Radaev (2001), studying the ability to gain access to more or less competitive agencies may even provide the foundations for a sociological typology of Russian enterprises. However, it seems that the best protection is grounded in both private and public spheres. In a big plant, for instance, having its own private security department with people directly benefiting from privileged connections with law enforcement agencies seems to be highly competitive. It means that benefiting from "administrative resource" (as it is called in today's Russia) is a *sine qua non* condition for efficient protection. In other words, while state law enforcement agents might exclusively provide highly reliable protection, private protection agents cannot guarantee such efficiency on their own.

Administrative resources indeed benefit from a comparative advantage. As a result, the state is not a provider of policing like any other, because having privileged access to law enforcement agents represents comparatively the most precious resource. This explains the fact that some private security agencies accept cooperation with the police in maintaining public order (e.g., during mass meetings, sports, cultural events, city fairs, etc.). This cooperation is on a free-of-charge basis, and though it is not clear whether it is an option or a "legal obligation",[11] private agencies have to comply with these kinds of missions, which attests to the key function of state police as an administrative resource for private security agencies. It allows the latter to maintain good relations with state police agents, the managers of private agencies very often being former colleagues. It also protects private agencies from tightened control on their activity or accounts, and consequently from the possible risk of closure.

In fact, the relevance of the public-private dichotomy for studying the multi-lateralization of policing in post-soviet Russia is quite difficult to assess. Bayley & Shearing (2001: 8) recognize that, in other contexts, the boundary between public and private sectors may be hard to distinguish. However, this assertion is particularly exemplified in post-Soviet Russia for several reasons. First, hidden dynamics of informal appropriation of policing were found under the reputedly all-state form of policing in the late-Soviet era. Second, since the latter half of the 1980s, authorizing and providing policing has become a constitutive resource to gain power and/or legitimacy. The Russian state was not able to build a legal and institutional framework and control all kinds of innovative interactions that occurred between the public police and private interests. Policing in Russia represents a patchwork of situations that have resulted from dialectical tensions and articulations between two ways (bottom-up and top-down) of making rules and regulations. Finally, private interests are best secured when they benefit from privileged access to administrative resources, which gives a comparative advantage to state law enforcement agencies over its competitors. As a result, the overlapping of private and public resources and interests represents the normal way to gain power and/or legitimacy in post-Soviet Russia. In order to protect property rights, for instance, the most valuable providers are not situated clearly in the public or private sectors, but rather benefit from a multi-positional situation.

Controlling State Law Enforcement Agencies

As the ability to provide policing possibly constitutes a resource for maintaining or gaining power, the Russian Ministry of Internal Affairs (MVD) should not be considered a homogeneous body, but rather a set of more or less autonomous agencies. We have already seen that the territorially based bureaucratic organization of the Ministry matters as a source of autonomy for police agents. However, we would like to emphasize that the division of work between various departments has led to the fragmentation of both authorizing and providing policing inside state law enforcement agencies.

It should be noted that the tax police (a new law enforcement agency institutionally not belonging to the Ministry of Internal Affairs) was created during the 1990s and dismantled in 2003. During its short existence, the tax police gained importance in the Russian law enforcement system, as can be seen in the increasing number of penal code articles that referred to this agency (Gregory & Brooke, 2000). The tax police acted as a criminal investigation agency, organizing impressive armed raids in firms and banks, and attracting some notoriety and prestige. Yet its field of work rendered tax police agents particularly vulnerable to corruption, patronage, political instrumentalization and collusion with entrepreneurs.

Inside the MVD, the anti-organized crime directorate has gained considerable autonomy during the 1990s. First, it is separate from other criminal investigation directorates, which means that its budget is directly discussed with the Minister. Second, its territorial organization is specific: as the anti-organized crime directorate is supposed to fight against collusions between local elites (including local law enforcement officials) and the underworld, its presence is limited to 13 (then 7) of the 89 regions of the Russian Federation. In this configuration, each agency is supposed to struggle with organized crime in several regions. As a result, in the post-Soviet context, each law enforcement agency, at any territorial level, has tended to develop its own interests and patronage relationships.

The history of post-Soviet police corruption scandals shows that none of these agencies has remained untouched. Since Vladimir Putin became President of the Russian Federation, controlling law enforcement agencies seems to represent a crucial issue. Among other measures, the liquidation of the tax police in 2003 may be seen as a major step in this direction. The widely publicized disbanding of a criminal police network in Moscow in June 2003 should be interpreted as another step, exemplifying the government's determination to tackle police corruption. Nevertheless, many observers consider this operation reflects only pre-electoral matters (Kopylov, 2003). However that may be, these steps are connected to a general Russian police reform project that tends to centralize the struggle against crime and municipalize public security missions.

Since the beginning of the 1990s, the public security branch of the police has faced problems in trying to position itself in the new Russian policing landscape. Always described separately from the criminal branch, it is often referred to as the "local police", though it is not really the case since the department in charge of public security—the MOB (*Militsia obshchestvennoi bezopasnosti*)—remains under the control of the state. The involvement of regional and municipal authorities—which is real—is mainly the result of various arrangements and combinations also varying in place and time. The most common way for municipal or regional bodies to contribute to public security is by helping to finance staff from local budgets. In Omsk, many of the local agents—though they are members of the state police and wear state police uniforms—were once paid from the city's autonomous budget that offered them extra bonuses and free housing in exchange for the promise to stay in the neighbourhood. When the region won the long-running conflict between city and regional authorities, payment of these agents was transferred to the regional budget. In 2001, the whole public security staff was a supplementary one entirely subsidized by the region as the result of a regional political decision to devote the entire state quota[12] to criminal investigation departments. In this case, regional authorities act clearly as an auspice of policing by deciding where and how to allocate the police resource.

Since the early 1990s, regional authorities have been sharing the prerogative to nominate the head of the regional public security department together with the Ministry of Internal Affairs. This has always been a real lever in the hands of regional leadership at a time of actual or potential conflict with the centre. This was particularly the case in Moscow, where the city police department has tried to gain greater autonomy since the autumn of 1999, especially in terms of residents' control.[13] In late 2001, President Putin won the battle over Luzhkov, and the "local police" was reintegrated into the state staff; but the police battle was clearly part of a broader conflict between the two men and, behind them, two main lobbies. During the Yeltsin era, all attempts to create genuine municipal police bodies failed (Kononov, 1997; Granat, 1998).[14] The policing issue seems to reflect in a salient way the weak institutionalization of relations between federal and regional levels.

Since 2000, President Putin has been attempting to regain general control over regional authorities and weaken the governors' powers. In May 2000, he announced the appointment of seven special representatives (often called "super-prefects") in charge of supervizing the 89 administrative regions (*oblast*) through seven new territorial entities (Gazier, 2001; Petrov, 2003). In June 2001, a presidential decree (Decree No. 644 of 4 June 2001; see also *Russian Regional Report 6(23)*, 11 June 2001 and *6(24)*, 19 June 2001) significantly reorganized the Ministry of Internal Affairs, giving more competence to "super-prefects", while President Putin tried to get the law amended in order to deprive governors of the right to participate in the nomination of regional police heads (*RFE/RL Security Watch* 1(1), 24 July 2000; 2(23), 11 June 2001; 2(27), 19 July 2001; and *Russian Regional Report* 6(19), 23 May 2001; 6(25) 3 July 2001). In the summer of 2002, Minister B. Gryzlov announced plans for a more radical transformation in the future: the two main functions of policing would be fully separated, criminal investigation departments remaining under the auspices of the federal state, while the public security branch would be fully transferred to municipalities. The former would be called "police" [*politsia*] and the latter would remain militia [*militsia*] (Demechko, 2002). In addition, a National-Guard-type federal structure would head the special units and militarized troops of the MVD.

Conclusion

> During transitions to democracy, democratic reform of the police is likely to be less important to emerging democratic governments than security. The emphasis on security in policing arises from two sources. The first is the political interest of emerging democratic regimes. ... The second source consists of the national interests of foreign donors. (Bayley, 1997: 60–61)

Foreign donors' involvement in defining post-Soviet policing is indeed a crucial issue, albeit one that should be studied separately. Nevertheless, the current willingness of Putin's government to centralize criminal investigation agencies, and establish and control the rules of a top-down process of municipalization of public security agencies may lead to two different interpretations. On the one hand, it is an illustration of a process of "normalization"—or, more exactly, of the Russian government's wish to bring together policing with Western standards,[15] as can be seen in the use of Western terms ("police", "guard") in recent projects of police reform. Yet, on the other hand, this process might also lead to an authoritarian form of policing. Many observers consider recent police reforms a sign of the increasing influence of Russian security services (FSB, ex-KGB) over the Ministry of Internal Affairs (see, e.g., *The NIS observed: An analytical review*, available online at: www.bu.edu/iscip).

Such interpretations might be misleading because, in our view, considering attempts "to maintain [government's] monopoly ... and discourage groups from acting as either auspices or providers of policing" (Bayley & Shearing, 2001: 27) as a pathway to authoritarianism may be too simplistic. As we have seen in the Cossack case, for instance, the spontaneous emergence of local auspices and providers of policing may meet a desire to defend non-democratic values. This is why connections between forms of policing and forms of political regime should be examined carefully. We have shown that, in the Soviet and post-Soviet context, authorizing and providing policing as a resource for power and/or legitimacy has been a source of enduring rivalry for over 30 years.

The identity of auspices and providers may evolve without changing the nature and functions of policing in Russian society as long as there is no open debate about security as a public good. Whether they are public or private, local or federal, all players in the field of policing tend to define themselves in the names of those for whom they act, set their own goals, and decide what there is to secure and protect. The confiscation of the process by which demands for policing are defined by those who claim their ability to authorize and provide policing remains the most crucial issue in today's Russia.

Notes

[1] See, e.g., the outline of the last penal code in Soviet Russia, the first and second chapter of which were devoted to "offences against the state" and "offences against socialist property".

[2] Reviving earlier attempts in the 1920s, Nikita Khrushchev created the *Dobrovol'nye narodnye druzhiny* in 1959. These were auxiliary citizen police units formed of volunteers (*druzhinniki*) in both residential communities and working collectives. In exchange for additional days off, these volunteers patrolled the neighbourhoods at night in search of tramps, drunks or any kind of "*khuligany*" (the Soviet term for petty offenders).

[3] We can add to the *druzhiny* their counterparts in the field of social and prevention work with young deviant people. Public inspectors and other bodies were volunteer citizens who, in many cases, played the role of social workers.

[4] In the same way, being a *druzhinnik* was a way of gaining access to otherwise unauthorized resources or goods (for companies brigades) or simply to some privileges (e.g., not being stopped by traffic police to show your license is known to be the main motivation to be member of traffic volunteer squads).

[5] As it is well known, crime in the Soviet ideology was seen as a result of class struggle in capitalist societies. Therefore crime was to be eradicated in the Soviet Union. This propagandistic vision of crime explains why official information on crime is so scarce. Yet, at the same time, it was permanently refuted by other sources of knowledge for Soviet people, such as satirical cartoons in newspapers, popular jokes, songs or movies.

[6] A kind of local neighbourhood watch in a more formal way, the public security council is a volunteer body created under the auspice of local self-management committees acting jointly with local police agents and dealing with petty offences, neighbour disputes, alcoholism-related problems and the like.

[7] This material is based upon research conducted by Anne Le Huérou for IHESI, Paris, in 2001–2002: "Vers l'invention d'une co-production de la sécurité: Evolutions institutionnelles et mode de cooperation des acteurs locaux, étatiques et non étatiques de la sécurité locale dans l'Europe post-communiste". Field work was undertaken mainly in Omsk and St Petersburg in cooperation with Dr Y. Gilinskii and Y. Kostyukovskii of the Centre of Deviance of the Institute of Sociology in St Petersburg (Russian Academy of Sciences) and with the expert office *Gepitsentr* in Omsk.

[8] Human rights organizations have extensively reported these violations, especially during the "foreigner" campaign during the summer of 2002. Authorized by Governor Tkachev, it was

conducted by Cossack paramilitary groups who were to search and expel illegal migrants (see, e.g., United Nations Committee on Elimination of Racial Discrimination, 2002; Glasser, 2002).

[9] Interviews and personal observation, Omsk, November 2001. This positive image was reflected in the results of a marketing survey conducted for the UVVO in the city of Omsk.

[10] In the neo-institutional studies, "private enforcers tend to appear as abstractions and are seen as sharing the same set of attributed behavioural assumptions as economic subjects [as if they were] merely passive providers of a commodity the selling of which wholly depends on the level of demand and available choices. ... While plausible theoretically, such assumptions tend to underestimate the actual capacity of force-wielding organizations to determine choices available to economic subjects" (Volkov, 2002: 19–20).

[11] Various state police officers and private securities managers with whom we met had different opinions on that point.

[12] In addition to the staff allocated to each region by the federal budget, regional authorities can hire additional personnel paid from their own budgets (Interviews with experts, Omsk, November 2001).

[13] The *propiska*, or internal residence permit system, that existed throughout the Soviet era as a means of control of the circulation of citizens and internal immigration is supposed to have disappeared in today's Russia. However, it still exists in the major cities, especially Moscow, and registration rules have become a very sensitive issue since the 1999 apartment house bombings and the beginning of the second war in Chechnya.

[14] In 1996, a presidential decree authorized (as an experiment) a few cities to set up their own police agencies, with their own staff. It was considered a failure and the experiment closed in 2001 (Interview with V. Smirnov, deputy head of public security department of the Ministry of Internal Affairs, Moscow, 15 November 2001; see also Kruessman, 1999).

[15] We do not ignore the fact that these standards are not shared by all Western countries, as some states are reluctant to give too much autonomy to the cities in this field.

References

Bayley, D. (1997), Who are we kidding? or developing democracy through public reform, in: National Institute of Justice (ed) *Policing in Emerging Democracies: Workshop Papers and Highlights*, National Institute of Justice, Washington, DC.

Bayley, D. & Shearing, C. (2001), *The New Structure of Policing: Description, Conceptualization and Research Agenda*, National Institute of Justice, Washington, DC.

Connor, W.D. (1972), *Deviance in Soviet Society*, Columbia University Press, New York.

Demechko, V. (2002), "Militsionerov podelyat na 'mentov' i 'kopov'" [Police agents will be split into "menty" and "cops"], *Izvestya*, 25 September.

Favarel-Garrigues, G. (2000a), *La lutte contre la criminalité économique en Russie soviétique et post-soviétique (1965–1995)*, PhD dissertation, Institut d'Etudes Politiques de Paris, Paris.

Favarel-Garrigues, G. (2000b), Implementing struggle against economic crime in Russia: Bureaucratic constraints and police practices, in: Pagon, M. (ed), *Policing in Central and Eastern Europe: Ethics, Integrity and Human Rights*, College of Police and Security Studies, Ljubljana.

Favarel-Garrigues, G. (2002), "Le policier soviétique et les politiques pénales (1965–1986)", *Revue d'histoire moderne et contemporaine*, Vol. 49, no. 2, pp. 54–77.

Galeotti, M. (1990), "From Gorky to Tol'yatti: New models for the police", *Report on the USSR*, 31 August.

Galeotti, M. (1993), "Perestroïka, perestrelka, pereborka: Policing Russia in a time of change", *Europe-Asia Studies*, Vol. 45, no. 5, pp. 769–786.

Gambetta, D. (1993), *The Sicilian Mafia: The Business of Private Protection*, Harvard University Press, Cambridge, MA.

Gazier, A. (2001), "La mise au pas des régions russes? La réforme institutionnelle de V. Poutine", *Le Courrier des pays de l'Est*, Vol. 1015 (May), pp. 4–14.

Glasser, S.B. (1998), "More racism in Russia", *The Washington Post*, 13 June.

Granat, N.L. (1998), Mesto i rol' mestnoi militsii v sisteme organov mestnogo samoupaavleniya [The role of the local police in the self-administration bodies' system], in: *Mestnoe samoupravlenie, Teoriya i Praktika [Local Self-administration: Theory and Practise]*, Akademiya MVD Rossii, Moscow.

Gregory, F. & Brooke, G. (2000), "Policing economic transition and increasing revenue: A case study of the Federal Tax Police Service of the Russian Federation 1992–1998", *Europe-Asia Studies*, Vol. 52, no. 3, pp. 433–455.

Grossman, G. (1977), "The second economy of the USSR", *Problems of Communism*, Vol. 26 (September–October), pp. 25–40.

Hendley, K. (1999), "Rewriting the rules of the game in Russia: The neglected issue of the demand for law", *East European Constitutional Review*, Vol. 8, no. 4, pp. 89–95.

Hendley, K., Murrell, P. & Ryterman, R. (2000), "Law, relationships and private enforcement: Transactional strategies of Russian enterprises", *Europe-Asia Studies*, Vol. 52, no. 4, pp. 627–656.

Juviler, P. (1976). *Revolutionary Law and Order*. MacMillan, New York.

Katsenelinboigen, A. (1977), "Coloured markets in the Soviet Union", *Soviet Studies*, January, pp. 62–85.

Kononov, A. (1997), "Munitsipal'naya militsiya. Kakoi ei byt'?" [What should be a municipal police?], *Rossiiskaya Federatsiya*, Vol. 2, p. 24.

Kopylov, S. (2003), "Gryzlovskaya matritsa", *Russkii Zhurnal*, 25 June. Available online at: www.russ.ru/politics/20030625-kopil.html.

Korzhakov, A. (1997), *Boris Yeltsin: Ot rassveta do zakata [Boris Yeltsin: From Dawn to Dusk]*, Interbook, Moscow.

Kriminologicheskaya Assotsiatsiya (1994), *Izmeneniya prestupnosti v Rossii [Changes of Crime in Russia]*, Nauchno-Issledovatel'skii Institut Problem Ukrepleniya Zakonnosti i Pravoporyadka, Moscow.

Kruessman, T. (1999), "A tale of two cities: Municipal policing in Krasnoyarsk and Irkutsk", Paper presented at the AAASS 2000 Congress, Saint Louis.

Lampert, N. (1985), *Whistleblowing in the Soviet Union: Complaints and Abuses under State Socialism*, MacMillan, New York.

Le Huérou, A. (1997), "Pouvoirs locaux et pouvoirs régionaux à Omsk", *Nouveaux Mondes*, Vol. 7 (Winter), pp. 129–160.

Le Huérou, A. (2002), "Des pratiques locales de sécurité hybrides. Le cas de la Russie", *Les Cahiers de la sécurité intérieure*, Vol. 50, pp. 19–42.

Los, M. (1990), *The Second Economy in Marxist States*, Macmillan, Basingstoke.

Los, M. (2002), "Post-communist fear of crime and the commercialization of security", *Theoretical Criminology*, Vol. 6, no. 2, pp. 165–187.

Nelson, L. & Kuzes, I. (1995), *Radical Reform in Yeltsin's Russia: Political, Economic and Social Dimensions*, M.E. Sharpe, Armonk, NY.

Oleinik, A. (2001), *Prison, criminalité organisée et sociétés post-soviétiques*, L'Harmattan-Italia, Turin.

Petrov, N. (2003), "Federal reform, two and a half years on", *Russia and Eurasia Review*, Vol. 2, no. 1. Available online at: www.jamestown.org/pubs/view/rer_002_001_001.htm.

Pokhmelkin, A.V. & Pokhmelkin, V.V. (1992), *Ideologiya i ugolovnaya politika*, INION, Moscow.

Radaev, V. (2001), "Entreprise, protection et violence en Russie à la fin des années 1990", *Cultures et Conflits*, Vol. 42 (Summer), pp. 47–68.

RFE/RL Security Watch (various dates). Available online at: www.rferl.org.

Russian Regional Report (various dates). Available online at: www.iews.org.

Shelley, L. (1996), *Policing Soviet Society: The Evolution of State Control*, Routledge, London.

Trehub, A. (1989), "Hard times for Soviet policemen", *Radio Liberty Report on the USSR*, Vol. 1, no. 23, pp. 18–21.

Tsypkin, M. (1989), "Workers' militia: Order instead of law", *Report on the USSR*, 17 November, pp. 14–17.

United Nations Committee on Elimination of Racial Discrimination (2002), *The Compliance of the Russian Federation with the Convention on the Elimination of All Forms of Racial Discrimination: An NGO Report to the United Nations Committee on Elimination of Racial Discrimination, 62nd Session, Moscow, March 2003*. Available online at: www.memo.ru/eng/hr/dscr0212e/.

Ustinov, V. (2002), "Doklad General'nogo prokurora RF Prezidentu Rossii I Federal'nomu Sobraniyu O sostoyanii zakonnosti, pravoporyadka v Rossiskoi Federatsii i rabote organov prokuratury za 2001 god po presecheniyu pravonarushenii" [Russian Federation General Procuror's report to the President and Federal Assembly on law enforcement in Russia and on *Prokuratura*'s involvement in struggling with crime in 2001], www.strana.ru, 30 April.

Vaksberg, A. (1992), *La mafia russe*, Albin Michel, Paris.

Varese, F. (2001), *The Russian Mafia: Private Protection in a New Market Economy*, Oxford University Press, Oxford.

Volkov, V. (2002), *Violent entrepreneurs: The Use of Force in the Making of Russian Capitalism*, Cornell University Press, Ithaca, NY.

Williams, J. & Serrins, A. (1993), "The Russian militia: An organization in transition", *Police Studies*, Vol. 16, no. 4, pp. 124–128.

Yeltsin, B. (1990), *Ispoved' na zadannuyu temu* [*Confession on a given subject*], Rukitis, Riga.

Pretrial detention in Russian criminal courts: a statistical analysis

Kirill D. Titaev

ABSTRACT

The article focuses on the topic of pretrial detention in the Russian Federation. Using a data set of 10,000 coded decisions of Russian criminal courts, the paper answers the following questions: what factors influence the likelihood of pretrial detention in the Russian criminal justice system? Does the fact of pretrial detention affects decisions regarding case dismissal, the type of punishment, and length of incarceration? The hypotheses are tested using the logit and ordinary least squares (OLS) regression models with standard control variables (such as gender, employment status, criminal history, procedural characteristics of the case). The analysis shows that the key predictors of pretrial detention are unemployment status, informal criminal records, and the non-confession of guilt. Furthermore, it is shown that the fact of pretrial detention significantly influences the likelihood of the non-dismissal of the case. The key predictor for the likelihood of choosing imprisonment as a type of punishment is pretrial detention. No significant connection was established between pretrial detention and the length of incarceration.

Introduction

In interviews, Russian lawyers claim that pretrial detention is one of the most important factors in sentencing in Russia. Pretrial detention is an important factor in the sentencing process in the United States and in other countries, as indicated by statistical studies of sentencing (see, e.g., Williams, 2003). Although empirical data about its role in Russia are unavailable, statements like "The key goal is to avoid pretrial detention. If your client is in jail, he will be sentenced for real incarceration" (interview with defence attorney) are a common occurrence during expert interviews with Russian lawyers. While pretrial detention has no formal influence on the sentence according to Russian criminal law, Russian judges have the right to take into account any extralegal factors in their sentencing decision. Using statistical data on court decisions, this paper presents evidence that the factor of pretrial detention plays a significant role in sentencing in Russia.

The Russian legal system is continental: coded law plays a central role and precedents are secondary. Russia's contemporary criminal justice is still under the significant influence of the Soviet past (see details in Solomon, 2002). Since the Soviet era, Russian courts have been producing very low levels of acquittal – less than 0.2% (excluding cases with private prosecution[1]). The system of criminal justice includes police detectives who have to find and detain the suspect. All formal legal operations in the preliminary investigation are done by investigators. It is also the investigator's prerogative to initiate the process of pretrial detention by requesting the court order. Courts approve these requests in more than 90% of cases (Trochev, 2012), which means that the decision about pretrial detention in fact largely depends on the investigator. The Russian Criminal Procedural Code prescribes some formal circumstances that necessitate pretrial detention. These circumstances include the defendant wanting to abscond, wanting to commit a crime, or wanting to have an influence upon the witness or victim. In addition to that, the defendant has to be a suspect in a crime with a maximum sentence length of more than 3 years of incarceration (5 years for underage defendants). Under special circumstances, pretrial detention may also be set for crimes with a smaller maximum sentence length. The defendant must either have no abiding place in Russia, have no identifying documents, or have a history of absconding or breaking some other form of restraint (CPC RF, 2001, art. 97 and 108).

It is a fact that – in the United States – detainment prior to trial may negatively affect the perception of the defendant by the judge and jurors (Williams, 2003). However, it is more important that the problem of pretrial detention is closely linked to the problem of general extralegal biases in the court system. This article will use the factor of pretrial detention to advance our understanding of the actual mechanisms of sentencing disparity.

While the seriousness of the crime remains the main factor in sentencing in Russia, there are many other factors that lead to an unequal treatment of the suspect. In other words, extralegal factors often influence sentencing, while the inequality in sentencing stems from the connection of said factors to the extralegal status of the accused (e.g., employment) (Spohn, 2008). Using the original data set, I will describe the role of pretrial detention (present in 20% of all cases) using a regression model with standard control variables (such as severity of crime, gender of the offender, plea bargain, and others).

This article addresses the following questions:

(1) What are the factors that increase the likelihood of pretrial detention?
(2) How strong is the influence of pretrial detention on sentencing decisions?

The second question will be answered separately for each successive stage of the Russian criminal procedure. In the Russian criminal procedure, choices have to be made regarding sentencing or case dismissal, the type of the punishment (actual imprisonment or not), and the length of imprisonment. These stages are described in Russian literature (see, e.g., a sociology-minded description in Volkov, Dmitrieva, Pozdnjakov, & Titaev, 2012) as key questions that have to be resolved in the process of sentencing. A brief description of the Russian criminal justice system will be given below.

Since July 2011, texts of sentences of courts of general jurisdiction (district courts) were made available online, allowing the Institute for the Rule of Law to collect data from district court websites. At the time of data collection, about 70% of all sentences were available. The empirical source of this research is a representative random sample of 10,000 criminal cases heard between 2010 and 2011 in district courts. District courts resolve over 75% of criminal cases. These 10,000 sentences were coded for 51 substantive variables. Based on the results of over 50 interviews with judges, investigators, prosecutors, and other lawyers, I will subsequently explain the social mechanism of judicial decision-making in criminal courts.

Literature review and research issues

The first statistical analysis of the problem of pretrial detention was conducted in the late 1960s (Ares, Rankin, & Sturz, 1963; also see an early review in Goldkamp, 1983). Since then, there have been two main topics in this research area. The first is focused on the legal and extralegal predictors of the probability of pretrial detention (see, e.g., Freiburger & Hilinski, 2010). The second topic is the effect of pretrial detention on the choice of the type and duration of punishment (e.g., Sacks & Ackerman, 2014). These two questions are often considered together in the same paper (as in Spohn, 2008). In this article, the questions about predictors of pretrial detention and about its influence on the punishment will be discussed in parallel. There are some groups of issues usually discussed in the context of pretrial detention, such as the problem of the effect of pretrial detention on post-punishment behaviour (especially for young offenders see, e.g., Frazier & Bishop, 1985). These issues are beyond the scope of this work. The effect of pretrial detention on sentencing is sometimes also explored when looking at the sentencing process in general (see review in Chiricos & Bales, 1991; the short description in Ulmer, 2012) or other problems of criminal justice (see, e.g., Humphrey & Fogarty, 1987; Oleson, Lowenkamp, Cadigan, VanNostrand, & Wooldredge, 2016). Contemporary authors emphasise that there are only few studies devoted to this subject (Reitler, Sullivan, & Frank, 2013).

The predictors of the probability of pretrial detention traditionally focused on the legal and extralegal formal characteristics of the convicted and used regression models (Spohn, 2008; Williams, 2003). Researchers found connections between the likelihood of pretrial detention and other factors. Unsurprisingly, these factors were formal legal predictors: criminal records and criminal history (Holmes, Daudistel, & Farrell, 1987; Oleson et al., 2016; Sacks & Ackerman, 2014, 2012), the seriousness of the crime (see review in Spohn, 2015; discussion in Wermink et al., 2016), and reports from the probation services (Oleson et al., 2016). The formal rules for decisions regarding pretrial detention vary in different jurisdictions, but the three factors specified above are frequently considered. In sum, decisions regarding pretrial detention are generally predictable: repeat offenders (or offenders with a long history of crime) who are convicted of more serious offences are frequently detained (Spohn, 2008).

However, the key testable hypotheses are not oriented to the influence of the legal factors. The scholars looked at the extralegal characteristics of the convicted person (Spohn, 2015). Discovering the inequality between formally equal groups was a main aim of these research endeavours (Mitchell, 2005; Spohn, 2015; Ulmer, 2012). During the last half-century, scholars tested the influence of many extralegal factors, such as race and ethnicity (Demuth, 2003; McIntyre & Baradaran, 2013; Spohn, 2008) and gender, age and its interactions (Demuth & Steffensmeier, 2004; Freiburger & Hilinski, 2010; Oleson et al., 2016). Therefore, the most discriminated groups (young men from minorities) are discriminated when it comes to pretrial detention too. They have much greater chances to be detained than representatives of other groups (Spohn, 2015).

The most difficult (and perhaps most important) issue is the question about the socio-economic status (SES) of the offender (Demuth, 2003; Spohn, 2008). Scholars tested the role of such predictors as employment status (D'Alessio & Stolzenberg, 2002), educational level (Spohn, 2008), and family ties (Demuth, 2003). Although most of the recent papers use various socio-economic variables as controllers in the regression models, different papers give conflicting answers regarding the effect of these variables on pretrial detention decisions. This could, however, be explained by different research designs and sampling (Spohn, 2015). In a recent article, Reitler et al. (2013) discuss the overlaps between legal and extralegal factors. They point out that if we take into account all recommendations for judges about family and social ties in the analysis, and take into account the fact that race and gender could be markers of lifestyle, scholars may conclude that there are not any extralegal characteristics. That said, these discussions are almost irrelevant in the Russian context. The reasons for this are discussed in the following section.

Consequently, this article will first address factors that influence the probability of pretrial detention in Russia. The discussion about legal vs. extralegal factors is not formally relevant for Russian law. Legally, the Russian Criminal Procedural Code (article 99) rules that the judge has to take into account "the seriousness of the crime, information about the personality of the defendant, his/her age, health conditions, family circumstances, employment status and other circumstances." The category "personality" in Russian legal discourses is explored further. So, in the Russian context, all extralegal factors can be interpreted as direct legal factors or proxy variables for them. However, this fact does not reduce the importance of the formal empirical model of pretrial detention in Russian criminal justice.

The next topic is the problem of the influence of pretrial detention on the trial outcome. In recent research, scholars have pointed out that "pretrial decisions determine mostly everything" (Sacks & Ackerman, 2014, p. 14). The influence of pretrial detention is usually analysed in relation to the verdict (Spohn, 2008, 2015; Williams, 2003), case dismissal (e.g., Spohn, 2015; Wheeler & Wheeler, 1980), the type of punishment (as a probability of incarceration – Sacks & Ackerman, 2014; Spohn, 2013), or the length of the sentence (Ibid). Research on pretrial detention (conducted with standard controls) indicates that pretrial detention significantly influences the decision concerning imprisonment. Its role in dismissing the case and the verdict is not so significant (Sacks & Ackerman, 2014; Williams, 2003). Furthermore, different studies show different effects on the length of incarceration.

Mariann Williams (2003) systematised and described the mechanisms of the influence of pretrial detention on the imprisonment decision. The first mechanism is the influence on the judge's position as a predictor of the defendant behaviour. Pretrial detention may be an artefact of economic bias, directly or through the access to a private attorney (see also Wheeler & Wheeler, 1980). Additionally, pretrial detention may be a marker of family and social ties (like employment, care of others, etc. – see Reitler et al., 2013). Naturally, all these mechanisms may also work in unison.

Extralegal factors play a large role in decisions about pretrial detention, and a lesser role in decisions about incarceration. Could it be that the fact of pretrial detention becomes a marker for the untrustworthiness of the defendant? Spohn (2013) described this complex set of relations as an indirect influence of extralegal factors (*if you were detained you are a more dangerous criminal*) on the incarceration decision and reviewed previous research on this subject.

Consequently, the second group of questions for this article is the following: does pretrial detention influence dismissal decisions, imprisonment decisions, and decisions about the length of the sentence? After considering these questions, we will turn to the discussion on the question of indirect influence in the last section.

One final aspect worth pointing out is country specific. All major quantitative studies are based on data from US federal courts (see Spohn, 2008) or on samples from a few state courts in different counties (see Sacks & Ackerman, 2012). The author of this article is not aware of any exhaustive research on this problem based on data from non-US countries, since only general descriptions without serious statistical analysis have been published on non-US pretrial detention (see Hafetz, 2002). There are only two exceptions – Israel (Gazal-Ayal & Sulitzeanu-Kenan, 2010) and the Netherlands (Wermink et al., 2016). At the same time, in spite of different characteristics of pretrial detention in different jurisdictions (Foglesong & Stone, 2011; Schönteich, 2013) the phenomenon of pretrial detention has similar meaning in different legal spaces (Domingo & Denney, 2013). Thus, these two articles (Gazal-Ayal & Sulitzeanu-Kenan, 2010; Wermink et al., 2016) demonstrate the applicability this model of analysis for non-US countries.

The present study

Context

The current legal system affords the Russian judge a considerable degree of discretion. There are no sentencing guidelines (only maximum and minimum punishments for each type of crime). However, the Russian criminal code rejects the principle of equal punishment for equal crime: it obliges the judge to take into account the personality of the offender (see further the description of personality in the Russian legal system). Judges are led to give different sentences to people who have committed the same crime. As shown in the introduction, Article 99 of the Russian Criminal Procedural Code establishes this rule for pretrial detention. Article 60 of the Russian Criminal Code (part 3; CC RF 1997) declares that in the sentencing decision, the judge has to "take into

CRIMINOLOGY AND CRIMINAL JUSTICE IN RUSSIA

account the character and measure of public danger presented by the crime and personality of the offender, including the aggravating and the mitigating circumstances, and also the influence of the punishment on the correction of the offender and on the living conditions of his (or her) family." The category of "personality" in Russian legal discourse has a very broad definition. Family and social ties, education, employment status – all these characteristics are interpreted as a part of "personality" in Russian legal discourse (see, e.g., Khun, 2010). So, the "personality" is a universal category for all extralegal and informal characteristics of defendant.

Methodology and data

A statistical analysis is more adequate for typical, routine cases. A crime that is rarely encountered by the judge or investigator will be resolved in a less predictable way. As was shown earlier (Holmes et al., 1987), there is a different degree of influence of pretrial detention for different crimes. Consequently, three typical crimes were chosen for this analysis, accounting for more than 22% of all Russian criminal cases (Sudebny department, 2013): theft, drug possession, and violent crime. These three crimes also refer to three different types of offences.

As of July 2010, all Russian courts of general jurisdiction are required by law to publish their decisions on websites. As it stands, courts publish approximately 37% of their decisions (Rezultaty monitoringa, 2012; Pozdnyakov, 2013). Moreover, courts do not tend to place any specific types of decisions and these 37% can be used as a basis for a representative sample (Pozdnyakov, 2013). Unfortunately, many important variables are not available for analysis. They are removed from the decision text as stipulated by Russian data protection and privacy law. These variables include, for example, information about age (date of birth), place of residence (type of settlement), and others. Models including this information will be analysed using another data set.

In 2011 and the first half of 2012, the Institute for the Rule of Law at the European University at St. Petersburg (Russia) collected 10,000 decisions of Russian criminal courts. The research design has been exhaustively described in Titaev (2011).

A two-stage simple random sample was used. At the first stage, 200 courts were randomly selected. Russian courts have different sizes, with between 5 and 40 judges per court. This method of selection gives some preference to smaller courts. However, current research indicates that there are no significant differences between bigger and smaller courts, allowing us to neglect this bias (Skougarevsky, 2014; Volkov, 2014). At the second stage, the dates between 1 January 2011 and 31 December 2012 were randomly selected, separately for each court. Subsequently, the coder used 50 cases that were resolved closest to this date. For approximately 20% of the selected courts, 50 cases were not available and were chosen from the courts in the reserve sample.

After the selection, every case was coded for 50 sustainable variables. The data set is human coded. It is not available for machine coding because Russian courts do not have a unified method for describing similar facts and there is no one technique or single file format for uploading the documents. The variables can be aggregated into several groups: personal characteristics of the defendant (gender, presence of dependents, criminal records, employment, and other), characteristics of the crime (article of the Criminal Code, number of crimes in the case, and number of defendants in the case), information about the behaviour of the victim (civil claim resolved together with the criminal case), parameters of the process (plea bargain, gender of the judge, public prosecutor, and defence attorney), and information about the behaviour of the defendant during the pretrial investigation (confession of guilt, compensation given to victims, and other factors). All these characteristics are described in Russian court decisions (verdicts, sentences, and other decisions).

The explanations of the variables are presented in Table 1. Some of these variables have common meanings (like gender) and do not need any special description. However, some variables (like a non-Slavonic last name) need special notations, which are presented below. Together, they are used as standard predictors for pretrial detention and standard controls for measuring the influence of pretrial detention on the sentence.

CRIMINOLOGY AND CRIMINAL JUSTICE IN RUSSIA

Table 1. Description and coding of variables.

Variable	Code
Dependent variables	
Pretrial detention	1 – defendant is imprisoned before first hearing, 0 – defendant is not imprisoned
Actual decision (not dismissal of case)	1 – case is not dismissed (real decision), 0 – case is dismissed
Real incarceration	1 – sentenced to incarceration, 0 – other sentences
Length of imprisonment	Years
Personal characteristics	
Gender of accused	1 – male, 0 – female
Non-Slavonic last name	1 – the accused has non -Slavonic or other "discriminated against" last name, 0 – other
Unemployed	1 – the accused is unemployed, 0 – other
Criminal records	1 – reference to informal criminal records (sudimost) in the sentence, 0 – no reference
Formal criminal records (recidivism)	1 – reference to formal criminal records (recidivism) in the sentence, 0 – no reference
Dependents	1 – the accused has an underage child (children), 0 – no children
The characteristics of the crime	
Number of accused in the case	Number
Number of charges in the case	Number
The behaviour of accused and victim	
Reconciliation of parties	1 – in the sentence there is a reference to reconciliation or active remorse in the sentence, 0 – no reference
Confession of guilt	1 – the accused has pleaded guilty
Certificates of good conduct	1 – reference to certificates of good conduct in the sentence, 0 – no reference
Extenuating circumstances	1 – important (according Criminal Code) extenuating circumstances (surrender, giving oneself up or assistance provided to a victim after crime) in the sentence, 0 – no reference
Civil claim	1 – separate civil claim in the case, 0 – no claim
The characteristics of the hearing	
Special order (plea bargain)	1 – the case after plea bargain, 0 – other
Gender of judge	1 – male, 0 – female
Gender of prosecutor	1 – male, 0 – female
Gender of defence attorney	1 – male, 0 – female

As in all similar studies (e.g., Williams, 2003), data about the sentence (type and dimension of punishment) and imprisonment are used as dependent variables. In Russia, one cannot use the verdict as a dependent variable because the number of acquittals is too small. The characteristics of the crime, hearing, and defendant are used as independent variables. The fact of pretrial detention is used as an independent variable when analysing the predictors and reasons for punishment.

The "Non-Slavonic last name" variable is used in this research as a proxy variable for ethnicity. Even though Russian criminal statistics do not register ethnicity – instead registering only citizenship – potential ethnic discrimination of Russian citizens with non-Slavonic ethnicities (especially from the Caucasus and Central Asia) will be discussed.

In the Russian legal system, there is a significant difference between the usual criminal records (*sudimost*), which can only be used as being characteristic of the personality or personal qualities of the accused and recidivism – a formal characteristic for several serious types of criminal records. Some years (from 1 year for non-serious crimes to 10 years, for, e.g., murder) later the discharge the criminal has the formal criminal record and new crime will be a case of recidivism. But after these period, new crime should be interpreted as a first-time violation. Judge has to take into account the recidivism but only may take into account the "sudimost" (criminal records). Table 2 shows that 41.4% defendants accused of theft have criminal records, but only 24.6% are recidivists in the legal sense.

The reconciliation of parties is a uniquely Russian legal technique. It means that the victim formally declares that the offender has compensated all damages and the victim does not have any claims. The reconciliation of parties is one of the formal preconditions for dismissing the case.

Certificates of good conduct are endorsements from relatives, colleagues, neighbours, officials, and others. This is a special mechanism for characterising the accused, inherited from Soviet times. The certificates have to describe the accused as a "good person" in real life (law-abiding, responsible, not prone to drinking). For the purposes of this paper, we will assume that these certificates are proxy variables for social capital, the sum total of "social connections" of the accused.

Extenuating circumstances in Russian law are formal parameters meant to affect the length of the sentence. They encompass nine points in total, including it being the defendant's first offence, voluntary surrender, and others. Some of extenuating circumstances in this model (like having dependents) are registered separately. In Russian law, there is no fixed measure for the effect of all extenuating circumstances on the sentence. These circumstances reflect good relations between the defendant and investigator. This is because it is usually the investigator who registers these circumstances in the case file.

A civil claim is a form of resolving the question about compensation paid to the victim within the legal criminal procedure. It indicates, first, the presence of an actual victim in said case and, second, the fact of real damage having been done to the victim.

A plea bargain (or special order) is slightly different from the American model (see details in Solomon, 2008). In the Russian version of the plea bargain, the defendant accepts the legal qualification of the crime and the list of crimes presented in the case. However, he or she cannot influence the sentence length. That said, the sentence has to be shorter than two-thirds of the maximum sentence length for the given crime. The presence or absence of a plea bargain is a very important legal characteristic of the case. For that reason, it will be used as a control variable in the regression model.

Findings

Demographic characteristics

There are two important decisions to be made in the strategy of exploration the extralegal factors in the court behaviour. First, one needs to choose the analytical approach. We can analyse the case pool together, including all types of crimes and all types of accused. In this type of research, all case types are "mixed." However, according to the law of large numbers, we can still see the main effects of the independent variables. This approach is often used in economics (for an example of data on Russia, see Skougarevsky, 2014; Volkov, 2014). An alternative strategy is to only consider frequently occurring crimes (e.g., theft) and to analyse several types of frequent crimes separately. This way, research is protected from the juridical doubt about the "common or regular crime."

In addition to the above decision, we may choose to study the effects of our predictors separately or together. The first method usually employs various techniques (e.g., regression analysis). This way, all complex and linked effects can be isolated. The second method is based on pair dependence and puts greater emphasis on the role of each separate factor. In this paper, only three types of crimes and some groups of factors are analysed together.

Descriptive statistics and of the variables are presented in Table 2.

Three legally defined crimes have been chosen for the study (in line with the main idea about the different effects of the same predictors for different crimes (Holmes et al., 1987)). These three crimes account for around 22% of all sentenced crimes in Russia and belong to three different types of crimes. In the Russian Criminal Code (CC RF 1997), there is a difference between an article and a part of an article. An article describes the crime in general (e.g., theft). A "part of the article" specifies the exact corpus delicti – for example, burglary as a form of theft. The Russian

CRIMINOLOGY AND CRIMINAL JUSTICE IN RUSSIA

Table 2. Descriptive statistics for key variables.

Variable	Violent crime (p. 1 art. 111 RCC)			Theft(p.2 art 158 RCC)			Drug possession (p. 1 art. 228 RCC)		
	N	Mean	Standard deviation	N	Mean	Standard deviation	N	Mean	Standard deviation
Dependent variable									
Pretrial detention	526	0.194	0.396	2799	0.166	0.373	791	0.121	0.327
Non-dismissal	518	0.994	0.076	2771	0.817	0.386	791	0.992	0.087
Real incarceration	528	0.375	0.485	2815	0.261	0.439	795	0.243	0.429
Length of imprisonment	198	2.508	0.981	733	1.550	0.604	192	1.430	1.232
Personal characteristics									
Gender of accused (Male)	527	0.732	0.443	2813	0.865	0.342	794	0.917	0.276
Non-Slavonic last name	521	0.036	0.188	2766	0.043	0.204	785	0.069	0.253
Unemployed	528	0.256	0.437	2815	0.299	0.458	795	0.247	0.431
Criminal records	528	0.225	0.418	2815	0.414	0.493	795	0.287	0.453
Formal criminal records	528	0.152	0.359	2815	0.246	0.431	795	0.172	0.378
Dependents	502	0.319	0.466	2551	0.241	0.428	756	0.282	0.450
The characteristics of the crime									
Number of accused in case	528	1.000	0.062	2815	1.263	0.571	795	1.019	0.145
Number of accusations in case	523	1.034	0.275	2435	1.419	1.499	791	1.114	0.421
The behaviour of accused and victim									
Reconciliation of parties	528	0.184	0.388	2815	0.259	0.438	795	0.064	0.245
Confession (self-admission) of guilt	528	0.970	0.172	2815	0.989	0.103	795	0.980	0.141
Certificates of good conduct	528	0.589	0.492	2815	0.433	0.496	795	0.652	0.477
Extenuating circumstances	528	0.640	0.480	2815	0.627	0.484	795	0.455	0.498
Civil claim	528	0.301	0.459	2815	0.215	0.411	795	0.004	0.061
Characteristics of the hearing									
Special order (plea bargain)	528	0.716	0.451	2815	0.730	0.444	795	0.854	0.353
Gender of judge	528	0.576	0.495	2815	0.520	0.500	795	0.546	0.498
Gender of prosecutor	481	0.611	0.488	2612	0.616	0.486	715	0.607	0.489
Gender of defence attorney	510	0.639	0.481	2721	0.608	0.488	763	0.516	0.500

Criminal Code includes less than 300 articles (excluding general section (articles 1–104) which describe basic rules of punishment) and around 1000 parts. In this research, three parts of articles (corpus delicti) were chosen.

- Part 1 of article 111 of the Russian Criminal Code (CC RF 1997). Infliction of damage to health without special circumstances. It describes a typical violent crime, including – for example – a fight or physical confrontation. Around 50,000 sentences are passed on this article every year. More than one-third of the accused are sentenced to incarceration. The maximum sentence is 8 years of incarceration.
- Part 2 of Article 158 of the Russian Criminal Code (CC RF 1997). Theft with aggravating circumstances (by a group, burglary, from clothing items or bags, causing substantial damage). This is a common property crime. The probability of sentencing to actual incarceration is 23.4%. Russian courts hear more than 150,000 of such cases annually. The maximum sentence is 5 years of incarceration.
- Part 1 of Article 228 of the Russian Criminal Code. The purchase, possession, transportation or production drugs without selling them. It is a typical drug-related, victimless crime. More than 50,000 individuals are sentenced under this article every year. Every fifth person is sentenced to incarceration. The maximum sentence on this article is 3 years of incarceration.

To interpret our models, additional qualitative data were employed. More than 50 interviews with judges, investigators, prosecutors, lawyers, and experts have been conducted (Paneyakh, Pozdnyakov, Titaev, & Shklyaruk, 2012; Volkov et al., 2012).

The likelihood of pretrial detention for suspects in Russia

In the following section, I will describe the factors of pretrial detention and the social mechanism for selecting the suspect prior to detention. The Russian Criminal Procedural Code gives the investigator 48 hours after arrest for making a decision and obtaining all necessary approvals for pretrial detention. Consequently, we have to describe the role of different factors in the order in which this information becomes available to the investigator. At the first stage in the typical case, the investigator learns all basic personal information a few hours after the arrest. We can check the role of these personal characteristics against the odds of pretrial detention. During the next stage of investigation, the detective prepares the preliminary legal qualification of the crime. It includes highlighting the relevant article of the Criminal Code, the number of the accused, and the number of accusations involved in the case. This description can be changed during the following stages of the pretrial investigation process, but, according to interview sources, this first description is important for deciding on pretrial detention. Throughout the process of the pretrial investigation and during the trial, the investigator tries to predict the behaviour of the parties. Although he or she may occasionally fail, he or she usually gains an understanding of the behaviour of the accused and the victim before deciding on pretrial detention. The results of binomial regression are presented in Table 3.

The relatively larger number of significant predictors for theft can be explained by the larger sample size for this crime. In general, there are two main predictors. The "unemployed" status of the accused connected with higher odds of detention (from 1.44 times for violent crime to 1.18 for theft). The chances of detention increase if there is a criminal record (more than 2 times for all types of crimes).

The influence of the "unemployed" status and criminal records is significant. The role of the number of accused and the number of charges is insignificant in cases of violent crime and theft.

In our research, the number of accusations is important for drug cases. A large number of charges are linked with higher odds of pretrial detention in drug cases (more than 1.7 times more likely). This difference between drug possession, theft, and violent crime indicates that there are separate models for different crimes.

We can see that the confession of guilt by the accused is a significant factor for cases of violence and theft. A confessing suspect is less likely to be subjected to pretrial detention (odds ratio 0.143–0.146). Investigators told in interviews that pretrial detention has two main objectives:

Table 3. Results of the binomial regression for dependent variable "pretrial detention."

Variable	Violent crime			Theft			Drug possession		
	B	S.E.	Exp. (B)	B	S.E.	Exp. (B)	B	S.E.	Exp. (B)
Gender of accused	0.650	(0.383)	1.915	0.122	(0.191)	1.130	0.332	(0.493)	1.394
Dependents	−0.289	(0.307)	0.749	−0.277	(0.142)	0.758	0.390	(0.288)	1.477
Non-Slavonic last name	0.650	(0.584)	1.916	0.516	(0.257)	1.675*	−0.062	(0.469)	0.940
Unemployed	0.731	(0.277)	2.076**	0.329	(0.121)	1.390**	0.689	(0.273)	1.992*
Criminal records	1.356	(0.409)	3.881***	1.622	(0.161)	5.065***	1.733	(0.336)	5.658***
Formal criminal records (recidiv)	0.422	(0.447)	1.525	0.255	(0.139)	1.291	−0.017	(0.349)	0.983
Number of accused in the case	21.261	(2.4×10^4)	1.7×10^9	−0.205	(0.114)	0.815	1.465	(0.573)	4.328*
Number of charges in the case	−0.238	(0.764)	0.788	0.237	(0.040)	1.268	1.134	(0.253)	3.109***
Extenuating circumstances	−0.685	(0.546)	0.504	0.336	(0.245)	1.400	−0.417	(0.408)	0.659
Reconciliation of the parties	0.427	(0.332)	1.533	−0.022	(0.171)	0.979	0.030	(0.508)	1.030
Confession of guilt	−1.924	(0.643)	.146**	−1.946	(0.464)	.143***	−1.030	(0.607)	0.357
Certificates of good conduct	−0.363	(0.270)	0.695	−0.252	(0.120)	0.778*	−0.153	(0.272)	0.858
Civil claim	0.261	(0.282)	1.299	0.539	(0.128)	1.714***	−0.168	(1.452)	0.845
(Constant)	−4.810	(1.081)	0.000	−1.314	(0.522)	0.269*	−4.810	(1.081)	0.008***
N		494			2417			744	
Nagelkerke R^2		0.260			0.249			0.253	

S.E. = standard error, *$p < 0.1$; **$p < 0.05$; ***$p < 0.01$.

to prevent escape and to obtain a confession. A criminal record and unemployment status, from their point of view, increases the likelihood of escape.

For theft cases, two proxy-variables are also important. The first one is the commencement of a civil claim within the criminal procedure (a specifically Russian mechanism for compensating the victim of the crime). It is not only representative of the size of damage but also an indicator of the social power of the victim. Socio-economically disadvantaged victims do not tend to know about this mechanism and consequently do not employ legal ways of pursuing compensation. The second important variable is the certificates of good conduct (however, their significance is not very substantial).

For all cases, there is an additional predictor of minor significance: the formal criminal record that defines the accused as a recidivist. The standard criminal records turned out to be more important than recidivism for Russian judges.

All predictors used explain around 25% of variance in all analysed crimes. In other words, these factors are responsible for 25% of the reasons for pretrial detention.

The role of pretrial detention in dismissal decisions

This section describes the effect of pretrial detention on the likelihood of dismissing the case in court. The dismissal of a case is a Russian legal technique (there are differences between Russian and US technique of dismissal. The judge can only dismiss the case if all of the following three conditions are met: if it is not major or serious, if the offender confesses guilt, and if he or she offers a compensation to the victim. There are many legal limitations for dismissal. In practice, however, there are only two important factors: the crime has to be comparably minor (maximum length of incarceration should not be more than 5 years) and the victim has to accept the deal (which removes this possibility for victimless crimes). In our sample, only theft meets these two conditions. Violent crime is too serious a crime for dismissal, while drug possession is a victimless crime. Consequently, only theft cases will be analysed in this section.

For this research, we have to analyse the general influence of pretrial detention described above. In this situation, we face the problem of endogeneity. In other words, we have to assume that the combined influence of pretrial detention and other control factors can actually be explained by other, "hidden" variables. The standard solution to this problem used in econometrics is to instrument key variables. However, in this – sample-based – research, we are unable to add any new variables to our data set and thereby control the sample. In fact, the Russian investigator, prosecutor, and judge do not possess any personal data about the defendant. At the first stage, the investigator describes a few formal characteristics and – at the next stage – he or she does not communicate or meet the accused. In many cases, the prosecutor sees the accused for the very first time in the courtroom. In the Russian system of criminal justice, contact between the prosecutor and the defendant before the trial is very rare. Consequently, according to our interviews and other qualitative data, we have to conclude that the investigator, prosecutor, and judge focus on a few simple markers in the offender's biography. All these factors are presented in our sample (excluding, as mentioned above, age, education, place of residence, and the type of settlement[2]). This point is important for all following sections, as the logic of the analysis will proceed along similar lines.

In analysing the role of pretrial detention in the chances for the case dismissal (Table 4), I controlled the role of pretrial detention by personal characteristics. All predictors, except a non-Slavonic last name, unemployment, and the formal criminal records are significant. Pretrial detention in this model reduces the likelihood of dismissal (1 in the dependent variable stands for the actual decision and 0 – for dismissed cases). The odds ratio for pretrial detention is 11.5 (more than 3.4 times likely) – only criminal records have a higher odds ratio. Defendants with children have a lower chance for dismissal.

Table 4. Results of binomial logistic regression for dependent variable "case is NOT dismissed."

Variable	Theft		
	B	S.E.	Exp. (B)
Pretrial detention	2.439	(0.795)	11.462***
Gender of accused	0.790	(0.266)	2.203***
Dependents	0.607	(0.244)	1.836**
Non-Slavonic last name	0.184	(0.503)	1.202
Unemployed	0.087	(0.220)	1.090
Criminal records	2.856	(0.454)	17.392***
Formal criminal records (recidiv)	16.524	(1290.851)	15001673.285
Number of accused in case	0.338	(0.183)	1.403
Reconciliation of the parties	−3.932	(0.213)	0.020***
Confession of guilt	−18.475	(6143.054)	0.000
Civil claim	18.408	(1409.338)	98694648.129
(Constant)	20.085	(6143.055)	528103314.008
N		2383	
Nagelkerke R^2		0.705	

S.E. = standard error, **$p < 0.05$; ***$p < 0.01$.

We can see that R-squared reaches 70.5%. Plea bargains are excluded from analysis. We interpret this as a sorting mechanism – in cases that have a chance of dismissal, plea bargains are not commonly employed: if the accused opts for a plea bargain in Russia, they lose all chances for dismissal.

According to this model, pretrial detention has a significant impact on the likelihood of case dismissal. Detained offenders have less chances for case dismissal. However, other factors also play a large role in this decision. In general, one can describe this situation as the judge's, prosecutor's, and investigator's choice (they all have to approve the dismissal), where there are several main factors (pretrial detention, criminal records, and the reconciliation of parties) and some less important ones.

Pretrial detention and the likelihood of imprisonment

The next stage of the Russian criminal procedure is the decision about the type of punishment. As the prosecutors and judges indicated in expert interviews, it is a choice between imprisonment and all other types of punishment. The differences between other types of punishment (non-imprisonment) are mainly technical and linked with social and economic conditions of the accused. For instance, the economic status of the offender plays a large role in the decision regarding fines or community service. In the following section, the influence of pretrial detention on the probability of imprisonment will be analysed.

From this stage and onwards, dismissed cases will be excluded from the sample. This is because no actual decision about the type of punishment has occurred in this type of a case.

Our predictors account for 57–64% of the variance (Table 5). The key factors are the criminal record (odds ratio of 9.3–10 for the imprisonment – 3.05–3.15 times) and pretrial detention (odds ratio of 6.7–16.1 for an imprisonment, risk ratio 2.6–4.1). Some factors are only important for theft and drug possession. They include non-Slavonic last names, formal criminal records and the number of charges in the case. Some factors are important for theft and – to a lesser extent – for the infliction of bodily harm. These include social connections (certificates of good conduct) and the reconciliation of the parties. Special orders (plea bargains) are only important for violent crime cases. Several characteristics of the accused and behaviour of parties are important for theft cases (however, this may be attributed to the larger sample size for cases of theft). These include extenuating circumstances and civil claims, confessions of guilt, and the gender of accused.

Table 5. Results of binomial logistic regression for dependent variable "imprisonment."

	Violent crime			Theft			Drug possession		
	b	S.E.	Exp. (B)	b	S.E.	Exp. (B)	B	S.E.	Exp. (B)
Pretrial detention	2.780	(0.447)	16.115***	1.909	(0.161)	6.744***	2.252	(0.414)	9.503***
Gender of accused	0.508	(0.354)	1.661	0.590	(0.220)	1,804***	−0,503	(0.555)	0.605
Dependents	0.021	(0.322)	1.021	−0.253	(0.154)	0,777	−0,212	(0.324)	0.809
Non-Slavonic last name	−0.841	(0.785)	0.431	0.779	(0.287)	2.180***	1.346	(0.459)	3.840***
Unemployed	0.059	(0.328)	1.060	−0.150	(0.140)	0.861	0.073	(0.322)	1.076
Criminal records	2.250	(0.519)	9.491***	2.232	(0.184)	9.316***	2.305	(0.381)	10.019***
Formal criminal records (recidiv)	1.303	(0.674)	3.682*	0.724	(0.149)	2.064***	1.634	(0.400)	5.125***
Number of accused in the case	−3.969	(3.201)	0.019	−0.222	(0.127)	0.801*	0.881	(0.792)	2.414
Number of charges in the case	1.352	(0.771)	3.863*	0.267	(0.060)	1.306***	2.010	(0.382)	7.462***
Extenuating circumstances	0.400	(1.014)	1.492	1.081	(0.317)	2.949***	−0.363	(0.491)	0.695
Reconciliation of the parties	−0.836	(0.414)	0.433**	−0.592	(0.200)	0.553***	−0.085	(0.518)	0.918
Confession of guilt	−1.233	(0.941)	0.292	−3.112	(0.701)	0.045***	−1.647	(1.030)	0.193
Certificates of good conduct	−1.051	(0.301)	0.350***	−0.675	(0.132)	0.509***	−0.481	(0.298)	0.618
Special order (plea bargain)	0.443	(0.320)	1.557**	0.532	(0.150)	1.702	−0.973	(2.108)	0.378
Gender of judge	−0.766	(0.336)	0.465	0.250	(0.182)	1.284	−0.610	(0.410)	0.543
Gender of prosecutor	0.110	(0.295)	1.116	0.087	(0.130)	1.091	−0.020	(0.288)	0.981
Gender of advocate	0.241	(0.304)	1.273	0.025	(0.135)	1.025	0.464	(0.297)	1.590
Civil claim	−0.096	(0.303)	0.909	0.050	(0.134)	1.052	−0.086	(0.289)	0.918
(Constant)	2.332	(3.490)	10.301	−1.562	(0.761)	0.210	−3.165	(1.542)	0.042**
N		426			2144			614	
Nagelkerke R^2		0.590			0.566			0.636	

S.E. = standard error, *$p < 0.1$; **$p < 0.05$; ***$p < 0.01$.

Pretrial detention and its influence on sentence severity

The last section of this paper tests the hypothesis concerning the influence of pretrial detention on the length of real imprisonment. Before discussing this question, two methodological points have to be considered. The first is the possibility of analysing cases with a violent crime and drug possession. They are presented only for illustrative purposes and will not be analysed, as the size of the sample (160 and 155 cases) makes it unsuitable for linear regression analysis. The second point concerns the character of the dependent variable. For better analysis, we should code this variable as a logarithm of the length of imprisonment. However, for the purposes of this preliminary discussion, I will sacrifice methodological precision in favour of a more interpretable model.

This model (Table 6) shows that the influence of pretrial detention on the length of imprisonment is insignificant. An important role is played by such predictors as formal and informal criminal records (+0.16 and +0.09 years for theft, respectively), plea bargains (−0.11 years for theft), and – ironically – the reconciliation of the parties and an additionally resolved civil claim (+0.11 and 0.087 years for theft, respectively).

Conclusions and discussion

As shown in previous sections, pretrial detention is a key factor when it comes to decisions about the type of punishment. Pretrial-detained offenders have an odds ratio of more than 6 for imprisonment in typical criminal cases. This tendency is significant with all important controllers (like criminal records, gender, and other). This is very similar to the American situation (Freiburger & Hilinski, 2010). In general, we can see that pretrial detention has a paramount influence on the decision about imprisonment: it is second in importance only to the criminal record.

We can offer a very straightforward explanation for this phenomenon. According to the research (Volkov, Dmitrieva, Pozdnjakov, & Titaev, 2015), the fact that the offenders whose

CRIMINOLOGY AND CRIMINAL JUSTICE IN RUSSIA

Table 6. Results of OLS regression for dependent variable "length of imprisonment."

Variable	Violent crime		Theft		Drug possession	
	B	Sig.	B	Sig.	B	Sig.
(Constant)		0.000		0.000		0.000
Pretrial detention	0.110	0.169	0.001	0.974	0.077	0.278
Gender of accused	−0.065	0.415	0.046	0.235	−0.111	0.101
Dependents	−0.110	0.172	−0.024	0.556	0.025	0.725
Non-Slavonic last name	0.015	0.846	0.040	0.318	0.146**	0.041
Unemployed	0.014	0.853	0.062	0.120	−0.008	0.909
Criminal records	0.383***	0.002	0.092**	0.037	−0.034	0.724
Formal criminal records (recidiv)	−0.060	0.610	0.165***	0.000	−0.013	0.882
Number of accused in case	−0.001	0.988	0.072*	0.072	−0.004	0.958
Number of accusations in case	−0.105	0.181	0.022	0.588	−0.034	0.630
Extenuating circumstances	0.007	0.931	−0.030	0.484	0.086	0.243
Reconciliation of parties	−0.065	0.395	0.111***	0.006	0.522***	0.000
Confession of guilt	−0.151*	0.082	−0.075*	0.080	−0.036	0.638
Certificates of good conduct	−0.052	0.501	−0.019	0.636	−0.046	0.509
Civil claim	−0.062*	0.423	0.087**	0.030	−0.043	0.534
Special order (plea bargain)	−0.217***	0.009	−0.110***	0.009	−0.257***	0.001
Gender of judge	0.087	0.264	−0.019	0.628	−0.066	0.330
Gender of prosecutor	−0.069	0.360	−0.024	0.534	−0.061	0.375
Gender of advocate	0.030	0.686	−0.022	0.587	0.042	0.540
N	160		619		155	
Adj. R^2	0.163		0.079		0.367	

$*p < 0.1; **p < 0.05; ***p < 0.01.$

punishment did not involve a deprivation of freedom were previously pretrial-detained means that the decision about pretrial detention had not been well substantiated. Sometimes, such decisions instigated an inquiry into the investigator's competence. Under circumstances where judges tend to cooperate with prosecution and investigation rather than take a fully independent position (Paneyakh et al., 2012), a decision about pretrial detention is in fact a decision about the type of punishment. The system of formal accountability of Russian judges is also based on such a formal criterion as the "legal quality" of the decision. This term mainly denotes restraint from repealing the decisions by the higher courts. All judges in interviews emphasise that this criterion is not only applicable to the main decision (the sentence) but also to intermediate decisions – including the decision concerning pretrial detention in the first place. The Russian system of repeal includes not only the two usual stages – appellation and cassation but also a "nadzor" or a second cassation or revision. This instance could take any decision for a check of its own will. This instance can choose to re-evaluate any previous decision. This institution is inherited from the Soviet model. In the 40s and 50s, most of the judges did not have a legal education, court practices varied significantly and the other parties involved were not trained in law. The Soviet Supreme Court created this stage in order to enhance formal control and unify the application of the law. It made formal control possible under the first instance courts, without involving any of the other parties (Pozdnyakov, 2015).

However, in the contemporary Russian court system, higher courts have formal limitations in employing this mechanism, though they may still occasionally make use of it The decision to not sentence a pretrial detained criminal to imprisonment provides grounds for a revision of the work of the judges who opted for pretrial detention in the first place. The typical size of the Russian district court comprises around seven judicial positions. One position is usually vacant; two judges are on vacation, on training, or "on sick leave." Thus, only four judges are present in court every day and only two specialise in criminal cases. Under these circumstances, the level of solidarity is very high. The judge has very strong motivation to confirm the previous decision, which was made by his/her colleague or by himself/herself.

That said, this explanation does not contradict the three classical explanations (Williams, 2003) such as economic bias (through the access to private attorneys), a judge's predisposition, and the effect of family concerns. In Russia, the usual "criminal" tends to be from a socio-economically underprivileged background and commonly employs a public defence attorney. The system of public defence attorneys in Russia is wholly dependent on the court and investigative structures. It is the latter who evaluate the quality of the defence attorney's work and make decisions about their salary. The mechanisms of public or professional control over the public defence attorney's work are largely ineffective. In this situation, the social characteristics of the accused play a dominant role, as the access to the private attorney is the determining factor of the actual position of the accused during the hearing. According to recent research (Khodzhaeva, Kazun, & Yakovlev, 2015), less than 5% of the standard cases in the district court outside of big cities involve private attorneys.

At the same time, pretrial detention is a very important predictor for the chances for the case dismissal. If we compare the influence of pretrial detention in Russia with the effect that it has on verdicts in the United States, we can see a significant differences (Williams, 2003). According to the interviews, in Russia, we have a fairly straightforward model. Dismissing the case in which the defendant has been detained pretrial is quite difficult, as this casts serious doubt on the validity of the original decision of pretrial detention. The difference in the American situation may be connected to the participation of laymen in the verdict in the United States – the jury is not bound by solidarity with the judicial corporation.

The pretrial detention (in Russia) is not important for the length of imprisonment. In the United States, the situation is different (Spohn, 2013). The explanation may be connected to the predominance of qualitative research (and the possibility of testing the results through further statistical research). The method of calculating sentence length used by Russian judges is very formal. Judges are well aware of the mean length of imprisonment for every routine crime and the formal markers for its adjustment (i.e., firearm use = +1 year, confession of guilt = −2 years, etc.). The detention status is not one of these markers, neither on formal nor on informal levels.

The key predictors of the pretrial detention in routine cases are the presence of a previous criminal record, unemployment, and the confession of guilt (excluding drug possession). Interestingly, classical social factors such as gender, dependents, and pseudo-ethnicity (non-Slavonic last name) do not play a significant role (compare Sacks & Ackerman, 2012; Spohn, 2008; Williams, 2003). In general, in Russian pretrials, the factors of the criminal biography (as informal characteristics) and unemployment are the most important grounds for pretrial detention. Admittedly, this model is not free from omitted variable bias (Mustard, 2003). In other words, we may have missed some important predictors explaining all other variance and also cancelling the effects of the analysed variables. However, there are two important considerations. The first is connected with the possibility of logical or theoretical hypothesising about other predictors. If we do not limit ourselves by this principle, we will never complete our analysis. From the interviews, expert positions and theoretical literature, we are aware of only one important predictor, which was not included in our model. It is the "homelessness" status of the accused. This information is not available because it is usually deleted from the texts of court decisions. All other important variables or their proxies are included in our model. The second consideration is more technical and connected with the problem of data collection. During the last century, all the studies that involved the creation of new data sets and sampling methods have been limited by the technical feasibility of the data collection process.

Finally, we have one more question. Is pretrial detention a mechanism of the indirect extralegal influence on the sentence? On the one hand – yes, but only for dismissing the case and the type of punishment, as the key role is played by such pseudo-legal factors such as unemployment and informal criminal records. On the other hand – no, because, in the Russian legal system, all these factors are part of "personal characteristics" or "personality," which the judge has to take into account. What is important is that the main role is played by factors which are very easy to define legally.

Notes

1. In Russian criminal law, there are two different types of cases. In private prosecution cases, accusations are presented by the victim without the participation of state officials. In public prosecution cases, accusations are presented by the official state prosecutor. The scope of this article does not include private prosecution cases.
2. These variables are highly significant (see Skougarevsky, 2014), but only in combination with our variables.

Acknowledgements

This text would have never been presented without the whole team of the Institute of the Rule of Law at the European University at St. Petersburg (Russia). The author is especially grateful to Vadim Volkov, Dmitry Skougarevsky, Ella Paneyakh, and Arina Dmitrieva, who have read, critiqued, and discussed drafts of this article. Additionally, I would like to extend my gratitude to the participants of the "Law and Society Annual Meeting (2013)" and "Changing the Russian Law: Legality and Current Challenges" conferences, where the earlier versions of the article were presented and discussed.

Funding

This work was supported by the John D. and Catherine T. MacArthur Foundation: [Grant Number 10-95485-000-GSS].

References

Ares, C., Rankin, A., & Sturz, H. (1963). The Manhattan bail project: An interim report on the pre-trial use of pre-trial parole. *New York University Law Review, 38*, 67–95.
CC RF. (1997). Criminal Code of Russian Federation, with amendments for 12/01/14.
Chiricos, T. G., & Bales, W. D. (1991). Unemployment and punishment: An empirical assessment. *Criminology, 29* (4), 701–724. doi:10.1111/crim.1991.29.issue-4
CPC RF. (2001). Criminal Procedural Code of Russian Federation, with amendments for 12/01/14.
D'Alessio, S. J., & Stolzenberg, L. (2002). A multilevel analysis of the relationship between labor surplus and pretrial incarceration. *Social Problems, 49*(2), 178–193. doi:10.1525/sp.2002.49.2.178
Demuth, S. (2003). Racial and ethnic differences in pretrial release decisions and outcomes: A comparison of Hispanic, Black, and White felony arrestees. *Criminology, 41*(3), 873–908. doi:10.1111/crim.2003.41.issue-3
Demuth, S., & Steffensmeier, D. (2004). The impact of gender and race-ethnicity in the pretrial release process. *Social Problems, 51*(2), 222–242. doi:10.1525/sp.2004.51.2.222
Domingo, P., & Denney, L. (2013). *The political economy of pre-trial detention*. London: ODI. Retrieved from http://www.odi.org.uk/sites/odi.org. uk/files/odi-assets/publications-opinion-files/8257.pdf
Foglesong, T. S., & Stone, C. (2011, April). Prison exit samples as a source for indicators of pretrial detention. *Safety and Justice, 2011*, 1–11.
Frazier, C. E., & Bishop, D. M. (1985). The pretrial detention of juveniles and its impact on case dispositions. *The Journal of Criminal Law and Criminology (1973-), 76*, 1132–1152. doi:10.2307/1143504
Freiburger, T. L., & Hilinski, C. M. (2010). The impact of race, gender, and age on the pretrial decision. *Criminal Justice Review, 35*(3), 318–334. doi:10.1177/0734016809360332
Gazal-Ayal, O., & Sulitzeanu-Kenan, R. (2010). Let my people go: Ethnic in-group bias in judicial decisions — Evidence from a randomized natural experiment. *Journal of Empirical Legal Studies, 7*(3), 403–428. doi:10.1111/ (ISSN)1740-1461
Goldkamp, J. S. (1983). Questioning the practice of pretrial detention: Some empirical evidence from Philadelphia. *The Journal of Criminal Law and Criminology (1973-), 74*(4), 1556–1588. doi:10.2307/1143065

CRIMINOLOGY AND CRIMINAL JUSTICE IN RUSSIA

Hafetz, J. L. (2002). Pretrial detention, human rights, and judicial reform in Latin America. *Fordham Int'l LJ, 26,* 1754.

Holmes, M. D., Daudistel, H. C., & Farrell, R. A. (1987). Determinants of charge reductions and final dispositions in cases of burglary and robbery. *Journal of Research in Crime and Delinquency, 24*(3), 233–254. doi:10.1177/0022427887024003004

Humphrey, J. A., & Fogarty, T. J. (1987). Race and plea bargained outcomes: A research note. *Social Forces, 66*(1), 176–182. doi:10.1093/sf/66.1.176

Khun, A. (2010). Uchet lichnosti vinovnogo pri naznachenii nakazanija. *Obshhestvo I Pravo, 5,* 94–99.

Khodzhaeva, E., Kazun, A., & Yakovlev, A. (2015). *Advokatskoe soobshchestvo Rossii.* Moscow: HSE.

McIntyre, F., & Baradaran, S. (2013). Race, prediction, and pretrial detention. *Journal of Empirical Legal Studies, 10* (4), 741–770. doi:10.1111/jels.2013.10.issue-4

Mitchell, O. (2005). A meta-analysis of race and sentencing research: Explaining the inconsistencies. *Journal of Quantitative Criminology, 21*(4), 439–466. doi:10.1007/s10940-005-7362-7

Mustard, D. B. (2003). Reexamining criminal behavior: The importance of omitted variable bias. *Review of Economics and Statistics, 85*(1), 205–211. doi:10.1162/rest.2003.85.1.205

Oleson, J. C., Lowenkamp, C. T., Cadigan, T. P., VanNostrand, M., & Wooldredge, J. (2016). The effects of pretrial detention in two federal districts. *Justice Quarterly, 33*(6), 1103–1122.

Paneyakh, E., Pozdnyakov, M., Titaev, K., & Shklyaruk, M. (2012). *Pravookhranitelnaya deyatelnost v Rosii: struktura, funktsionirovaniye, puti reformirovaniya Chast pervaya, Diagnostika raboty pravookhranitelnykh organov rf i vypolneniya imi politseyskoy funktsii* SPb, IRL EU SPb Retrieved from http://enforce.spb.ru/images/Fond_Kudrina/irl_pravookhrana_part_1_final_31_12_ich.pdf

Pozdnyakov, M. (2013). *Prakticheskaya realizatsiya printsipa otkrytosti pravosudiya v Rosyskoy Federatsii* SPb: IRL EU SPb. Retrieved from http://enforce.spb.ru/images/Isledovanya/otkrytost_pravosudiya_2013.pdf

Pozdnyakov, M. (2015). *Sistema osnovanii otmeny i izmeneniia sudebnykh aktov v rossiiskom ugolovnom protsesse.* Moscow: Yurlitinform.

Reitler, A. K., Sullivan, C. J., & Frank, J. (2013). The effects of legal and extralegal factors on detention decisions in US district courts. *Justice Quarterly, 30*(2), 340–368. doi:10.1080/07418825.2012.668925

Rezultaty monitoringa ofitsialnykh saytov federalnykh organov ispolnitelnoy vlasti (Reyting otkrytosti ofitsialnykh saytov FOIV). (2012). SPb, FSI. Retrieved from http://www.svobodainfo.org/ru/node/1613

Sacks, M., & Ackerman, A. R. (2012). Pretrial detention and guilty pleas: If they cannot afford bail they must be guilty. *Criminal Justice Studies, 25*(3), 265–278.

Sacks, M., & Ackerman, A. R. (2014). Bail and sentencing: Does pretrial detention lead to harsher punishment? *Criminal Justice Policy Review, 25*(1), 59–77. doi:10.1177/0887403412461501

Schönteich, M. (2013). The overuse of pre-trial detention: Causes and consequences: Martin Schönteich examines arbitrary and excessive pre-trial imprisonment. *Criminal Justice Matters, 92*(1), 18–19. doi:10.1080/09627251.2013.805368

Skougarevsky, D. (Ed.). (2014). *Ugolovnaja justicija v Rossii v 2009 g.: kompleksnyj analiz sudebnoj statistiki.* SPb: IPP EU SPB

Solomon, P. H., Jr. (2002). Putin's judicial reform: Making judges accountable as well as independent. *E. Eur. Const. Rev., 11,* 117–129.

Solomon, P. H., Jr. (2008). Assessing the courts in Russia: Parameters of progress under Putin. *Demokratizatsiya, 16* (1), 63–73. doi:10.3200/DEMO.16.1.63-74

Spohn, C. (2008). Race, sex, and pretrial detention in federal court: Indirect effects and cumulative disadvantage. *U. Kan. L. Rev., 57,* 879–1275.

Spohn, C. (2013). The effects of the offender's race, ethnicity, and sex on federal sentencing outcomes in the guidelines era. *Law & Contemp. Prob., 76,* 75–289.

Spohn, C. (2015). Evolution of sentencing research. *Criminology & Public Policy, 14*(2), 225–232. doi:10.1111/capp.2015.14.issue-2

Sudebny department (2013). Osnovnye svedenia o rabot sudebnoi sistemy. Retrieved from http://cdep.ru/index.php?id=79

Titaev, K. (2011). Kak sudy prinimayut resheniya: Isledovaniye vliyaniya vnepravovykh faktorov na rosyskiye sudy. *Ekonomicheskaya Sotsiologiya, 12*(4), 122–125.

Trochev, A. (2012). Suing Russia at home. *Problems of Post-Communism, 59*(5), 18–34. doi:10.2753/PPC1075-8216590502

Ulmer, J. T. (2012). Recent developments and new directions in sentencing research. *Justice Quarterly, 29*(1), 1–40. doi:10.1080/07418825.2011.624115

Volkov, V. (2014). *Socioeconomic status and sentencing disparities: Evidence from Russia's criminal courts* (Working paper IRL-01/2014) The European University at St. Petersburg, The Institute for the Rule of Law.

Volkov, V., Dmitrieva, A., Pozdnjakov, M., & Titaev, K. (Eds.). (2012). *Rossijskie sud'i kak professional'naja gruppa: sociologicheskoe issledovanie.* SPb.: IRL EU SPb. Retrieved from http://enforce.spb.ru/images/analit_zapiski/Jan_2012_NormsValues.pdf

Volkov, V., Dmitrieva, A., Pozdnjakov, M., & Titaev, K. (Eds.). (2015). *Rossijskie sud'i: sociologicheskoe issledovanie professii*. Moscow: Norma.

Wermink, H., Johnson, B. D., De Keijser, J. W., Dirkzwager, A. J., Reef, J., & Nieuwbeerta, P. (2016). The influence of detailed offender characteristics on consecutive criminal processing decisions in the Netherlands. *Crime & Delinquency*, 1–35.

Wheeler, G. R., & Wheeler, C. L. (1980). Reflections on legal representation of the economically disadvantaged: Beyond assembly line justice: Type of counsel, pretrial detention, and outcomes in Houston. *Crime & Delinquency, 26*(3), 319–332. doi:10.1177/001112878002600303

Williams, M. (2003). The effect of pretrial detention on imprisonment decisions. *Criminal Justice Review, 28*(2), 299–316. doi:10.1177/073401680302800206

Plea bargaining in Russia: the role of defence attorneys and the problem of asymmetry

Ekaterina Moiseeva

ABSTRACT

This research examines pretrial and trial negotiations in Russia's criminal justice system. It corroborates the statement that plea bargaining is a norm until it preserves the latter element – "bargaining." Negotiation skills are especially important for defence attorneys who take a mediator position between the legal community and civil society. The author claims that the nature of negotiations in Russia's criminal justice system is no different from that of other countries. Institutionally the weakest professional group in the Russian legal field, defence attorneys manage to play on the weaknesses of law enforcers and balance their own bargaining position. Yet, accusatory bias of Russian criminal process, managerial problems in law-enforcement agencies, and ineffective regulation of the appointed counsel system create a fertile ground for "shady" practices of defenders. In legal jargon, this phenomenon is labelled as "pocket defence attorneys" – a concept that embraces those actions of appointed counsels that benefit state officials but not defendants. Dependence of appointed defence attorneys on law enforcers is a top-of-mind problem for Russia. An examination of such extreme cases can shed some light on the extent to which organisational context shapes the way lawyers dispense justice elsewhere.

Introduction

The unbiased nature of the judiciary had been called into question by social scientists long ago. Cooperation between judges, prosecutors, and defence attorneys and the effects of plea bargaining on the final verdict are well-investigated phenomena (Abrams, 2011; Alschuler, 1968, 1975, 1976, 1983; Blumberg, 1967; Bibas, 2011; Burstein, 1980; Caldwell, 2012; Dubber, 1997; Easterbrook, 2013; Eisenstein & Jacob, 1977; Friedman, 1979; Heumann, 1975, 1978; Lichtenstein, 1984; Maynard, 1984; Milenski, 1971; Nardulli, 1978, 1979, 1986; Newman, 1956; Padgett, 1985; Schulhofer, 1984, 1992; Springer, 1983; etc.).

Scholars provide two different explanations of the nature of negotiations in criminal justice – structural and social. The former derives from the organisational analysis of courts: as other bureaucratic organisations facing certain administrative concerns, courts develop specific administrative answers. Negotiations are one of such solutions or techniques used by court members to reap some benefits, namely reduce caseloads, press weak cases, etc. The organisational structure of criminal justice can be changed in a way that the system of incentives will be reshaped and *plea bargaining will be reduced*, for instance, by increasing the opportunities for defendants to waive jury trials (Alschuler, 1983), by making plea bargaining less expeditious and hence less favourable (Schulhofer, 1984), or by increasing the prosecutorial screening function (Wright & Miller, 2002).

The social explanation of the nature of negotiations reposes on the idea that communication is an inherent element of any interaction and that *plea bargaining is a norm*. In this sense, whichever changes in organisational structure are implemented, negotiation will remain. Maintaining group cohesion and reducing uncertainty are at the core of any social interaction, and relations between court members are not an exception. Broadly speaking, plea bargaining is a commercial contract, an invisible hand that distributes benefits among market players according to their bargaining skills (Easterbrook, 2013). The problem here is that most negotiations are conducted underground; market transactions are invisible and unregulated. Suggested improvements include making plea bargaining more transparent and available to everyone, so that consumers' rights receive appropriate protection (Bibas, 2011).

This study rests mostly on the social explanation of the nature of negotiations, while the main arguments of the structural approach are also taken into consideration. Plea bargaining can be regarded as a norm, insofar as all parties have more or less equal power in negotiation and it results in a win–win outcome. Judges, prosecutors, investigators, and defence attorneys all represent one profession and embrace a common way of thinking like a lawyer. This encourages professional collaboration, a phenomenon that is present in any type of professional work. In some cases, however, cooperation between lawyers takes a "pathological" form and no longer relies on professional values. As a result, one party (the defendant) is invariably losing.

Hereafter, I explore the role of negotiations in Russian criminal process, where – unlike in several other countries – plea bargaining is a formalised procedure. First, I describe the theoretical model of courtroom workgroups and negotiations. Then, I analyse how Russian lawyers interact with each other at the pretrial and trial stages and describe the role of defence attorneys in negotiations. (Most studies on plea bargaining concentrate on the trial stage, but in the Russian context, it is highly important to analyse the pretrial stage, since that is when the verdict is de facto given.) Further, I characterise the professional situation of Russian defence attorneys in terms of institutional weakness and dependency and show how this leads to *asymmetry* and "pocket" practices – a problem occurring when "breaches" of adversariality emerge and when defence attorneys no longer protect the interests of their defendants. Finally, I present my own view on the relation between adversariality as a doctrinal position and plea bargaining as an objective reality.

Theoretical model: courtroom workgroups and the role of negotiations

Courtroom workgroups and its goals

In their seminal work, Eisenstein and Jacob (1977) introduced the analytical concept of "courtroom workgroup," which suitably addresses the character of interactions between court members. Further, I emphasise the key findings of the book.

First, Eisenstein and Jacob (1977) assert that defendants are sentenced not in a vacuum but in a certain social context: "Outcomes of the felony disposition process are not the result of singular efforts by judges, prosecutors, or defence counsel. Outcomes result from interactions among these courtroom members" (p. 294). Even if those actors serve different organisations, play different roles, pursue different tasks, and acquire different resources, they all work for the same *external goals* – doing justice and handling cases expeditiously. Despite the fact that the meanings of "doing justice" and the reasons for expeditious disposition may vary a lot for different members, shared obligations make court members dependent on each other and encourage them to develop *internal* goals of interaction, which are maintaining group cohesion and reducing uncertainty. Thus, the outcome of the case for the defendant greatly depends on stability of relations between courtroom members and on the established rules of interaction.

Second, the essential purpose of interaction is to find a *common ground on the case*, this is why information becomes the vital resource, and negotiating the primary technique of workgroup members. (The two other work techniques of court organisations, about which Eisenstein and Jacob do not discuss much, are unilateral decisions and adversarial proceedings.) Negotiations are an art of information manipulation: the prosecution normally knows more about the facts of crime, and the defence has more information on the characteristics of the defendant and the practice of handling similar cases in other courts. Both kinds of information are important with regard to the final judgment. Plea bargaining is only one use of negotiation; the various other legal aspects of the case and the practices of handling similar cases in other courts are also negotiated. In the course of negotiations, Eisenstein and Jacob propose, "both parties are likely to move from their original positions towards a mutually acceptable outcome" (Eisenstein & Jacob, 1977, p. 32).

Third, Eisenstein and Jacob present the system of justice as a *local phenomenon*. Just as if they were testing the proverb "Different strokes for different folks," they compare the way a same crime has been investigated and disposed in three different cities and three different organisational contexts – Baltimore, Chicago, and Detroit. Despite the fact that statistically conviction rates are identical everywhere, the way of doing justice is quite different, in terms of expediency of proceedings, disposition methods, proportion of bails, guilty pleas, dismissals, etc. Such discrepancies derive from the policies implemented by sponsoring organisations (courthouses, district attorney offices, bars), as well as from the role of media, civil society, political culture, and other factors of macro-environment. For example, differences in the rotation system create stable workgroups with high rates of plea bargaining in Chicago and, on the contrary, lead to lesser degree of familiarity and higher number of trials in Baltimore.

Fourth, Eisenstein and Jacob show that workgroups do not exacerbate injustice and inequality based on race and wealth. Regardless of the intensity of daily interaction between the court members in different cities, all defendants get *similar verdicts* for similar crimes. Authors suggest that, instead of searching for racial or economic biases, the question that should be asked is: How often do courts convict innocent defendants and why does this happen? Two of the possible problems that Eisenstein and Jacob indicate are associated with police perjury (we do not know how often policemen lie in court) and ineffective representation (we do know how often defendants plead guilty to a crime they did not commit). The authors do not go into details on how to improve the system of criminal justice but assert that any reform proposals should be first of all estimated in terms of their effect on workgroups. Structural solutions without social reasoning will not succeed due to adaptiveness among the courtroom organisations.

Eisenstein and Jacob's book (1977) offers a splendid analysis of micro-politics of criminal courts through the macro-context and extends our understanding of how justice systems work on the level of individuals' interaction. Both authors are political scientists and therefore perceive courtroom members mostly as parties lobbying their interests. Authors do not dwell on what exactly negotiations are. Also, they do not reveal advantages and disadvantages of the criminal justice model in each of the three cities. As a result, readers cannot say if negotiations are good or bad, nor if we should abolish or take them for granted. Prior to discussing if negotiations are a threat or an alternative to adversarial proceedings, it is important to clarify what we call "negotiations."

What are negotiations?

Plea bargaining studies is to a great extent a policy-oriented field of research. This leads the scholarship to focus on the *result* rather than the *process*: researchers are concerned more with the effects of plea bargaining on the outcome than with how negotiations really occur. The proof of such state of affairs is the wide range of different typologies of plea bargaining. Scholars assure us that plea bargaining can be explicit or implicit (Schulhofer, 1984); initiated by a judge, a prosecutor, or a defence attorney (Padgett, 1985); that it happens more often with particular kinds of crimes (i.e., less severe) and correlates to the judges' working experience (i.e., the more experienced the judge, the more prone s/he is to negotiate) (Abrams, 2011). Yet, nature of negotiations remains unclear; so what are negotiations as a process?

To start with, plea bargaining and negotiations are often used as synonyms. The concept of "plea bargaining" is typically applied as a generic term for all kinds of negotiations in criminal process – on charge, on type of process, on characteristics of defendants, on length of incarceration, etc. (Feeley, 1979; Maynard, 1984). Even though admission of guilt is the most decisive resource and the most desired goal of negotiations, not all bargains aim at achieving guilty plea.

In his book *Inside Plea Bargaining* (1984), Douglas Maynard made a very detailed and comprehensive analysis of negotiations from a "within perspective." He describes negotiations as an everyday practice of courtroom members, "an inside activity (...) carried on by professionals in bureaucratic manner" (p. 201). All lawyers work with legal facts. Negotiations are aimed at examining all legal facts that both parties consider valuable, which also involves making a decision on the suitability of the case and coming to a resolution on what to do further. As Maynard points out (1984), negotiations are "not so much an information exchange system nor a mechanism for reaching agreements about facts and character" as they are "a vehicle for assuming numerous kinds of postures that sustain the viability of a given case action" (p. 134). If during negotiations a defence attorney could make the case unviable, then a prosecutor should drop it before the trial, even if s/he is convinced of the guilt of the person.

Negotiations are not any kind of cooperative communication. They have a distinctive linguistic form: the bargaining sequence, the author argues, necessarily includes an opener and a reply. There are two types of openers: offers ("OK, there is an offer") and position-reposts ("I want you to dismiss it"). Replying to the opener parties can come to the three following resolution opportunities: (a) unilateral agreement (one party accepts a proposed offer/position of the other), (b) bilateral agreement (one party rejects an offer/position and makes a counter-proposal which is accepted by the other), (c) compromise (both parties come to an intermediate position). The ultimate purpose of negotiations for a lawyer is to find a common ground, to get one's arguments across, and eventually to construct a "viable" case.

Negotiations can proceed in a *more* or *less* adversarial discourse. In some cases, negotiation is a perfunctory discussion about procedures that goes very smoothly; in others, it is an exchange of controversial arguments about the moral character of the defendant and her/his prior records, which takes the form of adversarial conflict. Either way, negotiation is based on collaboration and mutuality. Lawyers use information contextually; they manipulate it according to their practical concerns. A defence attorney makes some characteristics of the defendant visible and leaves others neglected; the same is true for other participants. Ultimately, both parties bring to each other's attention all valuable information about the case – advantageous and disadvantageous. Even if they disagree about facts, they keep communicating and taking into account each other's arguments in order to achieve a mutually satisfactory outcome. In this precise, professional sense, defence attorneys, prosecutors, investigators, and judges are the members of workgroups: they all work on the construction of *collective product* that is a legal case.

Defence attorneys as effective negotiators

It is helpful to conceive *workgroup* as an analytical tool that encompasses different collaborative practices of repeated players, rather than as assemblies of people who conduct some sort of covert activities. The character of interactions within the workgroup depends to a large extent on the behaviour of the defence attorneys, who have less organisational pressure and whose range of action is much wider than that of judges and prosecutors.

Defence attorneys play a key role in workgroups since they act as *mediators* between state officials and civil society. On the one hand, defence attorneys work for clients, and the delivery of high-quality services today will guarantee their occupation tomorrow. On the other hand, defence attorneys work in everyday contact with other members of legal profession, with whom they aim at cultivating long-term relations. Blumberg (1967) referred to such institutional position as that of a "double-agent." This model has negative connotations as it portrays defence attorneys as fellows of the court, for whom defending client's interests is of secondary importance to being in good terms with judges and prosecutors. Such view is not convincing. Cooperation does not mean backdown or collusion: it is beneficial for defence attorneys just as it is beneficial for clients (Lichtenstein, 1984). At the same time, the alternative representation of defence attorneys as justice crusaders who alone oppose the system is also misleading.

Effective negotiator is another ideal model of professional role of defence attorneys that seems to be a compromise between attorneys as double agents and zealous crusaders. As Uphoff (1995) argues, an effective defence attorney is one who obtains all possible information about the defendant, formulates a negotiating strategy that is appropriate to the given situation, and gets the optimum result for the client through bargaining. Defence attorneys spend much of their time bargaining; their competence as negotiators includes the understanding of formal and informal incentives of the other participants. They can figure out when to negotiate, which offers to take and which ones to reject, when it is suitable to make counter-proposals, and what style of negotiations to use in a particular context. Simply put, they know how to have the best of a bargain. In order to change the prosecutor's initial disposition, defence attorneys underscore the legal and practical weaknesses in the prosecution's case and point out mitigating circumstances for the defendant's actions (Lynch, 2003, p. 1403).

A consulting profession, lawyering rests not only on acquiring expert knowledge of law but also on communication skills. The mediatory position of defence attorneys determines their two main areas of work: (a) socialising clients into the legal system, shaping their view on legal order, interpreting the actions of state officials; (b) transforming citizens' needs into legal categories, constructing the legal case, and presenting it to other lawyers. In sum, it is centred upon *translation* from everyday language to the language of law, and vice versa.

Clients usually think that the system of justice is predictable, impartial, and inerrable (Sarat & Felstiner, 1986). Defence attorneys dispel all these illusions by showing that the job of judges is hurried and routinised, that their mind is unfathomable, that the outcome of the case is unpredictable and depends on personal connections of the defence attorneys with state officials. To earn the confidence of the client, defence attorneys should promote themselves not only as experts in law but also as possessors of insider knowledge on how the system works. Socialisation of clients also benefits state lawyers: first, citizens with unfounded claims will not run to the courts since defence attorneys will filter them out; second, socialised and informed citizens know what to expect and have a realistic level of expectations.

Two concluding remarks are in order at this point. First, the work of lawyers is interwoven with negotiations, as these are an intrinsic property of any legal practice. Second, negotiations are cooperative and competitive at the same time. Having control over different kinds of information "makes the 'game' of plea bargaining a gamble for both sides" (Caldwell, 2012, p. 70). In other words, there is nothing wrong with plea bargaining, until there is "bargaining."

Evidence from Russia: pretrial and trial workgroups and the role of defence attorneys

Empirical data

The current study of workgroups in Russian criminal justice is a part of a bigger project on Russian advocates conducted by the Institute for the Rule of Law (IRL)[1] from 2012 to 2015.[2] The project has started with the following research question: What is the professional situation and institutional position of Russian defence attorney's vis-à-vis law enforcers and judges? Given the accusatory bias in Russia's system and the major role of state officials in handling criminal cases, Russian defence attorneys are often seen as the weakest players of the legal field, not having real

CRIMINOLOGY AND CRIMINAL JUSTICE IN RUSSIA

Table 1. Interviews with advocates.

Total number of interviews	54
Individual	51
Group	3
Total number of informants	58
Male	48
St. Petersburg	35
Specialisation on criminal cases	44

Table 2. Interviews with law enforcers and judges.

Total	110
Judges	19
Chiefs of the court	16
Prosecutors	11
Investigators	43
Police officers	14
Heads of police offices	7

power. In the course of interviewing Russian advocates, our research team found that this viewpoint is true only to some extent. For instance, subordinated position of defence attorneys to their counterpart can be perceived both as evidence of institutional dependency (more so for appointed counsels) and as a tactic that benefits a client (more so for hired counsels). Although less than 1% of court cases in Russia end in acquittal,[3] there are various ways to quasi-acquit a defendant; in such situations, the work of defence attorneys is of utmost importance. The *current paper* discusses the bargaining opportunities of Russian defence attorneys in the context of accusatory bias, and the modes of their cooperation with state lawyers.

The empirical database of the research consists of 54 semi-structured interviews with Russian advocates and 115 h of observations of criminal trials in district courts of St. Petersburg (see Table 1). Two-thirds of the interviews were taken in St. Petersburg and the rest in Moscow, Vladimir, Kazan, and Irkutsk. The majority of the informants were specialising in criminal cases; almost all of them had experience of working as appointed counsels, although only few of them were doing this job on a regular basis.

Observations in criminal courts became the logical extension of the project.[4] From 2014 to 2015, I observed more than 50 criminal cases (under 28 articles of the Criminal Code, with 29 judges, and in 9 district courts of St. Petersburg) focusing on how judges, public prosecutors, and defence attorneys handle criminal cases. Data from observation were recorded in a structured diary. General characteristics of the case; description of physical space; timing; type of procedure; actions and direct orations of different actors; patterns of interactions before, during, and after the hearing were tracked for every case. An increasing focus was on the difference between the work of appointed and hired counsels, as well as on the informal culture of the courts. To conduct the same observation at pretrial stage was literally impossible since police offices are completely closed to strangers. To describe the law enforcers' context of work and the role of negotiations at pretrial stage, a separate database was analysed (see Table 2). This includes more than 100 interviews with judges, prosecutors, investigators, and policemen, which were collected by the IRL from 2010 to 2013 within the frameworks of different research projects.[5]

Professional situation of Russian advocates

Throughout history, Russian advocates[6] were facing a wide range of problems typical of the phenomenon of professionalisation from above: ambivalent relations with the state, low prestige, lack of collective action, autocratic culture and inefficiency of professional associations. Advocates were mentioned as a professional group for the first time in the course of Alexander II's Judiciary Reform of 1864. Due to the high qualification standards for entering the profession, prerevolutionary advocates were small in numbers, but wealthy and respected. From the very beginning, the relations between the advocates and the state were ambivalent. On the one hand, self-regulation institutions of prerevolutionary advocates made them not much different from their Western colleagues (Mrowczynski, 2012). On the other hand, the limits of the professional autonomy were determined by the state's interests. The rather ambitious judicial reform of XIX century had been shortly thereafter rolling back: in 1874, the power to exercise disciplinary actions was handed back from the bars to the judicial authorities; in 1889, the government banned the formation of new local bars; in the meanwhile, pan-Russian congress had been held only once. Thus, autonomy *de jure* was not translated into de facto autonomy. As Levin-Stankevich (1996) notes, the state has always reminded advocates that being member of a free profession does not mean being a free professional (p. 237). Additional problems of prerevolutionary advocates were related to low reputation and lack of professional solidarity. As for the former, prerevolutionary advocates earned much public recognition by defending persons charged with political crimes in the end of XIX century (Barry & Harold, 1968). As for the latter, absence of national association and paternalistic guardianship of the local bars restrained natural mobilisation of professional community (Burbank, 1995).

In Soviet times, the judicial system underwent radical changes. The new government carried out a collectivist project of *advokatura*: the private practice and the market of legal services were abolished, and the advocates had been attached to state legal bureaus. The new role of the Soviet advocate was that of assistant of the court who helps judges and prosecutors to establish the objective truth (Undrevich, 1928). The Ministry of Justice controlled the policy of local bars and the elections of its presidium. Yet, advocates had not become part of the state hierarchy and still enjoyed a degree of autonomy that any other professional group in the USSR could only dream of (Huskey, 1982). For a long time, advocates were perceived in a negative light as representatives of bourgeois society and protectors of enemies of the people. But – just like a century before – they managed to recover their reputation by defending the Soviet dissidents in the 1970–1980s.

A new stage of professional project of Russian *advokatura* started after the collapse of the Soviet Union. The emergence of a market economy created new job vacancies in the legal sphere, which were filled mostly by former business counsels (*jurisconsults*) and younger lawyers. In the 1990s, Russian advocates were placed in an emerging context of market economy and faced the same problems as their Western colleagues – marketability of services and professional monopoly. Soviet advocates held exclusive monopoly on representation of individual clients in all cases at all stages. But as of the late 1980s, the situation was changing: advocates started losing their monopoly both to alternative bars and new law firms, which were taking incumbent positions on the market of legal services.

Only in 2002, a Federal Law on *advokatura* regulating the profession passed. As Burrage predicted (1993), the *advokatura* was "swamped by a host of wholly unregulated practitioners" (p. 585). The old bars' leadership had no capacity to mobilise the profession. The main discussion over the draft of the Law "has been less about building the *advokatura* as a self-governing legal profession in the Western sense and more about maintaining a legal institution whose main function is to provide legal aid to Russian citizens" (Jordan, 2005, p. 775). Obligation to provide indigent citizens with a free legal aid gave the state a cover for active involvement in decision of how the professional community should be organised. As a result, the only monopoly that advocates had retained was representation in criminal cases – their exclusive privilege and duty for the last 150 years. Advocates continue facing the exact same problems as before: low reputation, paternalism of the state, and lack of solidarity. Today, in civil cases, anybody (i.e., even one lacking a law degree) can work as a representative. Those legal representatives who do not specialise in criminal process often perceive an advocate licence as a burden rather than a privilege due to difficult qualification exam, higher taxes, ban on advertising, and ill reputation of appointed counsels that shed negative light on all professional community. Moreover, even though the control of the Party has vanished more than 20 years ago, advocates continue experiencing the pressure from the state, especially in criminal cases.

Further in this article, I will focus solely on criminal process; I will thus use the term *defence attorneys* when referring to advocates working on criminal cases. The following aspects are important for understanding the current position of Russian defence attorneys: (1) every citizen who is subject to criminal liability is provided with a free representative on pretrial and trial stages[7]; (2) if citizens do not wish to use services of an appointed representative, they can hire another one and pay her/him out of pocket; (3) only lawyers who are licenced as advocates[8] can be representatives (both appointed and hired) in criminal cases; (4) the work of appointed advocates is remunerated by the state and coordinated by the local bars. "Appointed counsel" and "hired counsel" in reality are two types of contracts that serve different goals.[9] Some defence attorneys work only by appointment,[10] others only by agreement with a client, but most of them conclude both types of contracts.

The common view on the professional situation of Russian defence attorneys throughout the history is that they are the weakest professional group in the legal field. As Rand (1991) puts it, advocates were always in a separate, minor league. Nowadays, Russian advocates are still subject to domination by law enforcers and their institutional incentives. Russia's system of law enforcement borrowed much from the Soviet times. The most important path-dependence effects relevant to the current situation of defence attorneys are (a) accusatory bias in the criminal process and (b) evaluation system of policemen, investigators, and prosecutors.[11,12]

As for the latter, the efficiency of law enforcers is estimated through formal indicators established by the higher authorities, namely the number of registered, detected, and prevented crimes (also in comparison with the previous period). This has been informally called "checkmark system" (*palochnaya sistema*) (Paneyakh & Titaev, 2011). A reflection of the Soviet planned economy, a checkmark system shifts the focus of police work from crime detection to plan fulfilment. Trying to match statistics, law enforcers become very skilled in selecting which reports should be registered as crimes, in wrongful qualification of criminal actions, and even in falsification of crime rates (Paneyakh, 2013; Shklyaruk & Skougarevsky, 2015).

Accusatory bias derives from the inquisitive nature of the Soviet system of justice (Solomon, 2015). Russian law enforcers and judges are compelled to produce only guilty verdicts since every acquittal draws special attention from the higher authorities and potentially bears career risks for everyone involved in the case (Paneyakh, Titaev, Volkov, & Primakov, 2010; Pozdnyakov, 2015). There is even such a Soviet legacy as "reinvestigation"[13] when a case that has a chance to end up with acquittal in court is returned at the pretrial stage to be reinvestigated but instead is getting dismissed right after.[14]

The easiest way to get a guilty verdict in courts is to have an *admission of guilt* during the investigation process. In Russia, admission of guilt is a formal procedure, which is embodied in two institutions. The first one is the so-called special procedure court hearings (*osobyi poryadok*),[15] which means a fast-track litigation without examination of evidence. It applies only to crimes with the maximum prison term (up to 10 years) and guarantees reduction of the term by one-third in exchange for plea guilty. The second institution is "pretrial settlement,"[16] which is usually associated with more serious crimes. It includes not only an admission of guilt but also the defendant's repentance and collaboration for crime detection. In exchange, the defendant gets a milder sentence.

Russian investigators seldom use pretrial settlement, while special procedure is applied in more than 60% of all criminal cases (according to the statistical data of Justice Department of Russian Federation). Some researchers (like Bibas, 2011) suggest that plea bargaining resembles transactions in the illegal markets, where the state does not control the terms of the contract or the quality of services and does not protect consumers' rights. From this point of view, "legalisation" of plea bargaining, by making it more transparent and formal a procedure, will benefit everyone, especially defendants. Interestingly, Russia's case proves the opposite: formalised contract of plea bargaining helps mostly judges and law enforcers. Even though the procedure of pleading guilty is formalised, the practice of its implementation is often flawed. Introduced in 2001, the legislation on special procedure aimed at fastening the proceedings of "simple" crimes. In fact, it reduced by much the average duration of criminal procedure[17] and increased court efficiency but, as Solomon (2012) notes, did not make judicial process more transparent and less inquisitorial as expected. In a context of accusatory bias, special procedure became a powerful weapon in the hands of state officials. A sentence delivered through special procedure cannot be appealed: this cuts potential risks for investigators and therefore induces them to abuse it. As Paneyakh (2013) says, legal professionals in Russia select the "easiest cases to process rather than serve larger goals of justice and equality" (p. 2). I do not infer here that contracted plea bargaining is not acceptable by default. For example, in Italy, it works proficiently: it does not undermine the adversariality of the process, and the accused sometimes do very well (Solomon, 2012). In Russia, however, it became yet another bureaucratic instrument that at the end of the day does not provide defendants with a better outcome.[18]

This brief introduction to some crucial aspects of the rule of law in Russia gives a general idea of the working environment of Russian defence attorneys. What defenders can obtain for their clients is determined by the interests of the state officials with whom they must deal (Solomon, 1987). Policemen, investigators, prosecutors, and judges are all accountable to the state and bound by a united system of institutional stimuli: one acquittal can simultaneously lead to reprimand of a judge and to the retirement of an investigator. Accusatory bias and the system of evaluation create demand for predictable and loyal defence attorneys who do not cause any delays or other problems. At the same time, defence attorneys are well informed about the working environment of law enforcement agencies and understand their institutional logic. (Some of them have worked there before.)[19] Hereafter, I show how defence attorneys adapt to the given professional situation and even manage to reap benefits from it.

Russian defence attorneys as members of workgroups

Criminal defence in Russia is weaker than investigation and prosecution in many respects. Besides the positional disadvantages described above, the recourses of defence attorneys are also scarce. Historically, Russian advocates had a restricted access to defendants and case files at the pretrial stage. In the Soviet period, there were particular types of cases, on which only few privileged advocated could work (Kaminskaya, 1982).[20] Access to cases (*dopusk*) allowed law enforcers to obtain informal control over defence counsels and was perceived by the latter as the most sensitive threat to their professional autonomy.

Contemporary advocates also experience difficulties at the preliminary investigation stage. The work conditions of defence attorneys and law enforcers are by no means equal (Khodzhaeva & Rabovski, 2016; Kramer, 2003; Pomorski, 2007). Russian defence attorneys are not able to conduct their own investigation. If they get the evidence, they have troubles to attach it to a case, since investigators are those who evaluate the evidence in terms of relevance, admissibility, and creditability[21]; in practice, they reject most of the advocates' motions. If evidence, nonetheless, was attached, at the trial stage, judges tend to give more credit to the proofs collected by investigation than by defence. Moreover, if defence attorneys signed an official pretrial settlement on collaboration with prosecution, judges are not obliged to follow the terms of the agreement and can adjust or cancel it at their own discretion. Also, during court hearings, the motions of the defence are more often declined than those of the prosecution. Consequently, defence counsels must make their best efforts to attain something that state agents get on a silver platter.

Russia is not an exception in this case. The problem of institutional weakness of defence attorneys exists in many other countries. Defence attorneys often have to work on another's territory - courts, police offices - and thus their initial position if often disadvantaged. In the

United States, public defenders also face insufficient institutional support by comparison with prosecutors (Blumberg, 1967; Bright, 1994; Uphoff, 1995) who tend to abuse their power and often overcharge the defendants in order to initiate "coercive plea bargaining" (Caldwell, 2012).

The organisational structure of criminal process generally places defence attorneys at disadvantaged position, but this does not lead directly to unfair treatment for defendants. Positional weakness does not translate into negotiating weakness. Since Russian investigators send to courts only those cases that have good chances to win, and verdict is de facto taken at the pretrial stage (Titaev & Shklyaruk, 2016), it is extremely important for defence attorneys to play well their cards before court hearings. Falling into investigator's trap of institutional incentives, Russian defence attorneys resort to the "weapons of the weak" (Khodzhaeva & Rabovski, 2016) or, as one defence attorney puts it, they "speculate on the problems of investigation." Defence attorneys use a variety of *tactics* that block investigators' work and turn accusatory bias against them. Namely, they search for procedural errors and misspellings in the documents that could lead to an acquittal in court; they control timing, which is essential for investigators and prosecutors; they bring independent experts; they teach witnesses how to pass through interrogation; etc. In the end, they manage to find ground for negotiations on equal terms.

In the theoretical part, I described negotiations as a professional way of doing justice: everyone is willing to cooperate since this reduces uncertainty and saves time. Interviews with Russian defence attorneys and observations in criminal courts confirmed that negotiations are an essential element of lawyering that occurs as a part of everyday discourse. Due to accusatory bias, the most important negotiations – on charge and sentence – usually happen before court hearings. The sooner a defence attorney enters a case, the more chances s/he has to get a fair treatment for the client. If pretrial negotiations with investigators are not successful, defence attorneys still have a chance to prove their position in court.

Maynard (1984) discerns two main layers of negotiations, which we also find in Russian criminal process. The *upper layer* is based on factual information. Admission of guilt and special procedure are at the centre of attention here. If the accused pleads guilty, the investigator promises him/her a milder sentence or withdrawal of some charges. People are usually prone to settle since they face the potential loss of years of freedom. The role of defence attorneys as mediators is very important here: (a) if the evidence does not support the charges, they should dissuade their clients from the admission of guilt; (b) if the evidence is exhaustive, they should use the admission of guilt as a resource in negotiation and gain maximum benefits out of it.

Russian defence attorneys understand that special procedure is not always a good deal for the accused. Therefore, those counsels, who refuse to work by appointment and represent white-collar clients, rarely agree to use it. One of our informants of that kind referred to special procedure as the way to "condemn yourself." Defence attorneys working with low-status clients, on the other hand, are more lenient to special procedure. The truth is that – as all lawyers like to say – circumstances alter cases. Below is a typical example of beneficial use of plea guilty.

> This is a normal plea bargaining. (...). We have a road traffic accident with deaths. If it's the defendant's first charge, then he will get a suspended sentence and a revocation of his driver's license. If parties negotiate – you give a suspended sentence and do not revoke the driving license, we plea guilty – the deal is done. The defendant keeps the license and continues driving. (defence attorney, Irkutsk, 5[22])

The *lower layer* of negotiations is built around the characteristics of a defendant; such bargain occurs when there is already a plea of guilty, mostly at the trial stage. During negotiations lawyers create a criminal self of the defendant (Sarat & Felstiner, 1986). For every case, there is a unique set of attributes of the defendant (prior records, marital status, employment, race, belonging to ethnic minorities, mental state, etc.) and circumstances of a committed crime. A defence attorney should bring the attributes that are relevant for the concrete case to the attention of the judge and the public prosecutor. Thus, the defence attorney's job is to look for uniqueness in every case, which will allow the judge to use her/his discretion and soften the sentence. As Luban (2001) describes it, using facts *selectively* to support favoured conclusions is what advocates do for a living, it is their occupation (p. 171).

> I said, "Imagine her [defendant] situation. She has two kids. If she gets a suspended sentence, the Child Protection Services will have a file on her. (...). But she is a good woman". And then the public prosecutor replied, "Let's dismiss the case". The judge was also supportive, because all work on the case was done well, all characteristics were collected. (...). My task was just to depict the situation in a favorable light. (...). The judge is also human, she sees what is happening, and meets the needs. So, we changed qualification and signed a peace treaty. What was impossible to do at pre-trial stage, we reached in court. (defence attorney, St. Petersburg, 10)

The choice of the type of procedure is a focal point and a key bargaining tool in both layers of negotiations. During pretrial negotiations, both parties can "threaten" each other with trials. Russian defence attorneys could say that if the case goes to trial, it will end up with acquittal, since a judge can see the case differently. In interviews, all defence attorneys were very excited to tell stories about their bargaining victories through such lever. For a Russian advocate, who most likely will have an acquittal only once or twice in his/her entire career, the more realistic definition of "victory" would be a dismissal at the pretrial stage.

> I managed to dismiss a case before the court hearings. I persuaded an investigator that (...) if he sends this case to trial, he is going to get an acquittal. (defence attorney, St. Petersburg, 13)

Besides the two aforementioned main layers of negotiations, there are numerous other forms of routine negotiations, which are often associated with timing. Some themes of such negotiations are, for instance, how to choose a date for the trial that works for everyone; how to conduct an examination without dragging the trial out too long, i.e., which questions should be asked and which can be skipped, which witnesses should and should not be interrogated, etc. These kinds of negotiations usually happen in the aisles of the courthouses before the trial or in the courtrooms while waiting for a convoy.

> There are situations when a police escort is late (...) and it happens that the judge, the defense attorney, the public prosecutor, and the secretary are sitting altogether in the courtroom. And they informally discuss different issues, such as what will be inquired, what the public prosecutor can drop, and how the judge sees the case. (defence attorney, St. Petersburg, 11)

Thus, negotiating is a natural process in Russian criminal process. As Maynard (1984) puts it, "bargaining talk is distributed systematically within work routines which relate prosecutors, defence attorneys, and judges to a series of activities occurring both before and after any episode of negotiation" (p. 140). This is why participants do not even perceive it in terms of cooperation but rather as "a working environment, whose goal is to save time and nerves of each other" (defence attorney, St. Petersburg, 34). Everyone is interested in having a cooperative counterparty and creating relations that are built on trust and creditability. Confrontation can be beneficial only in particular and rare situations.

> To work with a competent defense attorney is a big pleasure because you can always negotiate with him. (prosecutor, St. Petersburg)

> For me building trust with a counterparty – an investigator, in this case – is a necessary and inevitable condition. I must look for mutual trust because otherwise I will not start a dialog with him. I will not be able to get my position over to him. (defence attorney, St. Petersburg, 10)

Both parties are professional lawyers working on the construction of "viable" criminal cases. In order to do so, they should have all information related to the case to test the survivability of their own version. After all, even disagreement rests on the consideration of what the opponent has to say. One of the informants compared it to playing chess, "You play white, I play black. One of us wins but it doesn't mean that we cannot be friends" (defence attorney, St. Petersburg, 51). This quote is a good illustration of the nature of negotiations – they are cooperative and competitive at the same time. At the end of the day, lawyers play together the game of doing justice.

To the problem of asymmetry

Counsel from the pocket: who is it?

Negotiations rest on the idea of cooperation and competition. Defence attorneys play the role of counterbalance to state prosecution: they protect people's rights to liberty as zealously as law enforcers protect the state's right on legitimate use of violence. The problem of asymmetry arises when defence attorneys do not act as effective negotiators, when the interests of a defendant are being neglected, and when cooperation with prosecution takes a pathological form.

For Russia, inefficient representation is one of the most serious problems in criminal justice system. There is even a special expression in lawyers' jargon – *pocket defence attorneys* – which refers to non-professional behaviour of appointed counsels working in the interests of investigation and prosecution. Other epithets of the same phenomenon are "parasitising defence attorneys," "behind-the-closet defence attorneys," "on duty defence attorneys," and "corridor defence attorneys." In the 3rd International Legal Forum,[23] Russian Deputy Minister of Justice Elena Borisenko used the word "inquisitive defence attorneys," pointing out that they are a by-product of the accusatory bias.

The following example from the observation in district courts of St. Petersburg illustrates the issue. A defendant was a young migrant from an ex-Soviet republic of Central Asia who was indicted for armed robbery.[24] He admitted guilt at the pretrial stage but during court hearings retracted his testimony. The judge and the public prosecutor were purposely asking him suggestive questions (which is forbidden by law[25]), while the defence attorney did not protest and even helped them.

Judge:	Did you hold the knife close to the guard's neck?
Defendant:	No, I just held it in my hand.
Judge:	But could it be that it was also close to the neck?
	The defendant denies. The judge and the defense attorney reformulate the question several times. In the end, the judge says, "But you already admitted guilt". Finally, the defendant confirms his previous testimony, and the interrogation continues.
Judge:	Were you going to spend the money?
Defendant:	No, I did not even see it.
Judge:	But did you talk with your friend about it? Did you discuss how much money would you get?
Defendant:	No, I did not even know where I was going.
Judge:	But if he had shared money with you, would you spend it?
	The defendant confirms, and interrogation continues.
Judge:	Did you see that people were scared?
Defendant:	I do not know. It was far from me.
Judge:	But if someone threatened you with a gun, would you be scared?
	The defendant confirms, and interrogation continues. (2014, St. Petersburg, No. 14)

What does being "pocket" exactly mean? The definition is quite nebulous. Actors of Russian legal field relate it simultaneously to three different concepts: (a) a separate group of appointed defence attorneys who collude with law enforcers and judges, (b) particular "pocket" practices of appointed defence attorneys, (c) the whole system of free legal aid, where every defence attorney becomes "pocket" by default. In order to explain what being a "pocket" defence attorney means, it is useful to look at how this term is applied in concrete situations.

Analysis of interviews and disciplinary actions held by the bar shows that the following actions of criminal defenders are typically described as "pocket"[26]:

- affixing a signature on the protocols of the investigators *without* actual participation in investigative actions;

- *passivity* in situations when active measures are demanded (lawful arrest and detention of clients, indictment of severe crime without evidence, tortures, etc.);
- taking a position that *contradicts* the client's view (e.g., forcing the accused to plead guilty against his/her will);
- *collusion* with investigators and prosecutors; intimidating clients and inducing them to bribe law enforcers in order to get a better outcome;
- getting cases *directly* from fellow investigators or judges, i.e., bypassing the bar's appointment system;
- *unethical* behaviour, impertinence in relations with clients.

So, "pocket" behaviour is normally described through denial, i.e., what appointed defence attorneys are *not* doing (even if they should). The only action that a "pocket" counsel *does* is convincing the accused to plea guilty.

> This is a radically different category of defense attorneys. I consider them as parasitizing defense attorneys who go with the current. (...). They do not appeal, do not file motions. (...). Is this defense? (...). They are indifferent people who do not care about people's lives. (defence attorney, St. Petersburg, 42)

> I just had a situation when the defense attorney forced his client to admit committing a very serious crime, and made him sign a pretrial settlement. He promised him a reduction of charges. The defendant – upon the suggestion of the investigator and with the approval of his defense attorney – even signed a few blank forms. (defence attorney, Moscow, 39)

Many legal experts – including defence attorneys themselves – look at the problem of pocket counsels very simplistically picturing them as an organised group of people who are fed by investigators and judges. This is not accurate. Even if there are defence attorneys who receive 80% of their cases from fellow investigators, they get the remaining 20% through own social networks and serve them very zealously. The phenomenon of "pocket" defence attorneys refers more to practices than to people. There are defence attorneys who have never been "pocket," and there are some who performed that role many times. If the defence attorney has majority of appointed cases, it does not make him/her immediately "pocket."

A more comprehensive view on the problem of "pocket" defence attorneys would be to perceive "pocketness" as a stigma that is produced through the discourse of professionals, who try to separate themselves from non-professionals. This is thus a distinguishing category that defines what is professionally appropriate and what is not in a given particular role. In our case, it applies to a role of appointed defence attorney. There is no universal definition of professionalism. The analysis of interviews with Russian advocates shows that the notion of professionalism in the work of appointed defence attorneys differs from that of hired counsels. Appointed attorneys deal with specific forms of criminal deviation: 80% of Russian criminals have a marginal social status (Volkov, 2014); 30% of them are repeat offenders; most common crimes are related to theft, drugs, and beating (see Table 4, 6; Volkov et al., 2014). The wages in the appointment system are very low.[27] Thus, appointed defence attorneys do not usually empathise with their clients and have no incentive to wholly devote themselves to the case.

> When you are hired, you will do more for your client. (...). You will file more motions, meet more people. It is probably in human nature: when you have a good salary, you work better. (defence attorney, Moscow, 52)

No one expects extraordinary activity and eagerness from an appointed counsel – adequate minimum of rights protection is enough. This is what Caldwell (2012) refers to as "capable defence" in contrast to "zealous defence." Yet, if an appointed defence attorney is sure of the innocence of the client, s/he will switch to the role of zealous defender and confront law enforcers by "trying to destroy the case by all available means that are not prohibited by law" (defence attorney, St. Petersburg, 31). The discourse of "pocket" practices of appointed defence attorneys and the problem of asymmetry emerge when minimum rights protection is not granted, innocent

CRIMINOLOGY AND CRIMINAL JUSTICE IN RUSSIA

defendants plead guilty, or guilty persons get sentences disproportionate to their crimes. This is why we should look at the problem not from the perspective of the individual but from that of the system.[28]

Grounds for collusive behaviour of appointed defence attorneys

Several factors create conditions for "pocket" behaviour of appointed defence attorneys. First, heavy caseloads and pressures coming from *accusatory bias* make state officials concerned with efficient time allocation. Law enforcers and judges have much paperwork and other routine activities that should be done expeditiously and with minimal costs. (For judges, it can be delivery decisions on detention orders and hearing fast-track cases.) This creates demand for loyal defence attorneys who easily accommodate to the working routine of law enforcers and judges and do not create unwanted problems.

Second, appointed defence attorneys are not only institutionally weak in comparison with law enforcers (as described above), but also *financially* dependent on them. If an advocate works by appointment, s/he is paid only after an investigator (or a judge) signs the papers and confirms the number of investigative actions (or court hearings), in which the advocate participated.[29] Since state officials have control over appointed counsels' wages, this leaves room for manipulation; for example, investigators may be tempted to reward a fellow counsel by overstating the number of working days.

Third, "pocket" practices become possible due to poor organisation of the free legal aid system. Legally, law enforcers should not participate in distribution of cases between appointed defence attorneys; this is a privilege of the advocates' community. Each regional bar decides how to organise the provision of free legal counsel for defendants at its own discretion.[30] However, the official *case distribution system* lacks control mechanisms. Thus, investigators and judges can bypass it undisturbed to either invite their fellow defence attorneys by a direct phone call or exclude non-cooperative defence attorneys by creating a so-called black list. These decisions are taken informally and have no legal basis behind.

> The investigator hates me after that case. I am on a "black list" of appointed defense attorneys of the central district of St. Petersburg. No one invites me anymore. (defense attorney, St. Petersburg, 20)

> I see that in the majority of cases the schedule is not working. (...). When there is urgent need to invite an appointed defense attorney, judges call those with whom they worked before. (...). The bar is not able to control it, they have no resources, they cannot even get the information that the line was cut. (defence attorney, St. Petersburg, 10)

Fourth, for defence attorneys, the interest in "pocket" practices also derives from *insufficient state funding* to the legal aid system (a general problem for many countries). Because of their low wages, appointed defence attorneys are incentivised to make money by increasing caseload and disposing cases as speedily as possible. By doing so, they adapt to the bureaucratic logic of law enforcers and adopt their practices. According to Bright (1994), in the United States, the quality of representation is the lowest in capital cases, where people's life is at stake. Due to inadequate funding for the indigent defence system, lack of supervision, deficit of investigative and expert assistance, American public defenders do not provide even the required minimal standards of legal representation to those who need it the most. "Slaughterhouse justice" is a rough but true description of such litigation model (Bright, 1994) that is also present in Russia. In such conditions, the state legal aid system features less competent lawyers, some of whom learn how to benefit from it.

Fifth, there are no efficient deterrence devices and *sanctions* for "pocket" behaviour. Advocates' professional community reports that it regularly punishes those members who collaborate with investigators and revokes their licences, but the bars do not have sufficient political capital to push their agenda at the national level. As for investigators and judges, their sponsoring organisations are concerned only with the number of acquittals and dismissals. Bypassing the official case distribution system is not perceived as unethical, and law enforcers do not get punished for inviting their fellow defence attorneys.

Thus, the problem of "pocket" defence attorneys is a reflection of different problems inside the Russian criminal justice system. Widely discussed and criticised, this issue has remained unsolved for years due to lack of strong political will to address it.

Negotiations, adversariality, and inequality

Plea bargaining has been criticised by scientists and laymen for a long time – both for being not adversarial and for producing social inequality. As to the former criticism, plea bargaining was gradually being reconsidered as a natural extension of the adversarial system. Negotiations are viewed as instrumental and tactical devices, which facilitate daily interaction of lawyers and bring benefits for each participant (Lichtenstein, 1984). As Uphoff postulates, "The lawyer committed to providing quality representation, therefore, must learn to be an effective negotiator" (Uphoff, 1995, p. 134–135). In contemporary American criminal process, where 90% of cases contain plea guilty, negotiating becomes an art of representation. In Russian courts, the rates of people who plead guilty are comparable (Volkov & Titaev, 2013). Some scientists (like Roberts, 2013) even claim that the accused should have a constitutional right to effective plea counsel. "Plea bargaining is no sport, (...) it is a serious event that – depending on whether and how it is conducted – can result in a lifelong mark of a criminal record and loss of liberty or even life" (Roberts, 2013, p. 2674). The current paper is consistent with such point of view: negotiations are by nature competitive, and ability to negotiate is the most vital professional skill for lawyers.

As for the latter criticism, it is argued that extensive use of plea bargaining makes the outcome of the case dependent not so much on the factual information, but rather on the negotiation skills of a representative. Such situation produces social inequality: wealthier people are likely to get more qualified legal assistance. Scant assistance of appointed counsels and zealous assistance of private counsels are two worlds apart with different populations of defendants and quality standards (Luban, 1993). Appointed defenders represent the lower social class, investigation virtually does not exist, and the time spent for every case is measured in minutes, rather than hours. The opposite could be said about private defenders. But this does not necessarily mean that a defendant represented by appointed defence attorneys get more severe penalties. Statistical data show that the influence of the type of counsel (appointed or hired) on the outcome is contextual: in certain situations, attorneys who regularly work by appointment are able to get more favourable outcomes for their clients (Anderson & Heaton, 2012; Hartley, Miller, & Spohn, 2010).

Today, plea bargaining is more widely accepted by legal scholarship than it was a few decades ago. After years of slashing criticism, it is gradually viewed as an integral part of criminal process. Vanishing trials and growth of consensual forms of dispute solution led scholars to think of adversarial criminal process as a historical phenomenon that is slowly dying, which is not necessarily bad (Menkel-Meadow, 2004). Plea bargaining follows such common trend of historical development of the legal system. Yet, some changes in negotiation process should be made. Social scientists are concerned with the informal character of plea bargaining: lawyers negotiate behind closed doors, which makes it impossible to ascertain whether a defence attorney is representing his/her client's best interest. Possible improvements suggested thus far are to create a more transparent and less informal procedure of negotiations (i.e., legalisation of plea bargaining) (Bibas, 2011), and to involve the defendants into the negotiation process (Kitai-Sangero, 2015).

I endorse the idea that negotiations per se do not compromise adversariality and that legalisation of plea bargaining does not necessarily benefit the defendants. On the contrary, I argue that reduction of bargaining opportunities for defence attorneys might lessen chances for the accused to get a better judgment. Russia's "special procedure court hearings" is a good example. Special procedure is a form of written contract between the prosecution and the defendant, according to which the latter gets a milder sentence in exchange for admission of guilt and simplified procedure of court hearing. (A similar fast track exists in Italy, Germany, Spain, and other counties.) Several arguments lied behind the adoption of special procedure in Russia: (1) since many criminal cases already contain a negotiated admission of guilt, the question was not about creating a new institution but rather legalising an existing practice; (2) written agreements make the terms of plea bargaining more evident to the defendants and, thus, protect their rights; (3) applying special procedure to "simple" cases significantly reduces caseloads of judges and investigators (for more details and further discussions, see Fomin, 2011; Lazareva, 1999; Nazarov, 2015; Velikiy, 2005). In reality, special procedure did not lead to better rights protection of the accused but narrowed the margin of action for the defence attorneys. In context of accusatory bias, special procedure became a widely accepted tool for Russian investigators and judges, and a useful instrument supporting their demand for loyal counterparty. As Solomon notices, it became rather the return to Soviet style inquisitorialism – "a paradoxical result of a measure embedded in a Code meant to promote adversarialism" (Solomon, 2015, p. 168).

Before criticising plea bargaining for producing inequality and proposing solutions for its regulation – which are certainly needed – one should separate the wheat from the chaff and focus on the roots of the problem. Much confusion derives from the loose of understanding of what plea bargaining essentially is. Plea bargaining studies are often marred with unnecessary politicised and moralising views; "bargained" dispositions are frequently perceived as an undesirable element of criminal justice. In fact, most negotiations are simple discussions on the merits of the case and the order of proceedings, which allow both parties to avoid the worst-case scenario (Lynch, 2003).

The idea of "plea bargaining" is quite undefined. In particular, there is a huge difference between "plea bargaining" as a process of oral negotiations and "plea bargaining" as a written contract. These are phenomena of different sorts, which we define with the same term. Lawyers negotiate all the time – not only for getting an admission of guilt but also for reducing charges, releasing the defendant on bail, attaching evidence to the case, choosing the type of procedure, selecting the date of the next court hearing, visiting the defendant at the pretrial detention centre, creating the criminal self of the defendant, etc. Trying to make *all* negotiations transparent is utopian: formalising on paper the terms of an achieved agreement does not reduce negotiations per se and does not make the process of negotiating completely transparent. So, the wrong problems are being solved by inadequate means.

As for the Russian case, the real threat to equality and adversariality comes from institutional incentives of law enforcers and organisation of legal aid system for indigent people. If one compares the outcomes of plea-bargaining cases for appointed and private counsels, s/he might come to conclusion that there is no much difference. But it is impossible to estimate the number of cases when defendants were forced to plea guilty. Insufficient remuneration of appointed defence attorneys brings less qualified and less skilled advocates into the appointment system. Poorly paid and insufficiently supervised, Russian-appointed defence attorneys generally feel less responsible towards clients. Judges and investigators, in turn, see defence attorneys as obstacles; the institutional pressure they experience forces them to look for loyal counterparties. This leads to appointed counsels' malpractices and opens the door for the problem of "pocket" defence attorneys who serve the interests of the state officials. "Pocket" counsels fail to perform the role of effective negotiator by inducing defendants to plead guilty to their disadvantage. This dysfunction of Russian criminal process ought to be solved with changes in the institutions of criminal justice.

Conclusion

In this paper, I analysed the role of defence attorneys as negotiators in Russia's criminal justice system. This topic has not been thoroughly investigated before. Usually, legal scholars who are interested in Russia look at plea bargaining focusing on "special procedure court hearing" and leaving the core of the negotiation process aside. At the same time, the case of Russian *advokatura* is a good illustration of the importance of negotiations in criminal process in general. It shows to which extent defence attorneys can be effective negotiators without sliding into non-professional collusive practices, especially as they work in a very challenging environment of accusatory bias and mighty state prosecution.

In the beginning of this article, I mentioned two different approaches to negotiations. From the structural perspective, negotiations are viewed as an organisational problem that could be solved by patching the holes in social and institutional settings. The social approach shows that negotiating is not necessarily a problem but, on the contrary, it is essential to the professional work of lawyers. While negotiating, lawyers pursue the external goals of doing justice and constructing a viable criminal case, and the internal goals of reducing uncertainty and saving time. Familiarity between members often eases negotiations, since it can greatly improve mutual trust. The more lawyers interact with each other, the more they become acquainted, and the less time they need to realise when, how, and for what they can reach an agreement. By itself, familiarity does not imply asymmetry. Such problem arises instead from both institutional weakness and financially dependency of Russian defence attorneys.

Russian defence attorneys are institutionally weak due to the professional situation they work in, which derives from the Soviet inquisitional system. Institutional incentives of judges and investigators create demand for cooperative defence, while procedural rules and practices of its implementation limit the opportunities for defence attorneys to make their own investigation, attach evidence to the case, and present arguments in court. In addition to these disadvantages, Russian advocates' community is not unified and lacks control over its members. Russia's problem is not unique. For example, Caldwell (2012) highlights the issue of "coercive plea bargaining," a practice widely used by US prosecutors, who abuse their bargaining position to overcharge the defendant. Despite positional weakness, defence counsels in both countries have margins for negotiating on equal terms, for they have very important bargaining resources – access to the accused, admission of guilt, factual errors found in the procesutor's case, time control, etc.

Things get complicated when Russian law enforcers obtain devices for driving supply in order to satisfy demand for loyal counterparty. The most important of such tools is control of investigators and judges over the remuneration of appointed defence attorneys. Moved by economic interests, some appointed defence attorneys engage in the practices of "pocket" counsels: they become subordinated to state officials and leave the interests of clients unprotected and unrepresented. Thus, prosecution gets the possibility to hire the adversary; such an asymmetry violates the basic principle of fair justice.

Unlike negotiations, which are essentially a social phenomenon, the problem of "pocket" counsels can be solved by structural means. All individuals are different in regard to adherence to social and professional norms. The problem of non-compliance is present in any social context, but some formal and informal institutions make non-compliance more advantageous. Possible solutions to the existing problem in Russia are (a) exclusion of investigators and judges from the system of payment of appointed defence attorneys, (b) wage increase for appointed defence attorneys, (c) spreading computerised system of case distribution to all regions, (d) elaboration of ethics enforcement mechanisms for appointed defence attorneys (including ex-post evaluation), (e) introducing sanction for law enforcers who bypass official distribution system, (f) reconfiguration of the special procedure in order to open more room for negotiations. These measures would have better and faster effect if accompanied by changes of the incentives of law enforcers and strengthening of professional freedom of advocates.

The current paper is a short introduction to the major problems of criminal defence in Russia. More thorough investigation on the factors of collusive relations between law enforcers and defence attorneys, and on the concrete role that defence attorneys play in criminal process (both appointed and hired) offers promising avenues for further research. Moreover, my empirical data are limited to a few big Russian cities; there is no information on the work of defence attorneys in small cities and in the countryside, where the professional environment is quite

CRIMINOLOGY AND CRIMINAL JUSTICE IN RUSSIA

different and the process of workgroup formation is smoother. Studying rural criminal justice will significantly enlarge our understanding of the rule of law in Russia in general and of the Russian legal profession in particular.

Notes

1. The Institute for the Rule of Law (IRL) is part of the *European University at St. Petersburg*, Russia. The author takes the position of researcher in the IRL from August 2012. The primary projects of the IRL are focused on criminal justice system, law enforcement agencies, and judicial authorities in Russia.
2. The author thanks her colleagues Ekaterina Khodzhaeva and Julia Rabovski who were participating in the project from the very beginning and conducted a large part of interviews.
3. A percentage of 0.2 criminal cases end up with acquittals in court (see Table 28; Volkov et al., 2014).
4. Most trials in Russia are public; this is why to get into the courts was not a formidable obstacle. Nonetheless, since seldom people attend court hearings and most cases are handled with no audience, some judges were anxious about my presence. For example, they could ask for my ID and my status. In this case, I presented myself as a researcher who observed the work of defence attorneys. Usually, that was enough to be allowed to attend a hearing. I presume that in the majority of cases, when I was not asked about my status, the judge and other court members thought I was a law student.
5. The two databases of interviews have been analysed with the support of NVivo software. In the first data set of interviews with advocates, the following topics were in focus: relations with state lawyers, control over clients, work routine, tactics of defence, career trajectory, specialisation, professional values, etc. The second data set of interviews with judges and law enforcers has been used selectively; my interest had been limited to their relations with advocates and attitude towards the state system of free legal aid.
6. As in most of Europe, legal profession in Russia is segmented, meaning that judges, law enforcers, and counsels do not have a unified professional association (like the American Bar Association) and a unified code of ethics for all lawyers.
7. Articles 50, 51 of the Russian Criminal Procedural Code.
8. To be licenced, one needs to get a degree in law, have a 2-year internship, and pass the exam in a local bar.
9. These two types of contracts differ in many respects. In the case of appointed defence attorneys, a contract is concluded between the state and a lawyer; it applies only to criminal cases; the wages are determined by the state; the nature of a contract is compulsive (a defendant cannot choose an appointed defence attorney nor can a defence attorney choose a client); a contract is discontinuous, meaning that there is usually one defence attorney during investigation process and another one in court. As for hired counsels, contracts are concluded between a defence attorney and a client; they applies both to criminal and civil cases; their rates are negotiable; they are based on mutual agreement; a client can choose to sign a contract for one action, for one stage, or for a whole case. Appointed defence attorneys usually work with lower social classes, while private defence attorneys are hired by middle and upper social classes.
10. The likelihood to work as an appointed defence attorney on a regular basis is higher for those who are in the beginning or the end of their careers. Young advocates use the state system of legal aid as a chance to get experience, learn informal rules of interaction in police offices and courts, and train their professional skills. For aged defenders, appointment is often the only available option. Also, appointed counsels are more numerous in the countryside, and hired counsels in the cities.
11. Three types of law enforcers are involved in preparing criminal cases: (1) policemen, who register crimes and arrest suspects; (2) investigators, who do detective and paper work, i.e., look for evidence, interview witnesses, and prepare documents; (3) prosecutors, who control the work of policemen and investigators, append their signature on the case file before it goes to a court, and present the case in court hearings (public prosecution).
12. See Solomon (1987) for a detailed analysis of vanishing acquittals in the Soviet criminal justice. According to Solomon, accusatory bias and evaluation system of law enforcement agencies emerged in the 1940–1950s.
13. Article 221 of the Russian Criminal Procedural Code (prosecutor's discretion); Article 237 of the Russian Criminal Procedural Code (judge's discretion).
14. Dismissals at the pretrial stage also have negative consequences for investigators but to a lesser extent.
15. Articles 314–317 of the Russian Criminal Procedural Code.
16. Articles 317.1–317.9 of the Russian Criminal Procedural Code.
17. Most of the cases in special procedure that the author observed in district courts were resolved within an hour, while normally criminal cases are tried for few months.
18. Special procedure has been thoroughly investigated by the IRL. One of the most outstanding findings is that special procedure does not lead to a milder sentence: judges in general do not sentence defendants beyond two-

thirds of the maximum, regardless of whether the case is reviewed in normal procedure or special procedure (Titaev & Pozdnyakov, 2012). As Solomon (2012) commented it, "In Russia, like in the United States, once a majority of accused persons plead guilty, then their fate becomes the statistical norm" (p. 297).

19. Almost 40% of Russian advocates have previous working experience in law enforcement agencies (see Graph 3.1; Kazun, Khodzhaeva, & Yakovlev, 2015).

20. KGB, with the help of local bars, enlisted those advocates who were allowed to work on such cases. In Moscow, only 10% of advocates have passed test on political loyalty and were included in the list (Kaminskaya, 1982).

21. Articles 87, 88 of the Russian Criminal Procedural Code.

22. Article 162 (2) of the Russian Criminal Code.

23. Article 275 of the Russian Criminal Procedural Code.

24. Official documentation of the Disciplinary Committee of the Bar of Leningradskaya oblast' published on its website.

25. From 5 to 40 US dollars for each action depending on the circumstances (complexity of the case, time of day, number of accused people, etc.).

26. Hereinafter, the number of the interview in the NVivo database.

27. This is the most important platform for discussing legal issues in Russia. The 3rd International Legal Forum was held in St. Petersburg on 27–30 May 2015.

28. Of course, individual factor cannot be completely excluded. People are susceptible to external influences to different extents. The likelihood of taking the "pocket" role by defence attorneys will depend on their social capital, stage of career, previous experience, personal beliefs and preferences, etc.

29. It is called sudoden' – literally "days of trials," the number of days in which the advocate worked on one case, both at the pretrial and trial stages. Regardless the time that the appointed defence attorney spent for one case during the day, s/he gets fixed fee. At the same time, the advocate can serve several cases per day and get more money. For example, s/he can attend 10 investigative actions for 10 different crimes or 10 investigative actions for 1 crime – in the first case, the wages will be 10 times higher.

30. There are different ways to distribute cases among appointed defence attorneys: (a) through special divisions created inside the regional bars, where coordinators receive the requests from investigators and judges by phone and assign those advocates who are on duty at the moment (like in St. Petersburg); (b) through independent call centres, where employed operators take the requests from investigators and judges by phone and dispatch advocates automatically selected by computer (like in Samara); (c) through advocate firms who take themselves the requests from investigators and judges by phone and assign their members who have smaller caseloads at the moment or who usually work by appointment (like in Moscow).

Funding

This work was supported by the Russian Science Foundation: [Grant Number 14-18-02219] ("Sociological Study of Legal Profession in Russia").

References

Abrams, D. S. (2011). Is pleading really a Bargain?. *Journal of Empirical Legal Studies*, 8(S1), 200–221. doi:10.1111/j.1740-1461.2011.01234.x

Alschuler, A. W. (1968). The prosecutor's role in plea bargaining. *The University of Chicago Law Review*, 36(1), 50–112. doi:10.2307/1598832

Alschuler, A. W. (1975). The defense Attorney's role in plea bargaining. *The Yale Law Journal*, 84(6), 1179–1314. doi:10.2307/795498

CRIMINOLOGY AND CRIMINAL JUSTICE IN RUSSIA

Alschuler, A. W. (1976). The trial judge's role in plea bargaining. Part I. *Columbia Law Review, 76*(7), 1059–1154. doi:10.2307/1121673

Alschuler, A. W. (1983). Implementing the criminal defendant's right to trial: Alternatives to the plea bargaining system. *The University of Chicago Law Review, 50*(3), 931–1050. doi:10.2307/1599531

Anderson, J. M., & Heaton, P. (2012). How much difference does the lawyer make? The effect of defense counsel on murder case outcomes. *The Yale Law Journal, 122*(1), 154–217. Retrieved from http://www.jstor.org/stable/23528652

Barry, D. D., & Harold, J. B. (1968). The soviet legal profession. *Harvard Law Review, 82*(1), 1–41. doi:10.2307/1339293

Bibas, S. (2011). Regulating the plea-bargaining market: From caveat emptor to consumer protection. Faculty Scholarship. Retrieved from http://scholarship.law.upenn.edu/cgi/viewcontent.cgi?article=1329&context=faculty_scholarship

Blumberg, A. S. (1967). The practice of law as confidence game: Organizational cooptation of a profession. *Law & Society Review, 1*(2), 15–40. doi:10.2307/3052933

Bright, S. B. (1994). Counsel for the poor: The death sentence not for the worst crime but for the worst lawyer. *Yale Law Journal, 103,* 1835–1883. doi:10.2307/797015

Burbank, J. (1995). Discipline and punish in the Moscow bar association. *Russian Review, 54*(1), 44–64. doi:10.2307/130774

Burrage, M. (1993). Review: Russian advocates: Before, during, and after perestroika. *Law & Social Inquiry, 18*(3), 573–592. doi:10.1086/492436

Burstein, C. (1980). Criminal case processing from an organizational perspective: Current research trends. *The Justice System Journal, 5*(3), 258–273. Retrieved from https://www.ncjrs.gov/App/Publications/abstract.aspx?ID=69643

Caldwell, M. H. (2012). Coercive plea bargaining: The unrecognized scourge of the justice system. *Catholic University Law Review, 61*(1), 63–96. Retrieved from http://scholarship.law.edu/lawreview/vol61/iss1/2

Dubber, M. D. (1997). American plea bargains, German lay judges, and the crisis of criminal procedure. *Stanford Law Review, 49*(3), 547–605. doi:10.2307/1229343

Easterbrook, F. H. (2013). Plea bargaining is a shadow market. *Duquesne Law Review. 51,* 551–558. Retrieved from http://chicagounbound.uchicago.edu/cgi/viewcontent.cgi?article=5051&context=journal_articles

Eisenstein, J., & Jacob, H. (1977). *Felony justice. An organizational analysis of criminal courts.* Boston, Toronto: Little, Brown and Company.

Feeley, M. M. (1979). *The process is the punishment: Handling cases in a lower criminal court.* New York, NY: Russell Sage Foundation.

Fomin, A. V. (2011). Пути совершенствования института особого порядка судебного разбирательства [Ways of improvement of the institute of special procedure court hearings]. *Biznes V Zakone. 5,* 99–101. Retrieved from http://cyberleninka.ru/article/n/puti-sovershenstvovaniya-instituta-osobogo-poryadka-sudebnogo-razbiratelstva

Friedman, L. M. (1979). Plea bargaining in historical perspective. *Law & Society Review, 13*(2), 247–259. doi:10.2307/3053251

Hartley, R. D., Miller, H. V., & Spohn, C. (2010). Do you get what you pay for? Type of counsel and its effect on criminal court outcomes. *Journal of Criminal Justice, 38*(5), 1063–1070. doi:10.1016/j.jcrimjus.2010.07.009

Heumann, M. (1975). A note on plea bargaining and case pressure. *Law & Society Review, 9,* 515–528. doi:10.2307/3053170

Heumann, M. (1978). *Plea bargaining.* Chicago: The University of Chicago Press.

Huskey, E. (1982). The limits to institutional autonomy in the soviet union: The case of the *Advokatura. Soviet Studies, 34*(2), 200–227. doi:10.1080/09668138208411409

Jordan, P. A. (2005). *Defending rights in Russia: Lawyers, the state, and legal reform in the post-soviet era.* Vancouver – Toronto: UBC Press.

Kaminskaya, D. (1982). *Final judgment: My life as a soviet defense attorney.* New York, NY: Simon and Schuster.

Kazun, A., Khodzhaeva, E., & Yakovlev, A. (2015). *Адвокатское сообщество России* [Advocates' community in Russia (analytical report)]. St. Petersburg: Institute for the Rule of Law. Retrieved from http://enforce.spb.ru/images/Products/Other_Publications/2015_analit_obzor_Advokaty_web.pdf

Khodzhaeva, E., & Rabovski, J. (2016). Strategies and tactics of criminal defenders in Russia in the context of accusatorial bias. *Russian Politics & Law, 54*(2–3), 191–226. doi:10.1080/10611940.2016.1176840

Kitai-Sangero, R. (2015). Plea bargaining as dialogue. *Akron Law Review, 49*(1), 63–89. Retrieved from http://ideaexchange.uakron.edu/akronlawreview/vol49/iss1/2

Kramer, M. (2003). *Rights and restraints in Russia's criminal justice system: Preliminary results of the new criminal procedural code (PONARS policy memo no. 289).* Harvard University. Retrieved from http://www.ponarseurasia.org/sites/default/files/policy-memos-pdf/pm_0289.pdf

Lazareva, V. (1999). Легализация сделок о признании вины [Legalization of plea bargaining]. *Rossiyskaya Yustitsiya. 5,* 40–41. Retrieved from http://lektor5.narod.ru/proces/lazareva.htm

CRIMINOLOGY AND CRIMINAL JUSTICE IN RUSSIA

Levin-Stankevich, B. L. (1996). The transfer of legal technology and culture: Law professionals in tsarist Russia. In H. D. Balzer (Ed.), *Russia's missing middle class: The professions in Russian history* (pp. 223–250). Armonk, NY: M.E. Sharpe.

Lichtenstein, M. J. (1984). Public defenders: Dimensions of cooperation. *The Justice System Journal*, 9(1), 102–110. Retrieved from http://www.jstor.org/stable/20877732

Luban, D. (1993). Are criminal defenders different? *Michigan Law Review*, 91(7), 1729–1766. doi:10.2307/1289650

Luban, D. (2001). Legal scholarship as a vocation. *Journal of Legal Education*, 51(2), 167–174. Retrieved from http://scholarship.law.georgetown.edu/facpub/586

Lynch, G. E. (2003). Screening versus plea bargaining: Exactly what are we trading off?. *Stanford Law Review*, 55(4), 1399–1408. Retrieved from http://www.jstor.org/stable/1229606

Maynard, D. W. (1984). *Inside plea bargaining*. New York, NY: Springer US.

Menkel-Meadow, C. (2004). Is the adversary system really dead? Dilemmas of legal ethics as legal institutions and roles evolve. *Current Legal Problems*, 57(1), 85–115. doi:10.1093/clp/57.1.85

Milenski, M. (1971). Courtroom encounters: An observation study of a lower criminal court. *Law & Society Review*, 5(4), 473–538. doi:10.2307/3052769

Mrowczynski, R. (2012). Self-regulation of legal profession in state-socialism: Poland and Russia compared. *Journal of the Max Plank Institute for European Legal History*, 20, 170–188. doi:10.12946/rg20/170-188

Nardulli, P. F. (1978). *The courtroom elite: An organizational perspective on criminal justice*. Cambridge, MA: Ballinger Publishing Company.

Nardulli, P. F. (1979). The caseload controversy and the study of criminal courts. *The Journal of Criminal Law and Criminology*, 70(1), 89–101. doi:10.2307/1142969

Nardulli, P. F. (1986). "Insider" justice: Defense attorneys and the handling of felony cases. *The Journal of Criminal Law and Criminology*, 77(2), 379–417. doi:10.2307/1143338

Nazarov, A. D. (2015). Обвинительный уклон в деятельности субъектов, ведущих уголовный процесс, как фактор, способствующий появлению ошибок в уголовном судопроизводстве [Presumption of guilt of an offender in the activities of the subjects controlling criminal process as a factor causing judicial mistakes in criminal judicial proceedings]. *Aktual'nye Problemy Rossiyskogo Prava*, 9(58), 149–154. Retrieved from http://law.sfu-kras.ru/data/method/e-library-kup/Papers/%D0%92%D0%90%D0%9A/2015/Nazarov%20APRP9.pdf

Newman, D. J. (1956). Pleading guilty for considerations: A study of bargain justice. *The Journal of Criminal Law, Criminology, and Police Science*, 46(6), 780–790. doi:10.2307/1139978

Padgett, J. F. (1985). The emergent organization of plea bargaining. *American Journal of Sociology*, 90(4), 753–800. doi:10.1086/228144

Paneyakh, E. (2013). Faking performance together: Systems of performance evaluation in Russian enforcement agencies and production of bias and privilege. *Post-Soviet Affairs*, 30(2–3), 115–136. doi:10.1080/1060586x.2013.858525

Paneyakh, E., & Titaev, K. (2011). *От милиции к полиции: реформа системы оценки деятельности органов внутренних дел* [From militia to police: The reform of the evaluation system of law enforcement agencies]. St. Petersburg: Institute for the Rule of Law. Retrieved from http://enforce.spb.ru/images/analit_zapiski/wp_11_03_palki_v_mvd_final-3103-fin.pdf

Paneyakh, E., Titaev, K., Volkov, V., & Primakov, D. (2010). *Обвинительный уклон в уголовном процессе: фактор прокурора* [Accusatory bias in criminal process: The role of prosecutors]. St. Petersburg: Institute for the Rule of Law. Retrieved from http://enforce.spb.ru/images/analit_zapiski/pm_3_prok_final_site.pdf

Pomorski, S. (2007). Justice in Siberia: A case study of a lower criminal court in the city of Krasnoyarsk. *Communist and Post-Communist Studies*, 34(4), 447–478. doi:10.1016/s0967-067x(01)00017-4

Pozdnyakov, M. (2015). Суд и правоохранительная система – цена компромисса [Courts and law enforcement agencies: The price of a compromise]. In V. Volkov (Ed.), *Обвинение и оправдание в постсоветской уголовной юстиции* [Conviction and acquittal in post-soviet criminal justice]. Moscow: Norma.

Rand, R. (1991). *Comrade lawyer: Inside soviet justice in an era of reform*. Boulder: Westview Press.

Roberts, J. M. (2013). Effective plea bargaining counsel. *Articles in Law Reviews & Other Academic Journals*. (Working Paper No. 286) (2650–2674). Retrieved from http://www.yalelawjournal.org/essay/effective-plea-bargaining-counsel

Sarat, A., & Felstiner, W. L. (1986). Law and strategy in the divorce lawyer's office. *Law & Society Review*, 20(1), 93–134. doi:10.2307/3053414

Schulhofer, S. J. (1984). Is plea bargaining inevitable?. *Harvard Law Review*, 97(5), 1037–1107. doi:10.2307/1340824

Schulhofer, S. J. (1992). Plea bargaining as disaster. *The Yale Law Journal*, 101(8), 1979–2009. doi:10.2307/796954

Shklyaruk, M., & Skougarevsky, D. (2015). *Криминальная статистика: механизмы формирования, причины искажения, пути реформирования* [Crime statistics: How it is constructed, tampered with, and could be reformed (analytical report)]. Moscow: Norma. Retrieved from http://enforce.spb.ru/images/Products/Crimestat_report_2015_IRL_KGI_web.pdf

Solomon, P. (1987). The case of the vanishing acquittal: Informal norms and the practice of soviet criminal justice. *Soviet Studies*, 39(4), 531–555. doi:10.1080/09668138708411718

Solomon, P. (2012). Plea bargaining russian style. *Demokratizatsiya, 20*(3), 282–299. Retrieved from https://www. gwu.edu/~ieresgwu/assets/docs/demokratizatsiya%20archive/GWASHU_DEMO_20_3/UV4U1383U8830621/ UV4U1383U8830621.pdf

Solomon, P. (2015). Post-soviet criminal justice: The perspective of distorted neo-inquisitorialism. *Theoretical Criminology, 19*(2), 159–178. doi:10.1177/1362480614568746

Springer, J. F. (1983). Burglary and robbery plea bargaining in California: An organizational perspective. *The Justice System Journal, 8*(2), 157–185. Retrieved from http://www.jstor.org/stable/20877703

Titaev, K., & Pozdnyakov, M. (2012). *Порядок особый – приговор обычный: практика применения особого порядка судебного разбирательства (гл. 40 УПК РФ) в российских судах* [Special procedure – usual sentence: The practices of application of special procedure in Russian courts (analytical report)]. St. Petersburg: The Institute for the Rule of Law. Retrieved from http://enforce.spb.ru/images/analit_zapiski/pm_gl_40_UPK_fin.pdf

Titaev, K., & Shklyaruk, M. (2016). *Российский следователь: призвание, профессия, повседневность* [Russian investigators: Vocation, profession, and routine]. Moscow: Norma.

Undrevich, V. S. (1928). *Советский суд и защита* [The soviet court system and defense]. *Revolutsiya Prava. 5*, 14–31. Retrieved from http://new.naukaprava.ru/catalog/435/710/2305/18336

Uphoff, R. J. (1995). The criminal defense lawyer as effective negotiator: A systemic approach. *Clinical Law Review. 2*, 73–135. Retrieved from http://scholarship.law.missouri.edu/cgi/viewcontent.cgi?article=1384&context= facpubs

Velikiy, D. P. (2005). Особый порядок судебного разбирательства: теория и практика [Special procedure court hearing: Theory and practice]. *Zhurnal Possiyskoi Yustitsii. 6*, 74–80. Retrieved from http://cyberleninka.ru/ article/n/osobyy-poryadok-sudebnogo-razbiratelstva-teoriya-i-praktika

Volkov, V. (2014). Socioeconomic status and sentencing disparities: Evidence from Russia's criminal courts. (Working paper No. IRL-01/2014). Retrieved from http://enforce.spb.ru/images/Products/in_English/IRL_ Preprint_2014_01_Vadim-Volkov_Socioeconomic-Status.pdf

Volkov, V., Dmitrieva, A., Skougarevsky, D., Chetverikova, I., Titaev, K., & Shesternina, J. (2014). *Уголовная юстиция России в 2009 г.: комплексный анализ судебной статистики* [Russian criminal justice in 2009: Complex analysis of judicial statistics]. Moscow: Statut. Retrieved from http://enforce.spb.ru/images/ Issledovanya/2014.06_Report_Database_2nd_ed.pdf

Volkov, V., & Titaev, K. (2013, February 28). Лишь 8% обвиняемых готовы бороться за свое доброе имя [Only 8% of defendants are ready to fight for their reputation]. *Vedomosti*. Retrieved from http://www.vedomosti.ru/ opinion/articles/2013/02/28/zavedomo_vinovnye

Wright, R., & Miller, M. (2002). The screening/bargaining tradeoff. *Stanford Law Review, 55*(1), 29–118. Retrieved from http://www.jstor.org/stable/1229590

The Restriction of Judicial Investigative Remand in Russia: The Role of Cultural Values in Citizen Acceptance and Perceived Fairness

OLGA B. SEMUKHINA

K. MICHAEL REYNOLDS

In 2001, the Russian Criminal Procedure Code was substantially reformed and replaced the 1960 Criminal Procedure Code of the RSFSR. One major reform element was a revocation of the trial judge's authority to remand a case for additional investigation, which had been allowed by the Soviet criminal procedural code. Our study examined citizen support for limiting the judge's remand authority. A self-report survey was administered to a representative sample of the Russian Federation (N=1,640) during the summer of 2006. Structural-equation modeling was used to analyze the results. Two research hypotheses were evaluated: 1) citizens with a collectively-oriented value system would reject the reform as unfair, and 2) those with individualistically-oriented values would perceive it as fair; both were validated. More than one-half of respondents (62.3%) reported the reform as unfair. Collective social values still prevail in Russian society and influence citizen support for the adoption of adversarial criminal procedural reforms. However, we also found individualistic values are increasing in younger age groups and among males.

INTRODUCTION

Since the Russian Federation emerged, numerous criminal law reforms have been pursued in an effort to attain an effective and democratic criminal justice system. Increased judicial independence was one focus of the reform efforts. In 1992, the Federal Statute, "On the Status of Judges," provided political and economic guarantees for judicial independence.[1] In 1996, a Federal Constitutional Statute, "On the Court System of Russia," provided for new constitutional courts for each subject region or republic of the federation.[2] In 1998, the Federal Statute, "On Justices of the Peace," created new trial court levels designed to reduce circuit court caseloads.[3] In 2002, the Federal Statute on "Court Agencies" provided judges with additional staff and resources.[4] The reforms implemented from 1992 through 2002 did have some measure of positive impact on judicial independence and trial judge neutrality.

While the reforms created during the decade after 1992 were substantial, the 2001 Criminal Procedural Code (CPC) reforms affected judicial independence and adjudication neutrality more directly. One of the reforms restricted judicial power by virtually prohibiting the remand of criminal cases for supplemental investigation.[5]

The judge's authority to order supplemental investigation was restricted and was permissible only in the case of certain procedural violations. Thus, what had been a common inquisitional trial practice during the Soviet period was substantially curtailed. The principal objective of the reform was to minimize trial judge partiality and increase the defendant's right to a fair trial.

Surprisingly, citizen support for the judicial reforms seems to be less than favorable (WCIOM, 2007; ROMIR, 2005).[6] Little empirical research has been done to measure citizen attitudes related to the trial judge reforms. However, several research studies have indicated that citizens do not believe court processes are fair and generally do not trust the court system (Levada, 2006; ROMIR, 2005; Novik, 2004). Various public opinion surveys repeatedly found that criminal justice reforms, including the 2001 CPC, did not create high public approval ratings (ROMIR, 2006; FOM, 2001). For example, a recent national study by WCIOM (2007) reported that only 4% of citizens believe that modern Russian courts are working properly. The study concluded that 33% of citizens believed that individuals would not obtain fair protection of their interests (WCIOM, 2007). A public longitudinal study of citizens conducted between January 2006 and November 2008 found that less than 30% were satisfied with the Russian court system (WCIOM, 2008). The low ratings of court institutions could be a result of the poor quality of the Russian court system generally, but it is clear that judicial reforms did not result in an improvement of public satisfaction with the courts.

Criminal justice professionals were surveyed prior to the CPC's implementation regarding their expectations for improved judiciary independence. Only 8.97% believed the new CPC reforms would result in an improvement (Mizulina, 2006b). One year after the CPC reforms were implemented, the professionals were surveyed again. On average, only 21% of judges thought that public trust in Russian courts would improve after the CPC judicial reforms. The prosecutors and investigators were more pessimistic and reported that public opinion would improve by 3.4% and 3.6%, respectively (Mizulina, 2006a).

These research findings directly contradict one of the key judicial reform goals. Russian Supreme Court Deputy Chief Justice Zhuikov declared that "increasing the status and the role of the court in Russian society" was one of the major goals of the court reforms, which included implementation of the 2001 CPC (Zhuikov & Gessen, 2007: 11).

There is not much information available from the English or Russian literature to help explain citizen attitudes toward the Russian judicial reform. Several legal policy-oriented studies are focused on the adversarial reform elements. This research took a legal perspective and was more related to policy outcomes (Pomorski, 2001; Butler, 2003; Solomon & Foglesong, 2000; Hendely, 1996; Muniz, 2004). Others focused on the introduction of jury trials related to subsequent public participation, citizen trust, and the perceptions of fairness (Ma, 1998; Thaman, 1995; Thaman, 1999; Diehm, 2001).

There is little existing literature exploring factors leading to low public satisfaction of the Russian judicial reforms. Some simply report dissatisfaction levels for the criminal justice institutions and related reforms (WCIOM, 2007; ROMIR, 2006, FOM[7], 2001). Other studies posited explanatory factors, but did not offer empirical evidence to support the proposition. The factors most commonly discussed were distrust of the government, law, socioeconomic conditions, judicial system abuse and corruption, and consequential legacies of the Soviet totalitarian state (Stoiko, 2002; Novik, 2004).

Our research examines potential explanatory contextual factors that are related to Russian cultural values. We postulate that cultural values can explain the low public support levels for comprehensive judicial reforms in general, and specifically, the trial judge reforms. This study's purpose is to examine and develop a better understanding of how contextual cultural factors impact citizen attitudes about the CPC reforms, while focusing on the restriction of judicial remand. Personal experiences with the criminal justice system were included in the study. The intent was to examine the relationship between low levels of judicial reform satisfaction and preexisting perceptions of the court system.

Literature Review and Research Question

The idea that public support for judicial reform in Russia can depend on societal cultural values is grounded on several socio-psychological and legal concepts. One of the most important is the notion that judgments about procedural fairness depend on societal cultural values. This concept has been widely explored in social-psychological disciplines for the past several decades. Experiments have shown that people with different cultural backgrounds perceive fairness of the two main procedural types—adversarial and inquisitorial—very differently (Austin, et al., 1981; Bos & Lind, 2001; Cohn, White & Sanders, 2000).

Findings indicate that societal attributes (i.e., cultural values) have a strong influence on perceptions of and support for different types of criminal procedure (Hamond & Adelman, 1976; Leung & Lind, 1986; Lind, et al., 1978). Several different theories explain why cultural values play a significant role in perceptions of procedural fairness. In our research, the group-value theory of Lind and Tyler (1988) is used. The theory assumes that if a procedure is similar to the fundamental values of the group, it will be viewed as fair (Earley & Lind, 1987; Lind, 2002; Lind & Tyler, 1988).

A second significant notion relating to the relationship between cultural values and public support for judicial reform is that of a personal orientation among types of cultural values and types of criminal procedure. A substantial amount of research, both legal and sociological, indicates that individuals who hold predominantly individualistic values are more likely to view the adversarial criminal procedure as fair. Conversely, those who predominantly favor collective values tend to see the inquisitorial procedure as preferable (Benjamin, 1975; Landsman, 1984; Hofstede, 1990, 2001).

This phenomenon has been explained as a function of how much control both the defendant and the prosecutor have over the outcome of a particular procedure (Austin, et al., 1981; Cohn, et al., 2000; Folger, 1977). The adversarial procedure guarantees a high level of participant control that is consistent with the active and self-reliant beliefs of an individualistically-oriented person. The inquisitorial procedure restrains the individual's control over the outcome and delegates it to a third party (a judge or other government entity) with higher authority, who represents the common interest. Such a decision-making mechanism is more appealing for a selfless (non-egoistic) person who holds collective values.

A third important idea for this study is the restraint of an active judicial role by the CPC reforms as part of a larger legal conceptual evolution. The legal reform shift signifies the evolution of the Russian criminal procedure from an inquisitorial to an adversarial model. By adopting the CPC reforms, the Russian Federation is attempting to move away from the fully inquisitorial Soviet-era model and closer to an adversarial model (Spence, 2006). In this model, the judge is required to be neutral, impartial, and to not serve an investigative or inquisitional role.

The reform limits the role of the trial judge to the function of adjudication by partially banning judges from remanding cases for supplementary investigation (as was possible under the previous procedural guidelines). This restriction is an attempt to reduce any possible bias in favor of the prosecution's interest and to prevent the judge from altering the charges (Stoiko, 2002). Under Article 232 of the 1960 CPC of RSFSR[8], the trial judge had the right to remand cases for additional investigation when a case was deemed incomplete (Berman, 1972). In practice, judges were also expected to write a decision justifying the remand, which frequently contained directions to the prosecutor to alter, add, or drop criminal charges (Smirnov, 1970). The judge was also allowed to initiate a new criminal case during the trial if it was discovered that the defendant had committed a new offense and had not been previously charged with the crime (Article 225 of the 1960 CPC of RSFSR). After the initiation of the case, the judge also had an opportunity to remand the case for further investigation (Smirnov, 1970).[9]

The literature suggests that judicial remand was one of the legal mechanisms that supported a zero-acquittal policy during the Soviet era. Whenever the defendant could not be convicted based on the existing evidence, the trial judge could use the remand as an alternative to acquittal (Burnham & Khan, 2008). By ordering a remand, the trial judge also frequently provided the prosecutor with investigative guidelines that were necessary to obtain a successful conviction (Stoiko, 2006).

In comparison with the 1960 CPC of RSFSR, the role of the criminal trial judge was substantially altered as a result of the 2001 CPC implementation. However, the judicial investigative remand restriction was not comprehensive and exceptions were allowed. Article 237 of the 2001 CPC authorizes the trial judge to remand a case in specific situations where there are "procedural violations." This exception is listed directly in paragraph 1 (subparagraphs 1 through 5) of the same Article. Paragraph 2 of Article 237 established a 5-day deadline for the prosecutor to eliminate defects in the case.

In 2003, Article 237 was supplemented by paragraphs 4 and 5, which prohibited the prosecutor from conducting new investigative actions and also deemed evidence that was obtained in violation of the 5-day deadline inadmissible.[10] On December 8, 2003, the Constitutional Court of Russia adopted Ruling #18-P which found Paragraph 4 of Article 237 of CPC unconstitutional. The ruling concluded that by banning the prosecutor from conducting any investigative actions after the judicial remand, the 2001 CPC limits the "constitutional rights of the defendant for court protection."[11] Paragraphs 2, 4 and 5 of Article 237 were excluded in 2008 by the federal statute.[12] Now, after a judicial remand, the 2001 CPC imposes no time limit on the prosecutor. Also, there are no limitations on the types of post-remand investigative actions. Practicing defense lawyers have opined that the exclusion made it easier for trial judges to remand cases based on procedural violations.[13]

Despite these recent amendments, the 2001 CPC is still more restrictive in relationship to the 1960 CPC of the RSFSR judicial remand provisions. The major restrictions are concentrated in Paragraph 1 of Article 237 and based on the premise that the judicial remand is only possible in cases of "procedural violations" that are listed in subparagraphs 1 through 5. The idea is that technical violations do not require the judge to evaluate the evidence and do not produce an accusatory bias (Borisova, 2009). However, the difference between procedural and substantial violations is not always clear. It is hard to draw a line "between correcting procedural errors and supplementing incompleteness" (Burnham & Khan, 2008: 58).

By combining the three aforementioned concepts, we postulate that individuals with collective cultural views would find changes in judicial remand less fair than individuals with predominantly individualistic values. However, this alone does not provide a full understanding of Russian citizens' attitudes pertaining to the judicial reform.

Socio-psychological theories strongly suggest that perceived fairness of legal procedure is a key factor to understanding both public support for and compliance with the law. Public opinion studies on legal reforms have found that, when individuals have little knowledge about the outcomes of new reforms, perceived fairness becomes a proxy. The proxy then serves as a basis for making a personal decision regarding support of the reform (Milgram, 1965; Bos, et al., 1997; Caldeira & Gibson, 1992) and is strongly correlated with voluntary compliance of the law (Friedland, Thilbaut & Walker, 1973; Gibson, 1989).

Group-value consistency is another factor that affects compliance. As part of altruistic group-oriented behavior, those who perceive a legal procedure as fair and consistent with their group values tend to comply with the law (Lind &Taylor, 1988; Lind, 2002). This theory suggests that individuals with collective values would be less likely to support the judicial remand reform and exhibit noncompliance as well. Conversely, those with predominantly individualistic group values will be more likely to support the reform.

The idea of a society having a set of specific group values is not new. Empirical findings confirm that most societies develop a set of dominant values derived from their unique historical context, geographic circumstances, economic condition, and other factors (Schwartz, 1995; WVS, 1996). The level of value domination can be different depending on the society's social cohesion, but some prevailing core values can be identified for the majority of the members (Kalsto, 2005).

In many cases, societies with prevailing core values were classified via a scale of individualistic and collective values (Schwartz, 1992; Hofstede, 1990). Collective group values always played an important and predominant role in Russian society (Tower, 1997; WVS, 1996, 2000). Although the most recent information published about cultural values in Russia is nine years old, we assume that a majority of its members maintain predominantly collective-oriented values.

With this in mind, it is likely that collectively-oriented individuals will view judicial reforms as unfair and will not be supportive of the reforms. If such values are predominant in traditional Russian culture, this may explain why there is low public support for adversarial procedural changes discontent with reforms that limit trial judges' authority. The research hypotheses are:

1. Collectively-oriented individuals view the ban of judicial remand for additional investigation as unfair.
2. Individualistically-oriented individuals view the ban of judicial remand for additional investigation as fair.

Hypotheses 1 and 2 are visually presented on Figures 1 and 2 respectively.

Additionally, this study presumes that a majority of Russians hold predominantly collective values. This presumption is empirically examined. Russian population demographics and survey respondents' direct experiences with the criminal justice system are used to control the hypotheses.

Methodology

The concept of individualistic and collective values was measured through a set of indicators adopted from Schwartz (1995, 1999). His measurement of cultural values is considered one of the most comprehensive instruments and consists of more than 35 indicators. For the purposes of our research, the indicators selected were those related to legal reform. A number of indicators pertaining to the concepts of hedonism and self-achievement were omitted.

Following the logic of Schwartz's methodology, 22 of the indicators selected were reduced through the use of confirmatory factor analysis (CFA) to 6 variables. These variables are stimulation, self-orientation, power, tradition, conformity, and benevolence. These variables represent the two main concepts

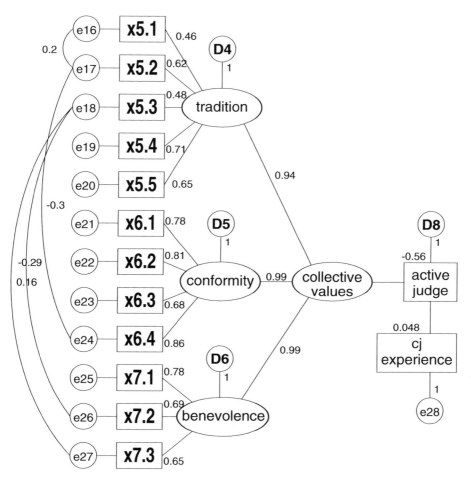

Figure 1. Structural equation model for hypothesis 1: Collective values and fairness of the restriction on judicial remand

of individualistic and collective values. The measurement models for collective and individualistic values are shown in Figures 1 and 2, respectively.

The evaluation of fairness related to the ban on judicial remand was measured directly via a self-explanatory survey item. The first part of the item stated the essence of the new policy in a simple format, and the second part inquired about the policy's fairness. To ensure the neutrality of the question and increase its clarity and comprehensibility, the questionnaire was pre-tested through 25 personal interviews and two pilot studies that were conducted in 2004 and 2005. See Appendix I to view the survey instrument in both Russian and English.

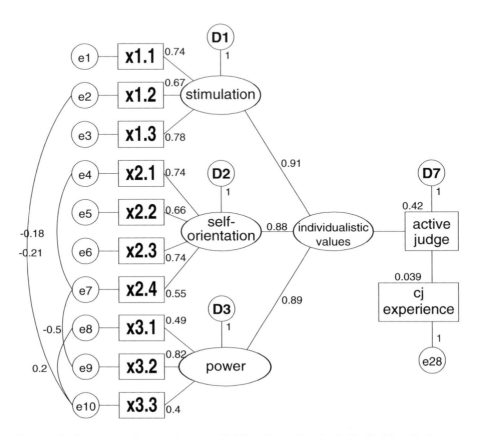

Figure 2. Structural equation model for hypothesis 2: Individualistic values and fairness of the restriction on judicial remand

The sampling was designed to obtain a national representative sample. Sampling was conducted in five stages. A list of regions within federal circuits was used as a sampling frame for the first stage. Regions were weighted using population demographics such as gender, age, professional occupation, average income, and proportion of rural to urban populations. Fifty of the 89 Russian regions were chosen from 6 of the 7 federal circuits. According to the Russian Constitution, the 89 regions are geographically grouped into larger units designated as "federal circuits."[14] At the time of the survey, there were 7 federal circuits in Russia. All 89 regions were grouped into 44 relatively homogenous clusters within the 7 federal districts. From this list, 22 clusters were randomly selected for sampling. These clusters consisted of 50 regions.

Cities, towns, and villages were selected from the clustered regions during the second stage of sampling.[15] From each of the 22 selected clusters, between 1 and 4 cities, towns, or villages were randomly selected for each of the 5 strata. The overall number of cities, towns, or villages selected within each circuit and stratum were controlled for by the Russian Federation population parameters. Table 1 provides details about the number of cities, towns, and villages selected within each circuit and strata.

Table 1. Number of cities, towns, and villages selected in each circuit for sampling

Circuits/Strata	> 1 million residents	500K-999K residents	100K-499K residents	< 100,000 residents	Villages	Total
Central	1	2	6	5	5	19
North-West	2	0	3	3	4	9
Volga	5	5	4	3	6	22
Southern	2	1	5	4	6	18
Ural	2	1	2	3	2	10
Siberian	2	2	4	3	4	15
Far East	0	2	2	2	2	8
Total	14	13	26	23	29	101

In the third stage of sampling, election districts were selected from the list of cities, towns, and villages.[16] The election districts were randomly selected with a probability proportionate to the number of registered voters. In each selected city, town, and village, 3 election districts were sampled. Thus, during the third stage, the sample consisted of 289 election circuits.

During the fourth stage of sampling, households registered with each election district were selected. This selection utilized a simple random method, wherein each household had an equal probability of being selected for the sample.[17] The total number of selected households at this stage was 2,000.

In the fifth stage of sampling, individual respondents were selected within each household. The selection was done using the quota requirements contained in the task list for each participating interviewer. The quotas were constructed based on age and gender parameters.

The sample size required to achieve a sampling error rate of +/- 5% was estimated to be 1,640 individuals. Subsequently, a sample size of 1,640 was achieved using a five-stage sampling process. The sample size estimate was based on a 95% confidence level, a medium-size effect, the homogeneity of the population, a statistical power of no less than 0.80, and a 2006 study population size of 142.8 million people (GKS, 2006). Table 2 provides a comparison of demographics for both the study sample and the Russian Federation population characteristics at the time of data collection. The comparison indicates that the study sample is representative of the national population in regards to age, gender, education, and residence.

Table 2. Comparison of the study sample demographic characteristics and Russian Federation Census data

Criterion	Study sample	2002 Census data
Age:		
18-24	14.6%*	14.6%
25-34	18%	17.8%
35-44	19.3%	20%
45-59	25.4%	23.7%
60+	22%	23.6%
Gender:		
Male	45.3%	46.6%
Female	54.7%	53.4%
Education:		
Incomplete school or lower	9%	23.1%
High school	21%	17.5%
Special professional education	47.5%	39.8%
Incomplete college degree	5%	3.1%
College degree	17.1%	15.7%
Graduate college degree	0.4%	0.3%
Place of residence:		
Urban	73.2%	73.3%
Rural	26.8%	26.7%

*-Percentages for age groups are calculated for population of 18 years old and older.

Sources: Age, gender, place of residence and education data are retrieved from the latest all-Russian Census conducted in 2002. Information available from the official web-site of the State Statistical Agency of Russia at www.gks.ru

Structural-equation modeling (SEM) techniques available in the Amos 5.0 application were used for the analysis. The choice of this statistical method was appropriate to accomplish the reduction of the numerous indicators of cultural values into the latent variables of peripheral and global cultural values (a second-order model). The adjusted goodness-of-fit index (AGFI), comparative goodness-of-fit index (CGFI), and RMSEA coefficients were applied as the criteria of goodness-of-fit statistics.

Table 3. First-order measurement model: Regression loadings for the cultural values indicators

Indicator	Label on SEM diagram	Regression loading	Standardized regression loading
Individualistic values			
Exciting life	x1.1	1.028	.737
Daring	x1.2	.895	.666
Varied life	x1.3	1.00	.776
Freedom	x2.1	.966	.741
Creativity	x2.2	.973	.663
Independent	x2.3	1.00	.743
Curiosity	x2.4	.702	.545
Capable	x3.1	1.00	.821
Ambitious	x3.2	.450	.400
Power	x3.3	.527	.491
Collective values:			
Humble	x5.1	1.00	.775
Accepting life	x5.2	.922	.687
Devout	x5.3	.857	.655
Respecting tradition	x5.4	.869	.624
Moderate	x5.5	.775	.480
Politeness	x6.1	.919	.648
Obedience	x6.2	1.00	.861
Self-discipline	x6.3	.661	.460
Honoring parents	x6.4	.988	.782
Responsible	x7.1	.958	.807
Forgiving	x7.2	.795	.676
Honest	x7.3	1.00	.707

*- all regression coefficients are significant at the 0.05 level.

Findings

Measuring Cultural Values in Russia

Guided by Schwartz's (1995) theory, the Russian cultural values were measured with a three-stage model. First, direct indicators related to specific cultural values were measured via the survey instrument. For this study, we used 22 direct indicators. Ten were related to individualistic values and 12 represented collective values (Table 3). Second, using confirmatory factor analysis (CFA), the indicators were reduced into 6 variables. The 6 variables were stimulation, self-orientation, power, tradition, conformity, and benevolence. The results of the first-order CFA are shown in Table 3. All 22 indicators have statistically significant factor loadings at an alpha level of .05. The values of standardized factor loadings for all 22 indicators range from 0.4 to 0.8, which indicates medium to strong relationships. These results suggest that all 22 value indicators are well-suited to measure the 6 variables.

Next, the 6 variables were reduced by the second-order CFA into 2 large value concepts: collective values and individualistic values. The results of the second reduction are shown in Table 4. The 6 variables had statistically significant regression loadings at an alpha level of .05. The standardized regression loadings for the variables of tradition, benevolence, and conformity were above 0.9. The results suggest that all 3 variables are excellent measures of the collective values concept. The standardized regression loadings for the variables of stimulation, self-direction, and power ranged from 0.8 to 0.9. The loading values indicate the 3 variables are good, or even excellent, measures for the individualistic values concept. Overall, the findings presented in Tables 3 and 4 support the model adopted from Schwartz as a valid way to measure the complex theoretical constructs of collective and individualistic values in a representative sample of the Russian Federation.

Table 4. Second-order measurement model: Regression loadings for the cultural values indicators

Variable	Concept measured	Regression loading	Standardized regression loading
Tradition		.928	.944
Benevolence	collective values	1.00	.987
Conformity		1.084	.990
Stimulation	individualistic	1.00	.908
Self-direction	values	1.118	.891
Power		.895	.876

*- all regression coefficients are significant at the 0.05 level.

The literature suggested that cultural values are strongly dependent on population demographics. Table 5 depicts the results of a non-parametric test that measured relationships among 8 demographic variables and cultural values. The results suggest that cultural values have statically significant relationships with the variables of age, gender, level of education, marital status, family size, household income, and employment status.

Table 5. Asymptotic significance for Kruskal-Wallis tests on cultural values variables

Variable title	Age	Gender	Education	Marital status	Residence	Family size	Income	Employment status
Exiting life	.000	.003	.000	.000	.001	.000	.000	.000
Daring	.000	.000	.000	.000	.051	.000	.000	.000
Varied life	.000	.007	.000	.000	.000	.000	.000	.000
Freedom	.000	.001	.000	.000	.000	.000	.000	.000
Creativity	.000	.950	.000	.000	.000	.000	.000	.000
Independent	.000	.004	.000	.000	.000	.000	.000	.000
Curiosity	.003	.997	.000	.000	.015	.007	.000	.003
Capable	.000	.340	.000	.000	.000	.000	.000	.000
Ambitious	.000	.001	.000	.000	.000	.000	.000	.000
Power	.000	.000	.000	.000	.000	.000	.000	.000
Humble	.034	.000	.086	.032	.002	.492	.214	.034
Accepting life	.000	.000	.034	.000	.631	.003	.226	.000
Devout	.000	.000	.289	.000	.001	.000	.050	.000
Respect tradition	.000	.008	.090	.000	.000	.362	.501	.000
Moderate	.107	.054	.017	.000	.136	.005	.578	.107
Politeness	.926	.000	.001	.434	.000	.572	.029	.926
Obedience	.205	.010	.015	.000	.001	.049	.011	.205
Self-discipline	.462	.004	.004	.008	.099	.456	.190	.462
Honoring parents	.082	.000	.120	.243	.007	.152	.144	.082
Forgiving	.019	.000	.041	.012	.139	.085	.138	.019
Honest	.000	.001	.001	.000	.247	.036	.054	.000
Responsible	.065	.024	.000	.001	.017	.095	.005	.065

Measuring Public Opinion about the Fairness of the Judicial Reforms

Descriptive information about public attitudes concerning the fairness of the judicial reforms is shown in Table 6. More then half of the respondents indicated the reforms were unfair (62.3%), and less than one-third (29%) reported the reforms were fair. Also, 16.9% responded that the reforms were absolutely unfair, in contrast to only 1.1% who reported the new policies were completely fair. Table 6 depicts the distribution of public opinion concerning the fairness of system. As seen in Table 6, no relationships are evident between actual experiences with the criminal justice system and public opinions pertaining to judicial remand reform fairness.

Table 6. Public opinion regarding the fairness of legal reform banning the judicial remand of cases for additional investigation by experience with the criminal justice system

Fairness judgment (responses)/ cj experience	Total Percent	No	Yes
Completely unfair	16.9%	20.1%	15.1%
Unfair	26.4%	22.3%	28.2%
Somewhat unfair	19%	24.9%	18.5%
Somewhat fair	21%	12.2%	23.8%
Fair	6.9%	8.6%	6.8%
Completely fair	1.1%	0.7%	1.7%
Don't know	8.8%	11.2%	5.9%
Total	100%	100%	100%

Hypotheses Testing

Tables 7 and 8 depict descriptive statistics for the concepts of collective and individualistic Russian values. Table 7 provides the proportion of responses to each of the 22 indicators, while Table 8 depicts average strength responses for the 6 importance indicator variables. Our research proposition that Russian society is dominated by primarily collective values can only be partially supported. Compared to previous research, we found there is a general attitudinal trend indicative of a shift from collective to individual values in contemporary Russia.

The collective values, conformity and benevolence, were perceived as having greater importance. The conformity response rate of "very important" was 74.6%, and the benevolence response rate was 75.6%. The remaining measure of collective values, tradition, was lower, with 57.9% rating it as "very important."

Table 7. The levels of importance of cultural values to Russian citizens based on direct indicators, 2006

Cultural value indicator	Proportion of "very important" answers	Proportion of "somewhat important" answers	Proportion of "not important" answers	Proportion of "contradict my values" answers
Exciting life	55.1%	27.9%	15.4%	1.6%
Daring	46.7%	34.1%	18%	1.2%
Varied life	51.6%	31.6%	16%	0.8%
Freedom	63.4%	25.3%	10.4%	0.9%
Creativity	52.5%	32.4%	13.9%	1.1%
Independency	65.1%	24.4%	9.6%	0.8%
Curiosity	58.9%	30.2%	9.9%	1%
Capable	64.8%	19.4%	10.6%	1.3%
Ambitious	51.6%	27.8%	19%	1.6%
Power	39.6%	37.6%	21.2%	1.6%
Wealth	56%	32.1%	11.4%	0.4%
Humble	56.6%	35.6%	7.2%	0.4%
Accepting life	54.4%	35%	8.7%	0.9%
Devoutness	45.1%	38.8%	15%	1.1%
Respecting tradition	68.3%	25.9%	5.4%	0.4%
Moderate	61.6%	33.3%	4.5%	0.6%
Politeness	75.6%	20.2%	4.1%	0.1%
Obedience	69.5%	24.9%	5.4%	0.2%
Self-discipline	68.9%	26%	4.9%	0.2%
Honoring parents	83.9%	12.7%	3%	0.4%
Responsible	78.1%	17.4%	4.2%	0.3%
Forgiving	80.1%	15.8%	3.5%	0.6%
Honest	69.2%	26.2%	4.4%	0.2%

The variables measuring the individualistic values, stimulation and power, were not as strong as the collective values, generally. Fifty-one percent (51.1%) of the respondents reported the simulation variable as "very important," along with 53% for the power variable. The self-direction variable was stronger than either stimulation or power, with 59.9% replying it was "very important."

A closer analysis of the cultural values indicators in Table 7 shows that some unexpected outcomes were observed in both the independence and

Table 8. The levels of importance of cultural values to Russian citizens based on aggregated variables, 2006

Cultural value indicator	Average of "very important" answers	Average of "somewhat important" answers	Average of "not important" answers	Average of "contradict my values" answers
Stimulation	51.1%	31.8%	16.4%	1.2%
Self-direction	59.9%	28%	10.9%	0.9%
Power	53%	29.2%	15.5%	1.2%
Tradition	57.9%	33.7%	9.1%	0.7%
Conformity	74.4%	20.9%	.3%	0.2%
Benevolence	75.8%	19.8%	4%	0.4%

devoutness indicators. The number of respondents that chose independence as their "most important" value was the highest among all individualistic values (65.1%). This outcome increased the overall ranking of the self-direction variable and made it look much more important than the other individualistic variables (Table 7). Conversely, 45% of respondents reported the value of devoutness as "very important;" this was the lowest value for all 12 collective indicators. This response rate lowered the "tradition" concept ranking considerably and partially contradicted our study expectations. There are also other indicators in both the individualistic and collective concepts that deviated from the expectation of collective value predominance. The collective indicators of being humble and accepting life reflect relatively low values. The individualistic indicators of freedom and being capable have somewhat higher values than other dimensions in their group.

Thus, the results of the descriptive analysis suggest that, while 2 out of 3 collective variables still are predominant in Russia, some individualistic values, such as independence and freedom, reveal a trend of greater importance. Some individualistic value preferences, combined with the rejection of specific collective values (i.e., devoutness and accepting life), are indicative of a cultural trend that is a departure from collective values. This trend was unanticipated and departs from our initial expectations. Our findings indicate that Russian culture is still primarily a collective value system but one that exhibits some observable exceptions and tendencies to espouse individualistic values. Some recent studies that examined Russian cultural elements support our observations of a recent shift in values (Ebert, 2004; Tuldum & Kalsto, 2005).

The results presented in Table 9 show that the latent variable, collective values, has a statistically significant and inverse relationship with the variable "judgment of the fairness of judicial remand." Standardized regression loading between these two variables is equal to -0.560, which is a medium-strength relationship. The respondents' cultural values can explain up to 31% of the variance in attitudes about the 2001 CPC judicial investigative remand reform.

CRIMINOLOGY AND CRIMINAL JUSTICE IN RUSSIA

Table 9. Structural model: relations between the type of cultural values and the judgment of fairness of the judicial reform.

Variable	Regression coefficient	R square
Collective values	-.560	.31
Individualistic values	.428	.18
Criminal justice experience in Hypothesis 1	0.048	.002
Criminal justice experience in Hypothesis 2	0.039	.001

*- all regression coefficients are significant at the 0.05 level.

Table 9 also indicates that there is a statistically significant medium-strength relationship between individualistic values and "judgment of the fairness of judicial remand." The standardized regression coefficient is equal to .0428 and the explained variance is 18%. The relationships in both hypotheses were controlled by the respondents' actual experience with the criminal justice system and 8 demographic variables (age, gender, level of education, marital status, family size, household income, place of residence, and employment status). None of the demographic variables had statistically significant relationships to the fairness of judicial remand. Consequently, these were removed from the model in compliance with the SEM methodology. The respondents' experiences with the criminal justice system had a statistically significant relationship with their perception of the fairness of judicial remand, but the regression weights were extremely low in both models (0.048 for hypothesis 1 and 0.039 for hypothesis 2).

Table 10 shows that data from our sample has a good fit for both structural equation models that are depicted in Figures 1 and 2. The goodness-of-fit statistics show good fit indices for both models (.894 and .904 accordingly). The values of RMSEA and CMIN/DF are not as high as the goodness indices (5.8 /0.74 and 6.2 /.079, respectfully), but do signify a modest and good fit.

Table 10. Goodness-of-fit statistics for research hypotheses 1 and 2

Hypotheses	CMIN/DF	AGFI	CFI	RMSEA
Hypothesis 1 (Collective values)	6.242	.837	.894	.079
Hypothesis 2 (Individualistic values)	5.850	.869	.904	.074

Based on the findings from Tables 8, 9, and 10, research hypotheses 1 and 2 are accepted. Russian respondents who hold predominantly collective values view the ban of judicial investigative remand as unfair. Conversely, respondents with mostly individualistic values view the ban as fair. Overall, about a quarter of the variance supporting a limitation of the trial judge's authority can be explained by cultural values.

Discussion and Limitations

The overall findings indicate that Russia continues to be a country with predominantly collective cultural values. The unusual pattern of the "devoutness" indicator is likely related to the recent Soviet period. The meaning of the word "devoutness" is closely associated in the Russian language and culture with religiosity and church authority. Soviet ideology strongly advocated atheism and suppressed religious values of any type. Therefore, it may follow that low values of the "devoutness" indicator do not signify an espousal of individualistic cultural values, but are instead a residual attitudinal influence from the Soviet period.

The unanticipated high rating of the "independence" value can also be explained by the recent historical developments in Russia. In a country where principal human freedoms (such as movement and speech) were restricted for several decades, independence became more than just a value. Independence in this context transformed into an ideal that people aspired to obtain. Therefore, as suggested by the traditional interpretation of Schwartz (1999), high values of the "independence" indicator may result from a desire to acquire a lost ideal rather than a preference for individualistic behavior.

It is also important to notice that, while the collective values have higher ratings in overall respondent preferences, the individualistic values also received relatively high ratings. The value percentages presented in Tables 7 and 8 for individualistic values are higher than 50%. This suggests that individualistic values are gaining popularity in Russia. Based on other empirical sources, one could logically assume that age and gender would be important factors regarding increases in individualistic value preferences (Hofstede, 2001; WVS, 1996). In our study all 8 demographic variables had statistically significant relationships with age, gender, level of education, marital status, family size, household income, and employment status. The younger generation, and male respondents, tended to have higher individualistic values than the older generation and females. The trend is consistent with findings on cultural values from other countries, reporting that individualistic values are preferred by younger generations and male respondents (Inglehart, 2003).

The study reveals the majority of respondents do not find the ban of judicial investigative and inactive judge as the only remedy against judicial bias (Kahn, 2002). It is evident that a majority of respondents do not see the benefits of such reforms. The study results do not allow an inference as to whether the respondents do not believe in the importance of an independent judge, or simply consider the possibility of judicial bias an adequate price to pay for "more effective" crime-fighting efforts. Some Russian legal experts believe the latter is the case (Baranov, 2002).

Based on the old Soviet tradition, the judge was not viewed by the public as a neutral arbiter of the facts or the law, but rather as a crime fighter (Berman, 1972).[18] Following this logic, one can see the ban of judicial investigative remand as just an unnecessary constraint for the judge to overcome in the complex world of increasing crime rates.

Our study found the demographic variables had no significance related to the fairness of judicial investigative remand. This is an indication that few differences exist in the population with regard to perspectives on remand reform; most do not support the judicial restriction and perceive it as unfair. The study found a statistically significant, but very weak relationship, between the respondents' criminal justice system experiences and their attitudes toward the fairness of the remand reform. It is possible that a relationship would be more evident and pronounced if experiences with the criminal justice system could be more accurately measured. Additional data collection is necessary in order to more fully understand why the respondents failed to support the judicial investigative remand reforms.

The data pertaining to perception of judicial reform fairness should be subjected to some scrutiny. The overall findings suggest that more than half of the respondents consider the judicial reforms unfair. Even though there is empirical support to conclude that cultural values can explain up to 31% of the respondents' views of judicial remand reform, other causes should also be considered to address the unexplained variance.

One can reasonably infer that issues related to overall trust in the criminal justice system, the government in general, and judges specifically, can influence public support for legal reforms. It is also logical to suggest that public attitudes toward judicial reform and trust of the court system are related to respondent assessments of the existing court system. However, in this study, direct experience with the criminal justice system had little impact on attitudes related to judicial remand. Therefore, it is possible that respondents' overall distrust of the Russian courts may explain the remaining variance in the judgment of fairness. However, the roots of this distrust should be examined more carefully since it could be a reflection of factors other than the court system's ineffectiveness in Russia.

Another important point is the complexity of the legal reform issues. Some respondents may have provided responses without an adequate understanding of the judicial reform policy changes or their impact on fairness. The questionnaire was designed to inform the respondent about the nature of the policy changes. Regardless, 8.8% of the respondents selected "don't know" in response to the item about legal reform fairness.

Nevertheless, this study provides evidence that cultural values are important factors in public acceptance of judicial reforms. Additional research to examine the relationship of demographics to government trust would be helpful to more fully explain why the majority of citizens do not accept the policy reforms.

CONCLUSION

The two research study hypotheses are accepted. The study's results confirm that an individual's set of cultural values (collective or individual) influences whether a respondent views the ban of judicial investigative remand as fair. Our initial research assumption that collective values would be prevalent in contemporary Russia was not fully supported. A descriptive data analysis revealed the majority of respondents hold predominantly collective values and view the ban on judicial investigative remand as unfair. However, all individualistic values ranked 50% or higher on the scale of importance. This indicates there is increasing support for individualistic values in modern Russia. It was found that a growing group of respondents who hold individualistic values support the judicial reform and consider the ban of judicial investigative remand equitable. There is also a strong relationship between those with predominant collective values and lack of support for the remand restrictions. Thirty-one percent of the variance related to legal reform fairness can be explained by the cultural values variables. This supports our assertion that cultural values in Russia play an important role in the acceptance of judicial reforms. Other factors that may relate to the disapproval of judicial reforms should be examined.

NOTES

1. The Federal Statute # 3132-1 "On the Status of Judges" was adopted on June 26, 1992, by the Congress of Soviets. The text is retrieved from www.consultant.ru. Consultant is a private company that maintains and provides access to the up-to-date official legal texts of all Russian documents. All legal documents in this article were retrieved from the Consultant database, available online at www.consultant.ru.

2. Federal Constitutional Statute "On the Court System of Russia" # 1-FKZ was adopted on December 31, 2006, by the State Duma. The text was retrieved from www.consultant.ru.

3. Federal Statute #188-FZ, "On Justices of the Peace," was adopted on december 17, 1998, by the State Duma. The text was retrieved from www.consultant.ru.

4. The Federal Statute # 30-FZ was adopted on March 14, 2002, by the State Duma. The text was retrieved from www.consutlant.ru.

5. The ban of judicial remand was originally declared in the Ruling by the Constitutional Court of Russia in 1999, which held that paragraph 1 of Article 232 of the CPC of 1960 is in violation of the Russian Constitution. For full details, please see Ruling #7P of the Constitutional Court of Russia issued on April 20, 1999. [Postanovlenie Konstitustionnogo Suda Rossiskoi ot 20.04.99 #7P "Po delu o proverke konstitutsionnosti polozhenii punktov 1 i 3 chasti pervoi statii 232"). [online]

Available www.consultant.ru. Accessed March 4, 2009. The CPC of 2001 expanded and detailed the ban originally declared by the Constitutional Court.

6. WCIOM is an abbreviation for the All-Russian Center of Public Opinion Research. It is a government research center created in the late 1980s. It is also sometimes spelled as "VtSIOM". However in this paper we use the abbreviation provided on the company's website: www.wciom.ru. The data was retrieved from www.wciom.ru. ROMIR is an abbreviation for Center for Russian Public Opinion and Market Research.

7. FOM is an abbreviation for the Foundation of Public Opinion, an independent non-profit research organization. The data is retrieved from www.fom.ru.

8. The abbreviation "RSFSR" stands for Russian Soviet Federative Socialist Republic.

9. These provisions were excluded from the CPC of 1960 by Statute #2869-1, which was issued on May 25, 1992.

10. Amendments were made by the Federal Statute #92-FZ issued on July 4, 2003.

11. The right of the defendant for court protection is guaranteed by Article 46 Par 1 of the Russian Constitution. This right resembles the right to a fair trial in US criminal law, but the two are not identical.

12. Federal Statute #226-FZ was issued on December 2, 2008. Retrieved from www.consultant.ru.

13. For example, refer to the opinion expressed by Panchenko in the article by Moskovskyi Komsomolets. Retrieved at http://www.mk.ru/blogs/MK/2008/12/18/society/386858/.

14. At the time of the sampling, Russia consisted of 89 regions. This number is currently reduced to 86 because several small regions have been merged together.

15. The following strata were developed: super-large cities with populations over one million people; large cities with populations from 500,000 to 999,000; middle-sized cities with populations between 100,000 and 499,000; and towns and villages with populations of less than 100,000.

16. The election districts are official territorial divisions of Russia within particular cities, towns, and villages that are used to organize all local and federal elections. Each election district has an identification number and a known number of registered voters. The number of registered voters per election district usually ranges from 100 to 1,000 people.

17. Due to the possibility of non-responses, the actual number of households selected was 25% higher than the sample size.

18. The "crime fighter" role of the trial judge in the Soviet Union should not be mistaken for the ideology of being "harsh on the crime." The trial judges in the SU were not simply expected to be harsh on criminal punishment, but also to participate actively in law enforcement efforts to combat crime.

REFERENCES

All-Russian Center of Public Opinion Research (WCIOM). (2007). Monitoring of the courts. [online] Available: http://wciom.ru/novosti/otkrytye-proekty/ocenka-dejatelnosti-sudov-v-rf.html   Accessed December 4, 2008.

All-Russian Center of Public Opinion Research (WCIOM). (2008). Monitoring of the satisfaction with the major societal institutions in Russia. [online] Available: http://wciom.ru/novosti/reitingi/odobrenie-dejatelnosti-obshchestven nykh-institutov.html   Accessed November 27, 2008.

Autsin, W., Williams, T., Worchel, S., Wentzel, A., & Siegel, D. (1981). Effect of mode of adjudication, presence of defense counsel and favorability of verdict on observer's evaluation of a criminal trial. *Journal of Applied Social Psychology, 11*(4): 281-300.

Baranov, A. M. (2002). Sovremennye problemy novogo ugolovno protsessa Rossii i ih reshenie v novom UPK [Modern issues of new criminal process of Russia and its solution in the new Code of Criminal Procedure]. Paper presented at the New Russian Code of Criminal Procedure and Its Application, Orenburg.

Benjamin, R. (1975). Images of conflict resolution and social control: American and Japanese attitudes towards the adversary system. *Journal of Conflict Resolution, 19*(1): 123-137.

Berman, H. J. (1972). *Soviet Criminal Law and Procedure*. Cambridge, MA: Harvard UP.

Borisova, B. (2009). Kommentarii k ugolovno-protsessual'nomu kdeksu RF 2001 [Commentary to the CPC of 2001]. Moscow: Knizhnyi mir. '

Bos, K. and Lind, E. A. (2001). The psychology of own versus others' treatment: Self-oriented and other-oriented effects on perceptions of procedural justice. *Personality and Social Psychology Bulletin, 27*(10): 1324-1333.

Bos, K., Lind, E. A., Vermunt, R., & Wilke, H. (1997). How do I judge my outcome when I do not know the outcome of others? The psychology of the fair process effect. *Journal of Personality and Social Psychology, 72*(5): 1034-1046.

Boylan, S. (1998). The status of judicial reform in Russia. *American University Law Review, 13*: 1327-1336.

Burnham, W., Maggs, P. B., & Danilenko, G. M. (2003). *Law and Legal System of the Russian Federation*. Huntington, NY: Juris Publishing.

Burnham, W. and Kahn, J. (2008). Russia's criminal procedural code: Five years out. *Review of Eastern and Central European Law, 33*: 1-93.

Butler, W. E. (2003). *Russian Law*. Oxford, UK: Oxford UP.

Caldeira, G. and Gibson, J. (1992). The etiology of public support for the Supreme Court. *American Journal of Political Science, 36*(3): 635-664.

Center for Russian Public Opinion and Market Research (ROMIR). (2005). Monitoring of attitudes towards the criminal law. [online] Available: http://www. romir.ru/news/res_results/11.html   Accessed October 1, 2006.

Center for Russian Public Opinion and Market Research (ROMIR). (2006). Public support of court system. [online] Available: www.romir.ru. http://www.romir. ru/news/res_results/14.html   Accessed October 1, 2006.

Cohn, E., White, S., & Sanders, J. (2000). Distributive and procedural justice in seven nations. *Law and Human Behavior, 24*(5): 553-579.

Diehm, J. (2001). The introduction of jury trials and adversarial elements into the former Soviet Union and other inquisitorial countries. *Journal of Transnational Law and Policy, 11*: 1-18.

Ebert, C. (2004). *Die Seele hat kein Geschlecht. Studien zum Genderdiskurs in der russischen Kultur*. Bern: P. Lang.

Earley, P. and Lind, E. A. (1987). Procedural justice and participating in tasks selection: the role of control in mediation justice judgment. *Journal of Personality And Social Psychology, 52*(6): 1148-1160.

Folger, R. (1977). Distributive and procedural justice: Combined impact of "voice" and improvement on experienced inequality. *Journal of Personality and Social Psychology, 35*(2): 108-119.

Friedland, N., Thibaut, J., & Walker, L. (1973). Some determinants of the violations of rules. *Journal of Applied Social Psychology, 3*(2): 103-118.

Fund of Public Opinion (FOM). (2001). Court system and jury. [Online] Available: http://bd.fom.ru/report/map/dd010628   Accessed October 4, 2006.

Gibson, J. (1989). Understandings of justice: Institutional legitimacy, procedural justice and political tolerance. *Law and Society Review, 23*(3): 469-496.

Hamond, K. and Adelman, L. (1976). Science, values and human judgment. *Science*, New Series, *194*(4263): 389-396.

Hendley, K. (1996). *Trying to Make Law Matters. Legal Reform and Labor Law in the Soviet Union.* Ann Arbor, MI: Michigan Press.

Hofstede, G. (1990). *Culture and Organization; Software of the Mind.* London, UK: McGraw-Hill.

_____. (2001). *Culture's consequences.* Thousand Oaks, CA: Sage Publications.

Inglehart, R. (2003). *Human Values and Social Change: Findings from the Values Surveys.* Leiden, Boston: Brill.

Kahn, J. (2002). Note: Russian compliance with articles five and six of the European Convention of Human Rights as a barometer of legal reform and human rights in Russia. *University of Michigan Journal of Law Reform, 35*(3): 641-694.

Kalsto, P. (2005). Nation-building in Russia: Value-oriented strategy. In Kalsto, P., *National Building and Common Values in Russia* (pp. 1-28). Lanham, MD: Rowman and Littlefield.

Landsman, S. (1984). *The Adversary System. A Description and Defense.* Washington, DC: American Enterprise Institute for Public Policy Research.

Leung, K. and Lind, E. A. (1986). Procedural justice and culture: Effect of culture, gender and investigator status on procedural preferences. *Journal of Personality and Social Psychology, 50*(6): 1134-1140.

Lind, E. A., Erickson, B., Friedland, N., & Dickenberger, M. (1978). Reaction to procedural models for adjudicative conflict resolution. *Journal of Conflict Resolution, 22*(2): 318-340.

Lind, E. A. (2002). Fairness judgment as cognition. In Ross M. and Miller D. (Eds.), *The Justice Motive in Everyday Life: Essays in Honor of Melvin J. Lerner* (pp. 416-431). Cambridge, UK: Cambridge UP.

Lind, E. A. and Tyler, T. R. (1988). *The Social Psychology of Procedural Justice.* NY, NY: Plenum Press.

Milgram, S. (1965). Some conditions of obedience and disobedience to authority. *Human Relations, 18*: 57-76.

Mizulina, E. B. (2006a). Reforma ugolovnogo pravosudiya v Rossi: god posle prinyatiya novogo Ugolovno-protsessual'nogo kodeksa Rossiaksoi Federatsii [Reform of the criminal justice system in Russia: A year after the adoption of the new CPC of Russia]. In Mizulina, E. B. and Pligin, V. N. (Eds.), Uroki Reformy Ugolovnogo Pravosudiia v Rossii [Lessons of Reforming Criminal Justice in Russia] (pp. 800-813). Moscow: Yurist.

Mizulina, E. B. (2006b). Rossiya nakanune vvedeniya v deistvie novogo ugolovno protsessual'nogo kodeksa Rossiskoi Federatsii [Russia on the eve of adopting the new Criminal Procedural Code of Russian Federation]. In Mizulina, E. B. and Pligin, V. N. (Eds.), *Uroki Reformy Ugolovnogo Pravosudiia v Rossii* [Lessons of Reforming Criminal Justice in Russia] (pp. 783-799). Moscow: Yurist.

Muniz, P. (2004). Judicial reform in Russia: Russia looks to the past to create a new adversarial system of criminal justice. *Willamette Journal of International Law and Dispute Resolution, 11*: 81-122.

Newcombe, K. (2007). Russia. In Bradley, C. M. (Ed.), *Criminal Procedure. A Worldwide Study* (pp. 397-470). Durham, NC: Carolina Academic Press.

Novik, V. V. (2004). *Judicial Reform Effective Activity of Court, Procuratura and Agencies of Preliminary Investigation in Russia*. St. Petersburg: Law Institute Press.

Pomoroski, S. (2001). Justice in Siberia: A case study of a lower criminal court in Krasnoyarsk. *Communist and Post-Communist Studies, 34*: 447-478.

Rokeach, M. (1973). *Beliefs, Attitudes and Values*. London, UK: Jossey Bass Publishers.

Russian Agency of Statistics. (2006). Demographic characteristics of Volgograd region. [online] Available: www.gks.ru   Accessed October 4, 2006.

Savitsky, V. M. (1979). Criminal Procedure. In Bassiouni, C. (Ed.), *The Criminal Justice System of the USSR* (pp. 45-92). Springfield, IL: Charles C. Thomas Publishers.

Schwartz, S. (1996). Value priorities and behavior: applying a theory of integrated value system. In Seligman, C., Olson J. M., & Zanna, M. P. (Eds.), *The Psychology of Values* (pp. 1- 25). Mahwah, NJ: Lawrence Erlbaum Associates, Publishers.

Schwartz, S. H. (1992). Universals in the content and structure of values: theoretical advances and empirical tests in 20 countries. *Advances in Experimental Social Psychology, 25*: 1-65.

Schwartz, S. H., Lehmann, A. & Roccas, S. (1999). Multimethod probes of basic human values. In Adamopoulos, J. and Kashima, Y. (Eds.), *Social Psychology and Cultural Context* (pp. 107-123). Thousand Oaks, CA: Sage Publications.

Schwartz, S. H. and Savig, L. (1995). Identifying culture-specifics in the content and structure of values. *Journal of Cross-Cultural Psychology, 26*(1): 92-116.

Smirnov, L. N. (1970). *Nauchno-Prakticheskyi Kommentraii Ugolovno-Protsessual'nogo Kodeksa RSFSR* [Scientific-Practical Commentary to the Criminal Procedural Code of RSFSR]. Moscow: Yuridicheskaya Literatura.

Solomon, P. and Foglesong, T. (2000). *Court and Transition in Russia. The Challenge of Judicial Reform*. Oxford, UK: Westview Press.

Spence, M. (2006). The Complexity of Success in Russia. In Carothers, T. (Ed.), *Promoting the Rule of Law Abroad* (pp. 217-250). Washington, DC: Carnegie Endowment for International Peace.

Stoiko N. G. (2002). *Questions of Criminal Process and Legal Reform*. Krasnoyarsk: Krasnoyarsk State UP.

Stoiko N. G. (2006). *Tipologiya Ugolvono Protsessa* [Typology of Criminal Procedure]. Krasnoyarsk: Krasnoyarsk State University Press.

Thaman, S. (1995). The resurrection of trial by jury in Russia. *Stanford Journal of International Law, 31*: 61-182.

Thaman, S. (1999). Europe's new jury trial system: The cases of Spain and Russia. *Law and Contemporary Problems, 62*: 233-250.

Tower, R. K., Kelly, C., & Richards, A. (1997). Individualism, Collectivism and Reward Allocation: A Cross-Cultural Study in Russia and Britain. *The British Journal of Social Psychology, 36*(3): 331-345.

Tuldum, G. and Kalsto, P. (2005). Value consensus and social cohesion. In Kalsto, P. and Blakkisrud, H. (Eds.), *National Building and Common Values in Russia* (pp. 29-58). Lanham, MD: Rowman and Littlefield Publishers.

World Value Survey Report. (1999). [online] Available: http://wvs.isr.umich.edu Accessed November 27, 2008.

_____. (1996). [online] Available: http://wvs.isr.umich.edu   Accessed November 27, 2008.

Yue, M. (1998). Law participation in criminal trials: A comparative perspective. *International Criminal Justice Review, 8*: 74-94.

Zhuikov, V. M., and Gessen, I. V. (2007). Sudebnaya reforma v proshlom i nastoyaschem [Court reform in the past and present]. *Statut*. Russian Academy of Justice: Moscow.

Appendix 1
Public Opinion of Ban of Judicial Remand in Russia
Questionnaire wording

A. Exact wording of questionnaire:

Пожалуйста, определите, насколько данные жизненные ценности, важны для Вас в качестве руководящих принципов в Вашей жизни

Увлекательная жизнь	Принятие своей доли в жизни
Смелость, храбрость	Религиозность
Разнообразная жизнь	Уважение традиций
Свобода	Умеренность
Творчество	Хорошо воспитанный
Независимость	Послушание
Любознательность	Самодисциплина
Быть способным	Уважение старших и родителей
Стремление к карьерному росту	Ответственность
Власть	Быть прощающим
Скромность	Честность

7 имеют наиважнейшее значение	6 очень важны	5	4	3 важны	2	1	0 не важны	-1 противоречат моим принципам

Согласно существующим уголовно-процессуальным законам в Российской Федерации, позиция профессионального судьи в суде отностиельно ограничена. Это означает в частности, что если в процессе суда выяснится что необходимо провести дополнительное расследование вновь открывшихся фактов, судья не может отправить дела на дополнительное расследование самостоятельно. Он должен подождать, пока прокурор или адвокат не потребуют этого. Если такие требования не были предъявлены, то судья обязан рассмотреть дело на основании тех доказательств, что уже имеются. С удья имеет право направить дело на новое рассмотрение только если допущены некотрые процессуальные нарушения

Скажите, считаете ли вы такое положение закона **справедливым**?

Абсолютно справедливо	Справедливо	В какой-то мере справедливо	В какой-то мере несправедливо	Не - справедливо	Абсолютно не- справедливо
☐	☐	☐	☐	☐	☐

B. Author's English translation:

How important are the following values in your life?

Exciting life	Accepting life
Daring	Devout
Varied life	Respecting tradition
Freedom	Moderate
Creativity	Politeness
Independent	Obedience
Curiosity	Self-discipline
Capable	Honoring parents
Ambitious	Responsible
Power	Forgiving
Humble	Honest

7	6	5	4	3	2	1	0	-1
of supreme importance	*very important*			*important*			*not important*	*opposed to my values*

According to the existing criminal procedural law in Russia, the role of the professional judge in court is relatively restricted. This means that if for example during the trial it would be established that the additional investigation of newly discovered facts is necessary, the judge cannot remand the case on his own initiative, unless the prosecutor or defense will request it. If the prosecution or defense does not request the additional investigation, the judge should proceed with the trial on the basis of existing evidence. The only time when the judge can remand the case for additional investigation is when certain procedural violations are found.

Using the scale provided in the card, please tell us, do you think that such a law **is fair**?

completely fair	*fair*	*somewhat fair*	*somewhat unfair*	*unfair*	*completely unfair*
☐	☐	☐	☐	☐	☐

Severity and leniency in criminal sentencing in Russia: the effects of gender and family ties

Iryna Chatsverykova

ABSTRACT

Using data on 5 million defendants prosecuted in Russian criminal courts in 2009–2013, I examine how sex, marital and parental statuses are related to sentencing decisions. The findings indicate that women face significantly lower likelihood of being incarcerated and a shorter length of incarceration than men. However, positive discrimination of women is not observed for drug-related crimes, where sex effect is not significant. Married offenders are less likely incarcerated than single persons. The effect of having children is inconsistent and varies depending on the type of offense and whether in/out or sentence length decisions are considered. When defendants face prison term, childcare responsibilities are associated with longer sentences, especially for females, which can be the "reverse side" of the child-caring role placed on women with children, but not on men. The paper demonstrates how gender order, as well as cultural and legal contexts of a particular society moderate the gender disparity in sentencing.

Introduction

Russian judges experience limited discretion when making sentencing decisions. Infamous political cases, such as the *Yukos* cases, in which the president of an oil company Mikhail Khodorkovsky and some other top managers were convicted twice (in 2004 for tax evasion, in 2010 for stealing oil) and put in prison, demonstrate the lack of "the rule of law" in Russia. The researchers explain the weakness of "the rule of law" by the persistence of "telephone law" (Hendley, 2009; Ledeneva, 2008). The practice of "telephone law" assumes the ability of governmental officials to influence the outcome of the adjudication when they have a strong interest in it. However, Russian criminal courts generally have to do with common crimes like domestic battery, corporal injury, theft, auto burglary, drug possession, drug sale or transportation, and so on.[1] Russian criminal justice deals mainly with offenders of lower socio-economic status (Volkov, 2014), who do not appear in the agenda of governmental officials or oligarchs. Thus, the independence from the governmental body is not the case in the vast majority of criminal cases.

The restrictions placed on judges by the criminal law (Volkov, 2015) and a major concern about the possibility of the decision being overturned by the appellate court (Pozdnjakov, 2012) are the most important factors that constrain the discretionary freedom of Russian judges. Every year Russian judges handle about 1 million criminal cases.[2] To my best knowledge, only a few empirical studies on judicial decision-making in Russian criminal courts emphasise social disparities in sentencing outcomes (Chatsverykova, 2014; Titaev, 2014; Volkov, 2014, 2015). The goal of this study is to analyse how sex, marital and parental statuses of the defendants are accounted for in sentencing decisions of Russian judges.

The Russian criminal justice system relies on federal statute laws, more specifically on the Criminal Code of Russian Federation adopted in 1996 (henceforth Code)[3] and on the Criminal Procedure Code of Russian Federation adopted in 2002 (henceforth CPC). According to Art. 4 of the Code, equality of all citizens before the law is one of the most important grounds of Russian criminal law. It specifies that a person who committed a crime should be held criminally responsible regardless sex, race, ethnicity, language, origin, income, official capacity, living place, religion, beliefs, participation in public associations, etc. Thus, judges should ignore such defendant's features while deciding on guilt of a crime.

On the other hand, individualisation of punishment is the underlying philosophy of the sentencing system in Russia and many other post-Soviet countries (see, e.g., Plesnicar, 2013). The concept of punishment individualisation is strongly related to the purposes of punishment. Art. 43 of the Code provides for the following purposes of punishment: restoration of social justice, rehabilitation of the convict, and prevention of future crimes. Art. 60 of the Code states that while choosing the type and size of punishment for convicted persons, judges are obligated to account for the dangerousness of the crime; the personality of the convicts, including mitigating and aggravating circumstances; and a hypothetical effect of the assigned punishment on the rehabilitation of a convict, and his or her family situation. The Code does not specify how exactly family situation of the defendant should be accounted for in the decisions about punishments. Moreover, the actual sentencing process still could be different from the described in the law on the books.

Previous research on sentencing in Russia demonstrated that, commonly, judges punish female offenders and married offenders more leniently (Chatsverykova, 2014; Volkov, 2015). The regression modelling of conviction and sentencing practices in Russia during 2009 – first half of 2010 indicated that married offenders are less likely to be sentenced and less likely to be incarcerated if they were sentenced while controlling for other social characteristics of offenders, their criminal history, the seriousness and type of offense, case processing characteristics (Chatsverykova, 2014). This study also showed that on average female offenders and offenders with children have lower probability to be incarcerated, but are more likely to be sentenced than male offenders and offenders without children. Using the data on sentenced offenders similar to the data in the research described above, Volkov (2015) explored legal and extra-legal origins of social disparities in sentencing in Russia. The study found that offenders with low social integration (unemployed, single, non-citizens, and non-locals) are more likely to be incarcerated and generally receive longer sentences (except for the married offenders sentenced for drugs) when charged with violent offenses, theft or drug-related offenses compared with their counterparts. The probability of incarceration as well as the sentence length was also lower for women sentenced for violent crimes or theft than for men. However, previous research did not account for possible interactions between offender's sex and family-related factors. I investigate how gender shapes sentencing process and provide evidence from Russia for the growing literature on the cultural aspects of judicial decision-making. This study contributes to the understanding of how gender and family-related effects on sentencing differ across countries.

Context for the present study

Literature on gender disparity in sentencing

The focal concerns perspective suggested by Steffensmeier, Kramer, and Streifel (1993) and elaborated on by other researchers (Doerner, 2015; Doerner & Demuth, 2012; Kurlychek & Johnson, 2004; Spohn & Holleran, 2000; Steffensmeier & Demuth, 2006) is widely used to explain social disparities in criminal sentencing decisions in the USA. According to this theory, three focal concerns influence judges in reaching sentencing decisions (Steffensmeier et al., 1993; Steffensmeier, Ulmer, & Kramer, 1998). The first concern, *blameworthiness*, is ordinarily associated with the retributive philosophy of punishment and supposes that the punishment fits the crime and corresponds with the degree of harm caused the victim. This perspective includes such measures as the seriousness of the offense and the defendant's criminal history. Employing this concern, judges can consider female defendants as less blameworthy and at a lower risk to reoffend compared with their male counterparts (Steffensmeier et al., 1998).

According to the second concern, *protection of the community*, judges make their sentencing decisions by confronting the goal of deterring recidivism in the context of high uncertainty about a defendant's future behaviour. The defendant's criminal history as well as other characteristics of the defendant, such as education, employment, family history, drug dependency, and the nature of the offense (e.g., violent or property), become important. Thus, judges who count the protection of children among their concerns can assign lenient sentences to women with childcare responsibilities (Griffin & Wooldredge, 2006).

These two concerns correspond to the idea of bounded rationality developed by Albonetti (1991). To decrease uncertainty, judges rely on stereotypes predicated by the age, sex, race, and socio-economic status of the defendant. The third concern, *practical constraints and consequences*, takes into account social costs, the relationship among courtroom actors, case flow, and an awareness of correctional resources. The main idea of the focal concerns framework is that judges apply different concerns – blameworthiness, protection of the community, and/or practical concern – when deciding on the proper punishment for a defendant.

Some researchers expand the focal concerns perspective to explain sentencing disparities outside the USA (Hartley, Kwak, Park, & Lee, 2011; Johnson, Van Wingerden, & Nieuwbeerta, 2010; Lee, Ulmer, & Park, 2011). Research on sentencing in South Korea discovers more lenient treatment of female narcotics offenders than their male counterparts (Hartley et al., 2011; Lee et al., 2011). The female-favourable sentencing outcomes in South Korea are interpreted through the differences in judicial perception of male and female blameworthiness and future crime risk. Moreover, from a practical concern, female methamphetamine offenders are seen to require rehabilitation rather than punishment (Lee et al., 2011). Depending on the social and legal contexts of a particular jurisdiction, focal concerns can imply various judicial considerations about significance of the committed crime, defendant's blameworthiness and dangerousness, and potential organisational and political consequences of a sentencing decision that judge considers to make.

However, the focal concerns framework is not a theory, from which specific predictions about social behaviour can be derived directly. Rather, it is a perspective (Hartley, Maddan, & Spohn, 2007) that shows general direction of the inquiry in empirical research on sentencing decision-making. To explain how exactly judges employ focal concerns, researchers rely on particular social theories developed to explain precise social disparities in judicial and law enforcement decision-making.

According to the chivalry and evil woman theses, *chivalry* or *paternalistic attitudes* of judges and other courtroom actors could favour female defendants through stereotypical perception of women as biologically weak and in need of protection (Crew, 1991; Nagel & Hagan, 1983; Visher, 1983; Zatz, 2000). In contrast, women are treated equally or even more harshly than men in cases of "masculine" violent crimes because of the so-called evil woman thesis (Nagel & Hagan, 1983; Rodriguez, Curry, & Lee, 2006). According to this perspective, women are treated in a protective and lenient manner if they are charged with typically "female" offenses. However, if they commit more serious crimes, such as violent or drug-related crimes, thus violating their sex-role expectation, they will receive more severe outcomes – possibly even more punitive than their male counterparts. Recent study demonstrates that selective chivalry and evil women explanations can be relevant when predicting sentences imposed on women with different criminal history (Tillyer, Hartley, & Ward, 2015). As Haney (2000) points out, contemporary criminology assumes the severity/leniency debate futile: the gender regime of sentencing can operate through both severity and leniency dependent on other social characteristics of offenders.

Another influential theory that explores gender disparities in sentencing is familial paternalism theory (Zatz, 2000) which highlights the importance of *family-related factors* for sentencing decisions (Daly, 1989). Daly called it "family based justice" (Daly, 1987, 1989). According to familial-based paternalism, defendants with children receive more lenient treatment and consequently have fewer chances to be incarcerated. Judges try to keep parents and children together in order to protect families from losing "sources of care and economic support" (Daly & Tonry, 1997, p. 232). However, many male defendants with children are fathers only biologically; they may not be providing economic support for families. Thus, female defendants with children receive more lenient sentencing outcomes because "court officials see more 'good' mothers than 'good' fathers" (Daly, 1987, p. 279).

The reported effects of parenthood dependent on sex vary across studies. Stacey and Spohn (2006) report that federal courts judges evaluate female convicts of drug offenses differently than male convicts, irrespective of their family situations or childcare responsibilities. Another study finds that family ties and childcare responsibilities predict punishment severity independently from offender's sex in all cases prosecuted in federal courts (Doerner & Demuth, 2012). However, Logue (2011) notes that sex modifies the effects of having family ties only for certain familied offenders convicted for drug crimes, and often it results in more punitive effects among women than among men. The research on sentencing process in special domestic violence courts in Canada demonstrates that presence of children is associated positively with sentence length – at least in the context of male defendants (Dinovitzer & Dawson, 2007). Sentencing research based on statistical data operationalises childcare responsibilities through formal criteria of having a child or children (Dinovitzer & Dawson, 2007; Doerner & Demuth, 2012; Kruttschnitt & Savolainen, 2009; Logue, 2011; Stacey & Spohn, 2006). Conducted in the Courts of Common Plea in the USA, surveys demonstrate that judges grant more leniency for those offenders who provide emotional (but not only financial) support in a family (Freiburger, 2010). Thus, familial paternalism theory finds only partial support in recent studies, and further research on sentencing and the effects on it of offender's parental circumstances is required.

Social control theory is another theory applied to interpret the interaction effect of gender and family-related factors on sentencing decisions (Zatz, 2000). As follows from the *social control* explanation, defendants with family ties are less likely to be incarcerated because they are subject to a higher level of social control through their daily responsibilities (Kruttschnitt, 1984; Kruttschnitt & Green, 1984). Based on the ideas of Donald Black (1976) on the behaviour of law, researchers assume that the quantity of law, or governmental social control, decreases with larger amount of informal social control (Dinovitzer & Dawson, 2007; Flavin, 2001). Thus, criminal justice system will treat people less severe if other forms of social control are available in their lives. One of the sources of informal social control specific to married women is economic dependence on their husbands and other relatives (Dinovitzer & Dawson, 2007; Kruttschnitt, 1984). Besides economic (and emotional) dependency, there is another cause for greater informal control provided to women through family – child-based social control which is mobilised through caretaking role performed by mothers rather than fathers (Dinovitzer & Dawson, 2007).

While analysing gender effects on sentencing in Finland, Kruttschnitt and Savolainen (2009) elaborate the feminist approach which underlines special attention to women's economic dependency and its accompanying social control or disparity in the division of labour between men and women. They find no evidence of preferential treatment of female defendants and explain these results with greater gender equality in labour, family rights, and responsibilities in Finland compared with the United States. The findings suggest that shifts in the gender order of the society may reduce gender disparity in sentencing. Thus, *cultural context* can moderate the influence of defendant's sex as well. However, as the authors point out, the results also can be explained by differences in legal systems such as the number of female judges compared with the

USA. Hence, gender order and features of a legal system moderate judicial decision-making and the effects of defendant's sex and family ties on it.

Gender order of Russian society

Different social roles performed by men and women in a family can impact on judicial perception of the defendant and his or her "family situation" (Kruttschnitt & Savolainen, 2009). Art. 60 of the Code states that family situation of the offender should be taken into account by Russian judges in order to choose a proper punishment. The post-communist transformation in Russia resulted in the reinforcement of traditional gender roles and women's growing dependence on men and family (Temkina & Zdravomyslova, 2003). Gender studies of a modern Russian society demonstrate differences in male and female functions in a family: men are usually supposed to provide financial support, while women are supposed to care for and to maintain the everyday functioning of the family, and to raise children (Ashwin & Lytkina, 2004; Zdravomyslova, 2003).

Inequity in family roles performed by women and men is often considered to be related to gender asymmetry in the division of labour (Connell, 1987; Kruttschnitt & Savolainen, 2009; Malceva & Roschin, 2006). At the same time, Russian women usually do not limit themselves to only family and household caretaking and have a high activity level within the labour market (Malceva & Roschin, 2006). This tendency can be attributed to strong continuity with Soviet norms and practices of the Russian gender order (Ashwin, 2006). The Soviet gender contract of "working mother" required women to become both wage earners and mothers (Temkina & Zdravomyslova, 2003). However, Russian women experience the effect of the so-called glass ceiling (Temkina & Zdravomyslova, 2003). In the civil service, it is apparent in the lack of women in positions associated with high responsibility (Roshchin & Zubarevich, 2005). Similarly, in the business sector, women frequently are in charge of small and medium-sized enterprises, but not larger ones (Malceva & Roschin, 2006). The researchers discovered that women's secondary position in the world of work is still taken for granted as it was in Soviet Russia (Kozina & Zhidkova, 2006).

As Schwartz and Steffensmeier (2008) mentioned, the gendered segregation of work and "glass ceiling" set different constraints on criminal opportunities for men and women, what indirectly can be resulted in sentence differences imposed on male and female defendants. Moreover, gender differences in family and labour produce different stereotypes of proper behaviour for women and men. Russian women are supposed to work, run a household, and take on the most of childcare responsibilities. Men should be the main breadwinners and mostly excluded from the household chores and everyday childcare. According to the focal concerns perspective on sentencing, judges can rely on stereotypes when evaluating defendant's blameworthiness and dangerousness, including his or her future behaviour and the risk to recidivate (Steffensmeier et al., 1998). Due to the different performances of men and women in the everyday life of a family in Russia, judicial decisions regarding punishing with incarceration and regarding sentence length can vary with the offender's sex and family situation.

Theoretical framework and hypotheses

Guided by the focal concerns perspective and the findings of past research on gender and criminal sentencing in the USA and other countries and taking into account gender aspects of culture and tradition of criminal justice in Russia, I put forward several hypotheses for the present study.

Empirical studies on sentencing in Western social context demonstrate that, generally, female offenders are recognised by the courtroom officials as less blameworthy and dangerous than their male counterparts and, thus, women receive more lenient sentences than men (Daly & Bordt, 1995; Doerner & Demuth, 2010, 2012; Johnson et al., 2010; Steffensmeier et al., 1993). Complimentary, the chivalry perspective suggests that women should be protected from prisons and therefore handled more leniently by the system (Crew, 1991; Nagel & Hagan, 1983; Zatz, 2000). There is no published research on attitudes of Russian judges on perception of female and male offenders. However, there are some reasons to think these sentencing practices can be the same among Russian judges.

Due to poor conditions of custodial institutions, judges try not to incarcerate convicts if the Code allows it and if there is a great chance that a convict will not impose a threat to other people (Paneyakh, 2012). Using semi-structured interviews with judges and other courtroom officials, Paneyakh (2012) shows that judges do not believe that Russian prisons can reform convicts and prevent future crimes. At the same time, interviews with present and former prisoners as well as with prison staff and local inhabitants reveal that the idea that "women offend against their nature" and their future behaviour should be corrected is persistent among people involved with law and order in Russia (Pallot & Piacentini, 2012). Thus, the incarceration of female offenders can be recognised as inappropriate punishment because custodial institutions are considered as inefficient for prevention and rehabilitation purposes. Judges can be concerned about these practical constrains.

Moreover, women compose only 15–16% of suspects yearly struck by the Russian police or other law enforcement agencies,[4] what corresponds to the universal pattern of "gendered gap" in criminal activity recorded by the police (Steffensmeier & Allan, 1996). Thus, women can be seen by the courtroom officials as less dangerous to the community at general. By following the community-protection and practicality concerns, Russian judges can impose more lenient sentences on female offenders than on male offenders.

Hypothesis 1: Generally, female offenders will be punished less severely than male offenders.

However, women can be treated differently dependent on the type of offense (Rodriguez et al., 2006). Selective chivalry or evil women theses are supposed to explain why judges provide greater leniency to those women who commit common, but not "masculine" crimes, specifically, violent crimes (Fernando Rodriguez, Curry, & Lee, 2006; Nagel & Hagan, 1983). Moreover, applying this perspective, researchers explore gender differences outside the USA not only among violent offenders (Lu, Liang, & Liu, 2012), but also among drug offenders (Hartley et al., 2011). Researchers hypothesise that female offenders in largely paternalistic society of South Korea will be treated more lenient than male offenders due to paternalistic attitudes towards women who are "weaker" sex and need to be protected by men (Hartley et al., 2011). Consequently, women who commit drug-related crimes violate traditionally prescribed role expectations and, thus, they do not worth protection.

At the same time, these studies do not test directly the main assumption of this theory about preferential treatment of female offenders who commit common, but not "masculine" crimes. To my best knowledge, this is a first study that tests the evil women thesis in the non-Western context. Since the collapse of the USSR, Russian society has experienced the reinforcement of traditional gender roles (Temkina & Zdravomyslova, 2003) that could lead to increasing gender prejudice among judges. Thus, I expect that Russian judges will punish female offenders less severe than their male counterparts when they charged with property crimes, but not violent or drug-related crimes.

Hypothesis 2: There will be more leniency accorded to women as opposed to men who commit property crimes.

Hypothesis 2a: Women who commit violent or drug-related crimes will be treated equally or even more severely than men.

Another major emphasis in the literature dedicated to the gender differences in sentencing is an attempt to discover how exactly gender conditions leniency. The difference in family situation seems to be one of the plausible explanations (Zatz, 2000). The importance of marital status as well as presence of dependents is emphasised in recent research on sentencing (Doerner & Demuth, 2012; Gaub & Holtfreter, 2015; Stacey & Spohn, 2006). From practical concern, incarceration of the offenders who have caretaking responsibilities may be unreasonable. One of the reason is that separation children from parents can result in greater costs for the society to provide childcare. Moreover, Art. 61 of the Code lists among other mitigating circumstances presence of children under age of 14 regardless offender's sex. Due to poor conditions of Russian orphanages[5] and with regard to Code's regulation, I assume that Russian judges will avoid punishing offenders with children by incarcerating them or by punishing them with large sentences in case of incarceration.

Hypothesis 3: Offenders with children will receive more lenient sentences than offenders without children.

I expect greater leniency granted by judges for parental offenders. However, the effect of children's presence on sentencing decisions can vary with offender's sex. Gender disparity in sentencing with regard to childcare responsibilities might base on different performances of men and women in the everyday life of a family in Russia. Women in Russia are believed to maintain the everyday functioning of the family as well as to work and gain some money, and men are only supposed to provide financial support (Ashwin, 2006; Zdravomyslova, 2003). Thus, judges can recognise the presence of children for female and male offenders differently during the assignment of punishment. Because judges can see women as less blameworthy than men and are guided by the idea of greater social costs for society, they will grant more leniency to female offenders with children than to their male counterparts. However, some female offenders can be excluded from those whom judges grant leniency with regard to offender's parental status. As research in the USA demonstrates (Roberts, 1991; Zatz, 2000), courtroom actors devaluate motherhood of poor, black, drug-addicted women. I expect that Russian judges will not grant leniency towards those female offenders with childcare responsibilities who are charged with drug-related offenses.

Hypothesis 4: Female defendants with children will be treated more leniently than their male counterparts when charged with property or violent offenses.

Hypothesis 4a: Female defendants with children will be sentenced equally or even more severe compared with male counterparts in drug-related cases.

Focal concerns framework presumes that judges evaluate future behaviour of the offender when they choose an appropriate punishment. The main consideration relates to the offender's risk to recidivate. Guided by the community-protection concern, judges make their predictions about future offender's behaviour based on attributions predicated on the nature of the offense, the offender's criminal history, other relevant-to-case information, as well as on offender's social characteristics, including family history (Steffensmeier et al., 1998). Social control theory assumes that individuals are equally inclined to engage in criminal behaviour, but they prevail over it due to the commitment to conventional social institutions (Gottfredson & Hirschi, 1990; Sampson & Laub, 1995). Marriage is one essential example of such institutions. The empirical literature generally finds that married people are less likely to commit crime and to reoffend (see review in Bersani, Laub, and Nieuwbeerta (2009). Married offenders can be seen by courtroom officials as at lower risk to reoffend than single offenders, because of the greater socialisation of married people and of their bonds to conventional social life.

Hypothesis 5: Married offenders will receive more lenient sentences than single people.

However, women and men in Russia perform different social roles related to marriage and family responsibilities, as it was discussed above. Due to different family roles performed by men and women in Russia (Ashwin & Lytkina, 2004; Zdravomyslova, 2003), I assume that married women experience greater social control in their lives than their male counterparts. Thus, judges will favour married women more than married men in sentencing decisions.

Hypothesis 6: Married female offenders will be sentenced more leniently than their male counterparts.

Modelling the sentencing process and data

To test these hypotheses, individual-level data on all defendants prosecuted in the Russian criminal courts in 2009–2013 is used. The data was provided by the Judicial Department at the Supreme Court of the Russian Federation (henceforth – Judicial Department). Russian judges are obliged to fill a statistical card on every defendant whose case is brought to court.[6] At first, data is collected by regional divisions of the Judicial Department. The data contains the information on all cases heard at federal courts or courts of peace. According to Art. 4 of federal constitutional law N1-FKZ from 31.12.1996 "On judicial system of Russian Federation" (last amended 05.02.2014), justices of the peace are part of unified Russian judicial body and in general rely on federal guides and regulations (for more detailed information on the Justice-of-the-Peace Courts in Russia see Hendley (2007)). Thus, they are obliged to fill statistical cards on defendants which are the same as in federal courts and upload them to the regional divisions of the Judicial Department. Every half a year regional divisions transfer gathered data to the Judicial Department.

Tried by special military courts, military cases are dropped from data. Cases against defendants under the age of 18 are heard at regular courts, but imply substantially different criminal justice procedures regulated by Chapter 50 of the CPC due to their juvenile status. Thus, cases against juveniles are excluded from the analysis.

Most cases are tried by one professional judge.[7] According to Art. 30 of the CPC, a tribunal of three judges hears the most serious offenses such as murder, acts of terror, armed mutiny, sabotage, and so on. Russia adopted a jury system for only the most severe, violent offenses. Within the time period covered by the data, offenders could opt for jury trial if they were charged with murder committed with cruelty; acts of terror resulting in people's deaths; murder of two or more people, or a child, or a pregnant person; and some other offenses specified in Art. 30 and 31 of the CPC.[8] Art. 30 of the CPC suggests that the case is directed to jury trial only if the defendant applies for it.[9] Sentencing process under jury trial is specially governed by Section XII of the CPC and differs in substantial way from that where the judge or judges act as triers of both fact and law. Thus, all cases resolved by jury are excluded from the final data.[10]

The public prosecutor's office plays an important role in the sentencing process as the prosecutor is the person who decides to bring a criminal case to the court and what charges to pursue. All possible reasons to dismiss a criminal case are listed in Art. 24 and 27 of the CPC. Prosecutors are not allowed to release certain offenders such as misdemeanants or first-time offenders without prosecution on the grounds of efficient case processing. Prosecutors are responsible for compiling the dossier, which contains all the reports from the pretrial and presentence investigations.

Unlike in most American jurisdictions, Russian prosecutors have little discretion when it comes to plea bargaining which is regulated by Section X of the CPC. Art. 314 and 315 of the CPC clarify that the offender can plead guilty when the dossier on criminal case is composed and ready to be sent to court or during pretrial hearing at the court if s/he faces 10 or fewer years of imprisonment by the Code. However, if the offender declares to provide a substantial assistance in criminal case investigation or in search of stolen property, then making an agreement with prosecution office on pretrial collaboration is possible. Following Art. 317.1 of the CPC, this can be done at any stage of the process after the start of criminal case investigation and before its end. Admitting guilt by plea bargaining or making an agreement on substantial assistance leads to a fast-track trial without the examination of evidence. In exchange, Art. 316 of the CPC guarantees that the sentence cannot exceed two-thirds of the maximum term of punishment provided by the Code.

The prosecutor's sentencing recommendation is always publicly announced at the end of the trial,[11] after which the judge determines the final sentence with regard to Art. 295 of the CPC. The prosecutorial recommendation does not legally bind the judicial decision, but stark deviation from it without reasoning can result in appellation of the decision by the prosecutor and, consequently, in an appellate court overturning the decision on the grounds of incorrect application of the Code or unfairness of the verdict with accordance to Art. 389.15 of the CPC. Regarding Art. 389.1 of the Code, both the prosecutor and the defence can appeal the decision. Unfortunately, analysed data does not contain any information on prosecutor or defence attorney. When modelling the sentencing decision-making, I cannot control for prosecutorial sentencing recommendations and, thus, separate the effects of judicial and prosecutorial discretions. However, this is common limitation in sentencing studies, and further research on the role of prosecution office (as well as presentence investigation office if it is present in criminal process of a particular jurisdiction) in sentencing is required.

Studies of sentencing disparities in the context of different guidelines in the USA expose the importance of adequate legal controls and accurate modelling of the sentencing process with respect to the law of a particular jurisdiction (Albonetti, 1997; Engen, 2009; Engen & Gainey, 2000; Engen, Gainey, Crutchfield, & Weis, 2003; Johnson, 2005). In Russia, the Code has individual indications for each offense and usually provides different types of punishment, among which the most frequent are real or suspended incarceration and fines. The Code contains maximum and minimum fixed terms for each offense (examples are provided in the Appendix, Table A1). Appropriate downward departures from the pre-scribed range are determined in Art. 61, 64, and 65 of the Code. Art. 60 of the Code declares that Russian judges are not allowed to impose more severe punishment than foreseen by the Code for the offense with which the defendant is charged. This rule cannot be violated under any conditions except for special cases of multiple charges that are all specified in Art. 69 and 70 of the Code. The original data does not contain information on maximum and minimum terms provided by the Code for each offense, but does specify the particular offense and the date of the verdict. My colleagues and I recorded missing data on the Code's regulations and merged it with our initial data on the defendants. This makes it possible to control for the one of the most crucial factors that determine the sentence severity – seriousness of the offense (Volkov, 2014) and upper and lower bounds of sanction for particular offenses.

All criminal offenses are ranked into four categories of seriousness according to Art. 15 of the Code: low, medium, high, and top high offenses. The upper-bound and seriousness-of-the-offense variables are highly correlated: according to Art. 15 of the Code, the first is the derivative of the last. Offenses without incarceration term and those with a maximum punish-ment of 2 years in prison (since the December of 2011–3 years) are of low severity. The seriousness of the offense is medium when the sentencing maximum for crimes without criminal intent is higher than 2 years of incarceration (since the December of 2011–3 years) and, for intentional crimes, is lower than 5 years. Offenses with a maximum punishment lower than 10 years in prison are top serious. Offenses with a punishment of 10 years and higher have top high seriousness.

Methods

Heckman's (1979) two-stage sample selection equation procedure with maximum likelihood estimation is used to estimate sentence length and the likelihood of being incarcerated. The Heckman correction procedure performs well in cases where the truncation sample is big enough. In the analysed data, only 18% of females and 32% of males are incarcerated (Table 1), and thus the potential for selection bias is serious. Average marginal effects[12] are computed for easier interpretation of the selection equation results (in/out decision). Sentence length is the number of years of incarceration and is naturally log transformed to address its skewed distribution. Log transformation of the sentence length and interpreting the anti-log of regression coefficients provide an evaluation of the proportional rather than absolute differences in sentence lengths, and thus avoids findings that are merely an artefact of differences between offenses in the sentences that are legally possible (Kurlychek & Johnson, 2004; Ulmer & Bradley, 2006).

Table 1. Descriptive statistics of dependent and independent variables by gender.

Variables	Codes or [min:max]	Female offenders		Male offenders	
		#	Mean	#	Mean
Dependent variables					
Incarceration (in/out)	0/1	516944	0.18	2838535	0.32
Incarceration length (years)	[0:28]	94726	3.54	904272	3.61
Ln(incarceration length)	[−2:3]	94726	0.97	904272	1
Independent variables					
Female	0/1	516944	1	2838535	0
Children	0/1	516944	0.44	2838535	0.31
Married	0/1	516944	0.26	2838535	0.24
Age (years)	[18:99]	516940	34.02	2838527	31.82
(Age centred)^2/100	[0:44]	516940	1.23	2838527	1.07
Russian citizen	0/1	516944	0.97	2838535	0.95
Local resident	0/1	516944	0.93	2838535	0.9
Higher education	0/1	516944	0.1	2838535	0.07
Unemployed	0/1	516944	0.71	2838533	0.67
Alcohol use	0/1	516944	0.19	2838535	0.27
Criminal history	dummy	516944		2838534	
No prior record/conviction	0/1		0.67		0.52
Convicted without record	0/1		0.01		0.01
Expired record	0/1		0.09		0.13
Non-expired record	0/1		0.15		0.16
Recidivism (habitual offender)	0/1		0.09		0.19
Plead guilty	0/1	516944	0.7	2838533	0.65
Criminal activity type	dummy	516944		2838535	
No group	0/1		0.9		0.84
Group	0/1		0.01		0.01
Gang	0/1		0.1		0.15
Leader of a group	0/1	515286	0	2829379	0
Accessory	0/1	515286	0	2829379	0
Number of charges	[0:5]	516944	1.18	2838535	1.24
Incomplete crime	0/1	515280	0.11	2829381	0.09
Offense severity	dummy	515115		2827466	
Low	0/1		0.49		0.37
Medium	0/1		0.27		0.36
High	0/1		0.19		0.22
Top high	0/1		0.05		0.06
Upper bound of sentence length	[0.5:20]	94666	7.99	903747	7.3
Lower bound of sentence length	[0.167:15]	94666	2.21	903747	1.73
Violent crime	0/1	515303	0.15	2829507	0.2
Property crime	0/1	515303	0.46	2829507	0.46
Drug crime	0/1	515303	0.12	2829507	0.15
Year of the verdict (dummy)	[2009:2013]	516944		2838535	
Region (dummy)	[1:89]	516944		2838535	
Type of crime (dummy)	[1:69]	515303		2829507	

The additional models of in/out and sentence length decisions for more frequently occurring offenses are estimated to check for consistency of the regression coefficients for variables of primary interest (descriptive statistics has been provided in the Appendix, Table A2). Probit function is used to evaluate incarceration decisions. Sentence length decisions are analysed with ordinary least squares (OLS) regression. I could not identify appropriate exclusion restrictions for separate offenses models. Meanwhile, the Heckman correction procedure does not execute well when exclusion restriction is not specified at all or specified incorrectly (Bushway, Johnson, & Slocum, 2007). Thus, I made a decision to estimate two-part models. The results of regressions as well as descriptive statistics regarded to specific offenses are provided in Appendix.

Dependent and independent variables

The dependent and independent variables as well as their codes and frequencies by gender are displayed in Table 1. Incarceration is dependent variable that coded "1" if defendant was sentenced to prison and coded "0" if other type of punishment (including suspended incarceration)[13] was imposed. The sentence length and its log-transformed derivative are continuous variables.

Social characteristics of the defendant include sex, parental and marital statuses, age, citizenship, residency, employment, and higher education. "Female", "children", and "married" are independent variables of primary interest. "Female" is coded "1" for female defendants and "0" – for male. The variable "children" means that the defendant has a child or children under the age of 18. "Married" indicates defendants who are officially married. "Russian citizen" represents that the defendant has Russian citizenship. "Local resident" means that the defendant's place of permanent registration is the district where the crime was committed. The alcohol variable indicates cases where defendants commit crimes under the influence of alcohol. The unemployed category includes those who officially registered for labour exchange services and those who were unofficially unemployed (defendants who could not confirm the recent presence of a permanent or temporary job).

The criminal history variable was defined along the 5 possible grades – (a) no criminal record (or first-time offender), (b) previously convicted without record, (c) previously convicted with record that was expired at the moment when crime was committed, (d) defendant with non-expired, active record, and (e) recidivism. The last three grades of criminal history are legally recognised by Russian criminal law.

Art. 86 of the Code clarifies that defendants are considered to be previously convicted without getting a record (b) when no punishment was imposed upon the defendant for a previous crime. This is possible on legal grounds such as dismissal of the case, which means that the offender was found guilty, but did not suffer any punishment. Being convicted without record has no legal consequences for the convict. A convict gets legally recognised criminal record (c and d) when sentenced to any type of punishment, thus, no legal circumstances or significant mitigating factors were found to release him or her from punishment. Conviction record is expired (c) when the probation (check) period after serving the punishment is over, otherwise the record is counted as non-expired (d). Defendants with no record or with expired prior records should not suffer any legal consequences, restrictions, or other types of discrimination because of their criminal past, because such consequences are not prescribed by the Code. No particular legal consequences in the Code are found for those offenders who have non-expired record (d). The exception is the cases when a previous conviction is counted as recidivate crime (e). According to Art. 18 of the Code, a crime is considered recidivate (and the offender is counted as habitual) only for defendants previously convicted with legally recognised record and newly charged for committing a crime with direct intent of wrongdoing. This means that defendants who repeated an intentional crime during the probation term[14] should receive with regard to Art. 68 of the Code no less than one-third of the maximum punishment provided by the Code for the offense. Moreover, habitual offenders who are recognised as high dangerous or top high dangerous have to fulfil some additional requirements in order to get a suspended sentence, according Art. 73 of the Code.

The analysis of in/out decisions includes, among legal controls, the seriousness of the offense, while the modelling of sentence length decisions accounts particularly for the upper and lower boundaries of the offense – maximum and minimum terms contained in the Code for each offense. According to Art. 56 of the Code, the general minimum for imprisonment is 2 months. In Russia, judges have the right to assign a punishment that is lower than a sentencing minimum with regard to Art. 64 of the Code, but not higher than a sentencing maximum.

Several additional variables are included to control for legally prescribed factors among which are the following: the number of charges, committing crime while being part of a group or a gang, criminal role, and stage of criminal act (accomplished or uncompleted). Models also take into account for defendants pleading guilty.

Descriptive statistics demonstrate that women are incarcerated more rarely than men (18% and 32%, respectively). Their prison terms are shorter by 0.07 years. Among sentenced women, the share of married defendants and defendants with childcare responsibilities is greater than among men. Female defendants are more likely employed. On average, they are older and more educated than their male counterparts. Women have more likely no prior criminal record and are charged with a less serious offense.

Results

Offender's sex has significant effect on sentencing decisions even after controlling for other social features of defendants and legally prescribed factors. In general, the probability of being incarcerated for female defendants is on 3.1% lower than for male even when dependent children and a spouse are not present (Model 1, Table 2) Moreover, women receive 8% shorter sentences than men (Model 2, Table 2). The results are in accordance with the hypothesis N1 regarding greater leniency for women than men.

The effects of marital and parental statuses are statistically significant, but the size of the effects is small. The probability of being incarcerated for male offenders is 1% lower if they have children and 1.6% lower if they are married (Model 1).Sentence length is 1% higher for men with children as well as for married men. These effects are similar or even stronger for female offenders. Hypotheses N3 and N5 suppose greater leniency to offenders with children or married offenders. The results confirm these expectations only in regards to in/out decisions.

The interaction term of having children and offender's sex is not significant in in/out decisions. Thus, presence of children associates negatively with incarceration decisions (−1%) regardless offender's sex. However, the effect of children presence on sentence length is positive and 4% stronger for women than for men. Hypotheses N4 and N4a suggest greater leniency towards women with children compared with their male counterparts when charged with property or violent offenses but not drug-related offenses. Further estimation with regard to the type of offense is needed to test these hypotheses.

The interaction effect of offender's sex and marital status is negative for the probability of incarceration (−1%) and positive for sentence length (+2%). Thus, when judges decide whether to incarcerate or not, women benefit from marriage more than men. However, in sentence length decisions, married women receive 2% longer sentences compared with married men. As predicted by hypothesis N6, marital status of female offenders has stronger negative effect on incarceration decisions compared with male offenders. However, it has opposite effect on sentence length decisions.

The analysis shows that family-related factors, including having children and being married, have weaker effects both on sentencing length and incarceration decisions than factors related to the type and seriousness of the offense, criminal history, offender's sex, residency, and citizenship

CRIMINOLOGY AND CRIMINAL JUSTICE IN RUSSIA

Table 2. Two-step Heckman models of incarceration and sentence length.

	Model 1	Model 2	
	In/out	Incarceration length	
	dy/dx	Ln (years)	antilog b
Female	−0.031**	−0.079**	0.92
	(0.001)	(0.003)	
Children	−0.010**	0.008**	1.01
	(0.001)	(0.002)	
Female × children	−0.003	0.038**	1.04
	(0.001)	(0.004)	
Married	−0.016**	0.009**	1.01
	(0.001)	(0.002)	
Female × married	−0.010**	0.023**	1.02
	(0.001)	(0.005)	
Age	0.000**	−0.001**	1.00
	(0.000)	(0.000)	
(Age centred)^2/100	−0.010**	−0.007**	0.99
	(0.000)	(0.001)	
Russian citizen	−0.127**	0.183**	1.20
	(0.004)	(0.009)	
Local resident	−0.067**	0.065**	1.07
	(0.002)	(0.005)	
Higher education	−0.002	0.029**	1.03
	(0.001)	(0.003)	
Unemployed	0.063**	0.009**	1.01
	(0.001)	(0.002)	
Alcohol use	−0.004**	−0.003	1.00
	(0.001)	(0.002)	
Criminal history (no prior conviction – ref. category)			
Convicted without record	−0.023**	−0.021*	0.98
	(0.003)	(0.009)	
Expired record	0.039**	0.024**	1.02
	(0.002)	(0.004)	
Non-expired record	0.283**	0.216**	1.24
	(0.001)	(0.005)	
Recidivism (habitual offender)	0.340**	0.219**	1.24
	(0.001)	(0.005)	
Plea bargaining	−0.060**	−0.141**	0.87
	(0.001)	(0.003)	
Offense severity (Low – ref. category)			
Medium	0.131**		
	(0.003)		
High	0.254**		
	(0.003)		
Top high	0.451**		
	(0.005)		
Upper bound of sentence length		0.102**	1.11
		(0.001)	
Lower bound of sentence length		0.026**	1.03
		(0.002)	
Observations	3342340	998327	
Rho	−0.251**		
Sigma	0.475**		

Other legal controls, dummies of years, regions, and types of crime are included. Column "antilog b" presents antilog-transformed coefficients (length equation), "dy/dx" shows average marginal effects (in/out equation). Clustered at court level standard errors are in parentheses. ** $p < 0.01$, * $p < 0.05$.

(Table 2). Russian citizenship associates negatively with the probability of incarceration (−12.7%) and positively – with sentence length (+18.3%). Residency at the place where the crime was committed and justice was provided has negative effect on the probability of incarceration (−6.7%) and positive – on sentence length (+6.5%). Unemployed offenders are on 6.3% more likely incarcerated and receive 1% longer sentences than employed (see Volkov, 2015 for more

CRIMINOLOGY AND CRIMINAL JUSTICE IN RUSSIA

details). Unexpectedly, when it comes to incarceration decisions, defendants with higher education do not benefit from it. In fact, they receive even longer sentences on 2.9% compared with less educated defendants in case of incarceration. Committing a crime under the influence of alcohol is negatively related to the possibility of incarceration (−0.5%) and is not significant at all in sentence length decisions. Pleading guilty and entering the fast-track mode of trial without evidence evaluation is related to less punitive sentences. Offenders who plead guilty are on 6% less likely to be incarcerated and receive on 14.1% shorter sentences.

Offense seriousness and offender's criminal history are among the strongest influences. Offenders are more likely incarcerated if they have prior criminal records, both expired (+3.9%) and non-expired (+28.3%), or who can be considered as habitual offenders (+34%) compared with those who have no record. Sentence length is 2.4% longer for the offenders with expired prior criminal records and 21.6% longer for those with non-expired record compared with first-time offenders. Habitual offenders receive 21.9% longer sentences than those who are convicted for the first time. Being previously convicted without record is associated negatively with both incarceration likelihood (−2.3%) and sentence length (−2.1%). Speculatively, these effects can be explained with the advantage of "repeated player" (the idea is based on Galanter's research (1974)), such as knowing the criminal process and higher chances of being in contact with well-qualified private attorney at the earliest stages of investigation. Meantime, previously convicted persons without record did not suffer legally from the consequences foreseen for those who have criminal record.

The probability of incarceration increases with offense severity by 13.1% for medium grave, 25.4% for high gravity offense, and 45.1%for top high gravity offense compared with low gravity offense. As expected, higher legal bounds of sentence length associate with longer sentences (+10.2% for upper bounds and +2.6% for lower bounds).

Turning to the findings related to our primary interest in gender and family-related factors, general sentencing model demonstrates mixed results and supports the hypotheses only partially. To further explore the hypotheses, I examine the effect of sex and family-related factors on sentencing separately for different types of crimes – violent, property, and drug-related. First, the results of incarceration decisions are reported (Table 3). After that, the results of sentence length decisions are presented (Table 4).

Hypothesis N2 predicts less severe treatment of female defendants charged with property crimes. Hypothesis N2a assumes harsher or equal sentences for women who committed violent or drug-related criminal acts. The analysis indicates positive discrimination of women charged with violent or property offenses (Model 3, Model 4) and the absence of preferential treatment of female defendants prosecuted for drug-related crimes (Model 5). Women are 5.9% less likely incarcerated for violent crimes and 4.9% – for property crimes than men. The difference in probability of incarceration between women and men is insignificant in drug-related cases

Table 3. Average marginal effects of being incarcerated, selection equation of Heckman two-stage models (in/out decisions).

	Model 3: violent	Model 4: property	Model 5: drugs
	dy/dx	dy/dx	dy/dx
Female	−0.059**	−0.049**	−0.002
	(0.002)	(0.002)	(0.003)
Children	−0.016**	−0.012**	−0.002
	(0.001)	(0.001)	(0.002)
Female × children	−0.003	−0.015**	0.007
	(0.003)	(0.002)	(0.004)
Married	−0.018**	−0.025**	−0.010**
	(0.001)	(0.001)	(0.002)
Female × married	−0.009**	−0.002	−0.012**
	(0.003)	(0.003)	(0.004)
Observations	647554	1530873	474318

Legal and social controls, dummies of years, regions, and types of crime are included. Clustered at court level standard errors are in parentheses. ** $p < 0.01$.

CRIMINOLOGY AND CRIMINAL JUSTICE IN RUSSIA

Table 4. Outcome equation of Heckman two-stage models (incarceration length decisions).

	Model 6: violent		Model 7: property		Model 8: drugs	
	Ln (years)	antilog b	Ln (years)	antilog b	Ln (years)	antilog b
Female	−0.131**	0.88	−0.086**	0.92	−0.029**	0.97
	(0.004)		(0.004)		(0.005)	
Children	−0.004	1.00	0.009**	1.01	0.012**	1.01
	(0.002)		(0.003)		(0.004)	
Female × children	0.008	1.01	0.065**	1.07	0.003	1.00
	(0.006)		(0.007)		(0.006)	
Married	−0.012**	0.99	0.010**	1.01	0.013**	1.01
	(0.002)		(0.003)		(0.003)	
Female × married	0.019*	1.02	0.040**	1.04	−0.003	1.00
	(0.008)		(0.008)		(0.007)	
Uncensored observations	251363		493765		204888	
Rho	−0.155**		−0.0417**		−0.332**	
Sigma	0.378**		0.484**		0.442**	

Legal and social controls, dummies of years, regions, and types of crime are included. Clustered at court level standard errors are in parentheses. ** $p < 0.01$, * $p < 0.05$.

(−0.2%). The findings are in line with hypothesis N2. However, hypothesis N2a is only partially supported. The results are robust and coincide with those from the evaluation of separate-offense models (Appendix, Table A3).

As hypothesis N3 predicts, the effect of parenthood is negative for probability of being incarcerated. Male offenders with children are less likely incarcerated by 1.6% for violent offenders (Model 3) and 1.2% for property offenders (Model 4). In case of property crimes, negative effect of childcare responsibilities on in/out decisions is stronger on 1.5% for mothers as directed by hypothesis N4 (Table 3). However, presence of children does not benefit offenders in violent (Model 3) as hypothesis N4 predicted. Hypothesis N4a states that female defendants with children will be sentenced equally or even more severe compared with male counterparts in drug-related cases what is confirmed by the empirical testing of the hypothesis (Model 5).

Models for separate offenses (Appendix, Table A3) indicate that the effect is robust except for drug-related offenses. Defendants with children sentenced for drug crimes (Model 5), including drug dealing (Appendix, Model 15), do not have any preferential treatment compared with those who does not have childcare responsibilities. However, having children is associated negatively with the probability of being incarcerated for defendants charged with drug possession (Appendix, Model 14), but the effect is weak. Thus, when it comes to in/out decisions, presence of childcare responsibilities has significant negative effect only for defendants charged with violent or property offenses. Hypothesis N3 predicts more lenience for offenders with children regardless type of offense. However, the results are consistent with this hypothesis only in violent or property cases. In property cases, women benefit from the parental status more than men do. The results support hypothesis N4a and partially – hypothesis N4 (for property cases).

Married defendants are less likely incarcerated as predicted by hypothesis N5. Marital status of defendants has more consistent effect on incarceration decisions within different types of crimes (Table 3) and specific offenses than parenthood (Appendix, Table A3). The probability of being incarcerated for married men is 1.8% lower for committing violent crime, 2.5% lower in case of property crime, and 1% lower for drug-related crimes compared with their unmarried counter-parts. The effects of marriage for female offenders do not differ substantially. Modelling the sentencing process for separate offenses confirms strong negative association between marriage and imprisonment in all cases.

The interaction effects of marriage and offender's sex are weak even if they are statistically significant (Table 3), for example, in models for violent offenders (−0.9%) or for drug offenders (−1.2%). Moreover, there are no significant interaction effects when separate models for specific

154

CRIMINOLOGY AND CRIMINAL JUSTICE IN RUSSIA

offenses are estimated (Appendix, Table A3). The findings provide no convenient evidence of greater leniency for married women than men as hypothesis N6 assumes.

To further test the hypotheses, I examine the effects of offender's sex and family-related factors on sentence length for violent, property, and drug-related crimes (Table 4). Female defendants receive sentences that are 12% shorter for violent offenses, 8% – for property offenses, and 3% for drug-related offenses than males even if no children or no spouse are present. The results are in line with the hypotheses N1 and N2. The findings do not support the evil woman thesis (hypothesis N2a) that assumes harsher sentences for women prosecuted for violent or drug-related criminal acts. Estimation of models for separate offenses shows similar results (Appendix, Table A4). Charged with personal injuries, female offenders receive 0.375 year (4.5 months) shorter sentences than male offenders (or 0.245 year shorter (2.9 months) if less serious bodily harm was caused to victim). Theft offenders are punished differently regarding offenders' sex as well: sentences for women are 0.092 year (1.1 month) or 0.219 year (2.6 months) shorter dependent on the amount of stolen property. However, the gender gap in sentence length is not significant in case of drug possession (0.3 month) and modest in case of drug dealing (0.7 month). Thus, offender's sex has weak effect on sentencing outcomes for defendants charged with drug-related crimes.

Hypothesis N3 predicts greater leniency towards defendants with children. The analysis of the effects of the defendant's sex and parental status on decisions regarding sentence length shows unexpected results. Contrary to expectations, having children has weak effect on sentence length decisions across different types of crime but rather associates positively with prison term. The exception is sentencing process in violent cases, where the effect of children is insignificant both for female and male offenders (Model 6). In drug-related cases, having children is associated positively with sentence length (+1%) regardless offender's sex (Model 8). In property cases, male offenders with children are punished with 1% longer sentences compared with males with no children present (Model 7). Moreover, sentenced to prison for property crimes, female defendants with childcare responsibilities receive 6.5% longer sentences than their male counterparts (Model 7). Separate analysis of specific offenses reveals that length for women with children is substantially longer than for men in all cases (Appendix, Table A4) except charges in personal injury that caused moderate bodily harm (Model 17). For example, while being charged with low serious theft, female offenders with children receive 0.148 year (1.8 month) longer sentences, and sentences for male offenders with children are 0.05 of a year (0.6 month) longer (Model 18). In case of more serious theft charges, having children associates with 0.183 year (2.2 months) longer sentences for women and only 0.035 year (0.42 month) longer for men. Thus, the gender gap in sentences for offenders with children is even bigger for more serious than less serious property crimes (0.148 and 0.098 year, respectively). Similar pattern is observed in violent cases. The analysis of separate drug-related offences also reveals that women with children receive 0.145 year (1.7 month) longer sentences for drug possession and 0.107 year (1.3 month) longer for drug dealing compared with men. In terms of length decisions, the findings contradict hypotheses N3 and N4 that predict greater leniency in sentences for offenders with children and especially for female offenders with children. The analysis of imposed sentences in case of different types of offenses as well as for separate offenses demonstrates rather longer sentences for offenders with children than for childless offenders. Moreover, positive effect of children presence on sentence length is even bigger for women than for men when sentencing outcomes for separate offenses are estimated.

Another family-related offender's characteristic is marital status. Besides property cases, marriage has extremely modest effect on length decisions and cannot be recognised as substantially significant regardless of defendant's sex. Married men receive 1% shorter sentences for violent crimes and 1% longer for property and drug-related crimes compared with single men (Table 4). In property cases, married females are sentenced to term 4% longer compared with males. The results contradict the initial expectations of this study in regards to more lenient sentences for married offenders and especially for women. Thus, hypotheses N5 and N6 do not find support in analyses of sentence lengths. The analysis of separate offenses demonstrates similar results with regard to hypotheses (Appendix, Table A4). Marriage associates negatively with sentence length for men when they are charged with personal injury offenses or drug dealing (Models 16, 17, 21) and correlates positively – for men prosecuted for theft or drug possession (Models 18, 19, 20). However, the effects are extremely small and mostly statistically insignificant. The effects of marriage on sentence length do not differentiate substantially between male and female offenders except for theft charges (Models 18, 19). Being charged with theft offenses of low and medium gravity, married female offenders receive 0.13 of a year (1.6 month) or 0.09 of a year (1.1 month) longer sentences than their male counterparts. Thus, the analysis of separate offenses reveals that marriage can result in increased sentences for offenders prosecuted for property or drug-related crimes. However, married male offenders can be treated by judges more leniently than their single counterparts in violent cases, but the effect is modest or even insignificant in the analyses of separate offenses. These results contradict hypothesis N5 that suggests shorter sentences for married compared with single offenders. Hypothesis N6 that predicts more lenient treatment of married women than married men does not find support in sentence length decisions. Moreover, in property or violent cases, marriage can be associated with harsher sentences for women than for men.

Summary

The analysis of sex and family-related factors in sentencing process can be summarised as follows. Generally, women are less likely to be incarcerated and receive shorter sentences, with the exception of being charged with drug-related offenses. The results support hypothesis N1, which assumes greater leniency for women. At the same time, hypotheses N2 and N2a, which are based on the evil woman or selective chivalry theses, hardly can be recognised as confirmed. These hypotheses suggest greater leniency accorded to women prosecuted for property crimes, but not violent or drug-related crimes, for which women can be treated even harshly than men. The results demonstrate that judges impose more lenient sentences, including possibility of incarceration and the size of prison term, on women in property cases as well as in violent cases. Moreover, in most of drug-related cases female and male offenders are treated equally. Thus, evil women and selective chivalry theories cannot explain fully the origins of gender disparity in sentencing process in Russian context.

Family-related factors have inconsistent effects on different levels of judicial decision-making. When it comes to in/out decisions, the findings partially support hypothesis N3, which suggests that defendants with children have lower odds of being sent to prison. The results show that defendants with children are less likely to be incarcerated when charged with common violent or property offenses. There is also strong support for hypothesis N5, which suggests more lenient punishment for defendants who are married. Indeed, married defendants are less likely to be incarcerated in general as well as across different types of crimes and particular offenses. However, hypotheses N3 and N5 are not supported by sentence length models in general as well as by most of the models estimated for different types of offenses or separate offenses. Incarceration length findings show that family-related factors, including children presence and being married, are often positively associated with punishment severity. However, these effects are modest.

There is no strong evidence for hypotheses N4 which suggested that dependent children would benefit female defendants more than their male counterparts in violent and property cases. As predicted by hypothesis N4a, there is no difference in sentencing outcomes for male and female offenders with children in drug-related cases. Only when charged with property offence, the interaction effect of sex and parental status is significant and can contribute to the idea of unequal treatment of female and male defendants with regard to the different childcare responsibilities expected from them. Moreover, average sentence length for women who have children is longer than for men. In separate analyses for different types of crime, these results are confirmed for property cases. Meanwhile, childcare responsibilities are related to more severe sentences for women compared with men charged with personal injury that caused heavy bodily harm, theft, drug possession, or drug dealing. Thus, when major legal characteristics of the case – severity of the offense, upper and lower bounds of prison term, the amount of damage caused by wrong-doing, – are equal, female defendants with children receive substantially longer sentences than their male counterparts. The results are unexpected. However, they can be explained using initial hypothesis N4 that is based on different female and male roles expected in children care what is discussed in the end of this paper.

Contrary to hypothesis N6, the analysis does not demonstrate substantial preferential treatment of married women compared with men both in incarceration and sentence length decisions. Interaction effect of defendant's sex and marital status is significant in in/out decisions in violent and drug-related cases and in sentence length decisions – in violent and property cases. However, after checking for consistency of the results within particular offenses, the interaction between sex and marriage remains significant only in sentence length decisions in property cases.

Conclusions

The findings on offender's sex effect on sentencing in Russia are consistent with much of the prior sentencing literature on sentences imposed in state and federal courts in the USA. Greater leniency is accorded to female offenders than male even after controlling for crime seriousness, the offender's criminal record, and other legally relevant factors (Albonetti, 1997; Daly & Bordt, 1995; Koons-Witt, Sevigny, Burrow, & Hester, 2012; Mustard, 2001; Spohn & Beichner, 2000; Stacey & Spohn, 2006; Steffensmeier & Demuth, 2006; Steffensmeier et al., 1998).

The findings indicate that women compared with men face significantly lower odds of being incarcerated and a shorter length of incarceration in general and in violent and property cases in particular. No gender disparity in sentencing was observed for drug-related crimes. Thus, the results do not support evil women or selective chivalry hypotheses that predict equal or even harsher treatment of females compared with males in violent and drug-related cases. However, gender studies in sentencing show that social characteristics of the victim, specifically sex, can interfere with sentencing outcomes in violent cases (Curry, Lee, & Rodriguez, 2004; Johnson et al., 2010). Unfortunately, this research as many others (for some exceptions see review in Ulmer, 2012) does not account for possible bias generated by victim's social characteristics that can be essential for estimating sex effects in violent cases. Thus, inclusion of victim's sex in sentencing modelling in future studies can help to reach an ending point in the discussion on the advances to explain gender differences in sentencing with evil women or selective chivalry theses. However, the results are in line with focal concerns perspective. Focal concerns perspective assumes that judges evaluate offender's blameworthiness and dangerousness, while making sentencing deci-sions, and take into account practical constraints. The findings demonstrate that Russian judges may see women as less blameworthy and less dangerous to the society than men except for drug-related cases.

The effects of family-related factors on sentencing are statistically significant, but much smaller than initially expected based on the Code regulation that allows judges to account for a defen-dant's family situation when imposing a punishment on a convicted person. Moreover, effects of having children and being married can differ drastically depending on whether in/out or sentence length decisions are considered.

Married people are less likely incarcerated regardless of their sex, even for drug-related cases where defendant's sex and parental status have little effects. Through the lens of the focal concerns perspective, more lenient treatment of married defendants can result from concerns for protecting the community and from practical constraints: as long as the family is capable of providing informal social control, the formal mechanisms of social control are not necessary and are related to greater social costs.

Unexpectedly, family-related factors, including being married and especially having children by female defendants, that are supposed to decrease penalty can result in longer sentences. When female defendants face prison term, sentences are longer when childcare responsibilities are present. This effect can be the "reverse side" of the child-caring role placed on women with children. Speculatively, judges try not to incarcerate defendants with children. However, when judges decide to impose prison term on defendants (which is rare among female convicts), sentences for women can be significantly longer when childcare responsibilities are present. One of the possible explanations that needs to be investigated in further research is that judges place on female offenders much higher expectations of good or "more appropriate" behaviour than on males. Speculatively, due to the child-caring role of women, they can be expected to adjust their behaviour to this role while men only have the duty to provide financial support for the family. This explanation is consistent with the idea that not all prosecuted women can be linked with a "good" mother attribution by court officials (Zatz, 2000). As a rule, white middle-class women benefit from motherhood. The treatment of poor black women can be substantially different. Cases prosecuting crack mothers in the USA in the late 1980s show the devaluation of motherhood for poor, black, drug-addicted women (Zatz, 2000). Similar to these women, female offenders in Russia who are sentenced to prison can be recognised by judges as those who do not deserve leniency due to their motherhood. Moreover, violation of mothering role may result in greater sentences because judges can perceive offenders sentenced to prison as those who do not perform parental duties well. Unfortunately, this research does not differentiate defendants with children who actually exercise parental duties or at least try to do so from those who do not. Neither do other statistical studies in gender and sentencing. However, this can be crucial for understanding of judicial discretion and judicial sense of justice. More differentiated approach to offender's family situation that will account for single parenthood, age, and number of children can be the area for further research.

Another limitation of this study should be mentioned and discussed. The data lacks measures of pretrial release status and, more importantly for this study, the identity or social characteristics of victims. Pretrial detention is positively associated with incarceration decisions in Russia (Titaev, 2014; Volkov, 2015) and, thus, can partially be responsible for some part of the estimated effects. However, the findings of this study are corroborated by Volkov's (2015) research that demonstrated that sex and marriage effects on sentencing decisions in Russia are significant after controlling for pretrial detention in incarceration models.

The present study shows that the focal concerns framework can be extended to predict sentencing outcomes in non-Western societies. However, the origins of judicial decision-making with regard to the local context require further research. Judicial concerns about offender's blameworthiness, protection of the community, and practical constraints should be investigated more closely by means of ethnographic research. Finally, future research may take into account social characteristics of judges, including sex, and their effects on decision-making.

Notes

1. Source: The official statistics published by the Judicial Department every half a year (Form N1 of the Reports on the performance of the general-jurisdiction courts to proceed criminal cases) on the official cite of the Judicial Department: http://www.cdep.ru/index.php?id=79.
2. Ibid.
3. All laws and regulations are cited from the ConsultantPlus database (http://www.consultant.ru/sys/english/).
4. Time period of 2009–2015 is covered. Source: The official statistics provided by the Ministry of Internal Affairs of the Russian Federation ("MVD") https://mvd.ru/folder/101762.
5. Human Rights Watch (2014) Abandoned by the State: Violence, Neglect, and Isolation for Children with Disabilities in Russian Orphanages. https://www.hrw.org/report/2014/09/15/abandoned-state/violence-neglect-and-isolation-children-disabilities-russian Accessed 27/04/16.

CRIMINOLOGY AND CRIMINAL JUSTICE IN RUSSIA

6. For more detailed information on the procedure of filling and submitting of statistical cards see the Directive on the maintenance of judicial statistics enacted in 2007 by the Decree N169 of the Judicial Department.

7. Source: official cite of the Judicial Department (Form N1 of the Reports on the performance of the general-jurisdiction courts to proceed criminal cases): http://www.cdep.ru/index.php?id=79.

8. A Federal law N321-FZ, adopted on 30 December 2008, has excluded some crimes, including terrorism and crimes against the state, from the jurisdiction of juries (Gurinskaya, 2015).

9. At the end of July 2013, the new amendment to the CPC (Federal Law N217-FZ) was introduced, according to which only those offenders who face life imprisonment without parole or death (there has been a moratorium on the death penalty acts since 1997) can request jury trial. Thus, people under age of 18 or over 65 as well as all women regardless age were automatically deprived of a right to trial by jury (Gurinskaya, 2015), as far as the Code guarantees no life imprisonment or death penalty to the offenders from those social groups. In 2016, the Constitutional court of Russian Federation recognised the regulation that outlaws female defendants from jury trial procedure unconstitutional and banned it (The Judgment N6-P from 25/02/2016).

10. The number of cases tried by juries is extremely modest and composes less than 1% of all cases yearly brought to courts in Russia. Additional analysis of data that included jury cases showed no substantial differences in estimated effects. Considerable dissimilarity in the process as well as small number of cases are the main reasons why the sentencing under jury trial is excluded from the present analysis.

11. Art. 246 of the CPC states that the prosecutor expresses his or her opinion on the sentence, but it does not specify a precise moment when he or she should do it. However, customary, the prosecutor recommends sentence during oral arguments at the end of trial.

12. Average marginal effects reflect to the change in probability per one unit change in independent variable averaged across the observed values of other independent variables.

13. Suspended incarceration is one of the possible and broadly used punishments (Paneyakh, 2012). Art. 73 of the Code clarifies that punishment, including incarceration for up to 8 years in prison, can be suspended by a judge if he or she comes to a conclusion that the convict can be reformed without actual execution of assigned punishment. When punishment is suspended, a trial period from 6 months up to 5 years is assigned. Judge can impose on the convict additional obligations that should be fulfilled during this period, such as an obligation not to leave a place of living without noticing authorised governmental officials, or an obligation to join special treatment programmes, and so on. In case of serious violations, judge can abolish the decision on punishment suspension and authorise an execution of previously assigned punishment.

14. Except for some cases specified in the Art. 18 of the Code such as low seriousness of the previous offence, age under 18, and some other.

15. The Legislationline.org is used for translating the Code in English (see http://legislationline.org/documents/section/criminal-codes/country/7). The source is provided by the OSCE and is available online.

16. The amendments that entered into force on 1 January 2013 are shown in *italics*.

Acknowledgements

The data was provided to the Institute for the Rule of Law, European University at St. Petersburg by the Judicial Department of the Supreme Court of Russian Federation. I am grateful to Vadim Volkov, Dmitriy Skougarevskiy, Kirill Titaev, and Mikhail Pozdnyakov who worked on data preparation and provided insightful comments that helped me to write this paper. I also thank anonymous reviewers for their helpful comments.

References

Albonetti, C. A. (1991). An integration of theories to explain judicial discretion. *Social Problems, 38*(2), 247–266. doi:10.2307/800532

Albonetti, C. A. (1997). Sentencing under the federal sentencing guidelines: Effects of defendant characteristics, guilty pleas, and departures on sentence outcomes for drug offenses, 1991–1992. *Law & Society Review*, *31*(4), 789–822. doi:10.2307/3053987

Ashwin, S. (2006). The post-Soviet gender order: Imperatives and implications. In S. Ashwin (Ed.), *Adapting to Russia's new labour market. Gender and employment behaviour* (pp. 32–56). Chippenham: Routledge.

Ashwin, S., & Lytkina, T. (2004). Men in crisis in Russia: The role of domestic marginalization. *Gender & Society*, *18*(2), 189–206. doi:10.1177/0891243203261263

Bersani, B. E., Laub, J. H., & Nieuwbeerta, P. (2009). Marriage and desistance from crime in the Netherlands: Do gender and socio-historical context matter? *Journal of Quantitative Criminology*, *25*(1), 3–24. doi:10.1007/s10940-008-9056-4

Black, D. (1976). *The behavior of law*. New York: Academic Press.

Bushway, S. D., Johnson, B. D., & Slocum, L. A. (2007). Is the magic still there? The use of the Heckman two-step correction for selection bias in criminology. *Journal of Quantitative Criminology*, *23*(2), 151–178. doi:10.1007/s10940-007-9024-4

Chatsverykova, I. (2014). Rol semyi, professionalnoy karyeri i pola podsudimih pri vinisenii prigovorov rossiyskimi sudyami. [The role of family, professional career and sex of offenders for the verdict outcome in Russian courts]. *Journal of Sociology and Social Antropology*, *17*(4), 101–123.

Connell, R. (1987). *Gender and power: Society, the person and sexual politics*. Amsterdam: Stanford University Press.

Crew, B. (1991). Sex differences in criminal sentencing: Chivalry or patriarchy? *Justice Quarterly*, *8*(1), 59–83. doi:10.1080/07418829100090911

Curry, T. R., Lee, G., & Rodriguez, S. F. (2004). Does victim gender increase sentence severity? Further explorations of gender dynamics and sentencing outcomes. *Crime & Delinquency*, *50*(3), 319–343. doi:10.1177/0011128703256265

Daly, K. (1987). Structure and practice of familial-based justice in a criminal court. *Law & Society Review*, *21*(2), 267–290. doi:10.2307/3053522

Daly, K. (1989). Neither conflict nor labeling nor paternalism will suffice: Intersections of race, ethnicity, gender, and family in criminal court decisions. *Crime & Delinquency*, *35*(1), 136–168. doi:10.1177/0011128789035001007

Daly, K., & Bordt, R. L. (1995). Sex effects and sentencing: An analysis of the statistical literature. *Justice Quarterly*, *12*(1), 141–175. doi:10.1080/07418829500092601

Daly, K., & Tonry, M. (1997). Gender, race, and sentencing. *Crime & Justice*, *22*(1997), 201–252. doi:10.1086/449263

Dinovitzer, R., & Dawson, M. (2007). Family-based justice in the sentencing of domestic violence. *British Journal of Criminology*, *47*, 655–670. doi:10.1093/bjc/azl078

Doerner, J. K. (2015). The joint effects of gender and race/ethnicity on sentencing outcomes in federal courts. *Women & Criminal Justice*, *25*(5), 313–338. doi:10.1080/08974454.2014.989298

Doerner, J. K., & Demuth, S. (2010). The independent and joint effects of race/ethnicity, gender, and age on sentencing outcomes in U.S. federal courts. *Justice Quarterly*, *27*(1), 1–27. doi:10.1080/07418820902926197

Doerner, J. K., & Demuth, S. (2012). Gender and sentencing in the federal courts: Are women treated more leniently? *Criminal Justice Policy Review*. doi:10.1177/0887403412466877

Engen, R. L. (2009). Assessing determinate and presumptive sentencing -Making research relevant. *Criminology & Public Policy*, *8*(2), 323–336. doi:10.1111/j.1745-9133.2009.00559.x

Engen, R. L., & Gainey, R. R. (2000). Modeling the effects of legally relevant and extralegal factors under sentencing guidelines: The rules have changed. *Criminology*, *38*(4), 1207–1230. doi:10.1111/j.1745-9125.2000.tb01419.x

Engen, R. L., Gainey, R. R., Crutchfield, R. D., & Weis, J. G. (2003). Discretion and disparity under sentencing guidelines: The role of departures and structured sentencing alternatives. *Criminology*, *41*(1), 99–130. doi:10.1111/j.1745-9125.2003.tb00983.x

Fernando Rodriguez, S., Curry, T. R., & Lee, G. (2006). Gender differences in criminal sentencing: Do effects vary across violent, property, and drug offenses? *Social Science Quarterly*, *87*(2), 318–339. doi:10.1111/j.1540-6237.2006.00383.x

Flavin, J. (2001). Of punishment and parenthood: Family-based social control and the sentencing of black drug offenders. *Gender & Society*, *15*(4), 611–633. doi:10.1177/089124301015004007

Freiburger, T. L. (2010). The effects of gender, family status, and race on sentencing decisions. *Behavioral Sciences & the Law*, *395*(October 2009), 378–395. doi:10.1002/bsl

Galanter, M. (1974). Why the "Haves" come out ahead: Speculations on the limits of legal change. *Law & Society Review*, *9*(1), 95–230. doi:10.2307/3053023

Gaub, J. E., & Holtfreter, K. (2015). New directions in intersections, inequality, and sentencing. *Women & Criminal Justice*, *25*(5), 298–312. doi:10.1080/08974454.2014.989299

Gottfredson, M. R., & Hirschi, T. (1990). *A general theory of crime*. California: Stanford University Press.

Griffin, T., & Wooldredge, J. (2006). Sex-based disparities in felony dispositions before versus after sentencing reform in Ohio. *Criminology*, *44*(4), 893–923. doi:10.1111/j.1745-9125.2006.00067.x

Gurinskaya, A. (2015). Trial by jury in Russia: From the cornerstone of the judicial reform to the constitutional history artifact. *VARSTVOSLOVJE, Journal of Criminal Justice and Security, 343*(1), 62–82.

Haney, L. A. (2000). Feminist state theory: Applications to jurisprudence, criminology, and the welfare state. *Annual Review of Sociology, 26*(1), 641–666. doi:10.1146/annurev.soc.26.1.641

Hartley, R. D., Kwak, D.-H., Park, M., & Lee, M.-S. (2011). Exploring sex disparity in sentencing outcomes: A focus on narcotics offenders in South Korea. *International Journal of Offender Therapy and Comparative Criminology, 55*(2), 268–286. doi:10.1177/0306624X09360966

Hartley, R. D., Maddan, S., & Spohn, C. (2007). Concerning conceptualization and operationalization: Sentencing data and the focal concerns perspective–A research note. *Southwest Journal of Criminal Justice, 4*(1), 58–78. Retrieved from http://swacj.org/swjcj/archives/4.1/Sentencing_data.pdf

Heckman, J. J. (1979). Sample selection bias as a specification error. *Econometrica, 47*(1), 153–161. doi:10.2307/1912352

Hendley, K. (2007). Are Russian judges still soviet? *Post-Soviet Affairs, 23*, 240–274. doi:10.2747/1060-586X.23.3.240

Hendley, K. (2009). "Telephone Law" and the "Rule of Law": The Russian Case. *Hague Journal on the Rule of Law, 1*, 241. doi:10.1017/S1876404509002413

Human Rights Watch. (2014). *Abandoned by thes State: Violence, neglect, and isolation for children with disabilities in Russian orphanages.* Retrieved from https://www.hrw.org/report/2014/09/15/abandoned-state/violencene glect-and-isolation-children-disabilities-russian

Johnson, B. D. (2005). Contextual disparities in guidelines departures: Courtroom social contexts, guidelines compliance, and extralegal disparities in criminal sentencing. *Criminology, 43*, 761–796. doi:10.1111/j.0011-1348.2005.00023.x

Johnson, B. D., Van Wingerden, S., & Nieuwbeerta, P. (2010). Sentencing homicide offenders in the Netherlands: Offender, victim, and situational influences in criminal punishment. *Criminology, 48*(4), 981–1018. doi:10.1111/j.1745-9125.2010.00210.x

Koons-Witt, B. A., Sevigny, E. L., Burrow, J. D., & Hester, R. (2012). Gender and sentencing outcomes in South Carolina: Examining the interactions with race, age, and offense type. *Criminal Justice Policy Review.* doi:10.1177/0887403412468884

Kozina, I., & Zhidkova, E. (2006). Sex segregationand discrimination in the new Russian labour market. In S. Ashwin (Ed.), *Adapting to Russia's new labour market. Gender and employment behaviour* (pp. 57–86). Chippenham: Routledge.

Kruttschnitt, C. (1984). Sex and criminal court dispositions: The unresolved controversy. *Journal of Research in Crime and Delinquency, 21*(3), 213–232. doi:10.1177/0022427884021003003

Kruttschnitt, C., & Green, D. (1984). The sex-sanctioning issue: Is it history? *American Sociological Review, 49*(4), 541–551. doi:10.2307/2095467

Kruttschnitt, C., & Savolainen, J. (2009). Ages of chivalry, places of paternalism: Gender and criminal sentencing in Finland. *European Journal of Criminology, 6*(3), 225–247. doi:10.1177/1477370809102166

Kurlychek, M. C., & Johnson, B. D. (2004). The juvenile penalty: A comparison of juvenile and young adult sentencing outcomes in criminal court. *Criminology, 42*(2), 485–515. doi:10.1111/j.1745-9125.2004.tb00527.x

Ledeneva, A. (2008). Telephone justice in Russia. *Post-Soviet Affairs, 24*(4), 324–350. doi:10.2747/1060-586X.24.4.324

Lee, M., Ulmer, J. T., & Park, M. (2011). Drug sentencing in South Korea: The influence of case-processing and social status factors in an ethnically homogeneous context. *Journal of Contemporary Criminal Justice, 27*(3), 378–397. doi:10.1177/1043986211412574

Logue, M. A. (2011). Downward departures in US federal courts: Do family ties, sex, and race/ethnicity matter? *Ethnic & Racial Studies, 34*(4), 683–706. doi:10.1080/01419870.2010.487568

Lu, H., Liang, B., & Liu, S. (2012). Serious violent offenses and sentencing decisions in China—Are there any gender disparities? *Asian Journal of Criminology, 8*(3), 159–177. doi:10.1007/s11417-012-9155-x

Malceva, I., & Roschin, S. (2006). *Gendernaja segregacia i trudovaja mobilnostj na rossijskom rynke truda* [Gender segregation and job mobility in the Russian labor force]. Moskow: Higher School of Economics.

Mustard, D. (2001). Racial, ethnic, and gender disparities in sentencing: Evidence from the US federal courts. *The Journal of Law and Economics, 44*(1), 285–314. doi:10.1086/320276

Nagel, I. H., & Hagan, J. (1983). Gender and crime: Offense patterns and criminal court sanctions. *Crime & Justice, 4*(May), 91–144. doi:10.1086/449087

Pallot, J., & Piacentini, L. (2012). *Gender, geography, and punishment: The experience of women in carceral Russia.* Oxford, UK: Oxford University Press.

Paneyakh, E. (2012). Practical logic of decision-making: Discretion under pressure and compromises at offender's cost. In V. Volkov (Ed.), *How judges decide: Empirical legal studies* (pp. 107–127). Moskow, Russia: Statut.

Plesnicar, M. M. (2013). The individualization of punishment: Sentencing in Slovenia. *European Journal of Criminology, 10*(4), 462–478. doi:10.1177/1477370812469858

CRIMINOLOGY AND CRIMINAL JUSTICE IN RUSSIA

Pozdnjakov, M. (2012). Smisl I dvusmislennost' obvinitelnogo uklona [Sense and ambiguity of the accusatorial bias]. In V. Volkov (Ed.), *Kak sudyi prinimayut reshenia: empiricheskie issledovania prava* [How judges decide: Empirical legal studies] (pp. 54–106). Moscow: Statut.

Roberts, D. (1991). Punishing drug addicts who have babies: Women of color, equality, and the right of privacy on JSTOR. *Harvard Law Review, 104*(7), 1419–1482. doi:10.2307/1341597

Rodriguez, S. F., Curry, T. R., & Lee, G. (2006). Gender differences in criminal sentencing: Do effects vary across violent, property, and drug offenses? *Social Science Quarterly, 87*(2), 318–339. doi:10.1111/j.1540-6237.2006.00383.x

Roshchin, S., & Zubarevich, N. (2005). *Gendernoe ravenstvo i rasshirenie prav i vozmozhnostey v Rossii v kontecste razvitia tysjachiletia* [Gender equality and expansion of women's rights and possibilities in Russia in the context of the millennium development]. Moscow: UNIC Moscow.

Sampson, R. J., & Laub, J. H. (1995). *Crime in the making: Pathways and turning points through life.* Cambridge: Harvard University Press.

Schwartz, J., & Steffensmeier, D. (2008). The nature of female offending: Patterns and explanation. In R. T. Zaplin (Ed.), *Female offenders: Critical perspectives and effective interventions* (pp. 43–76). Sudbury, MA: Jones and Bartlett. Retrieved from http://www.jblearning.com/samples/0763741159/Ch2_Female_Offenders_2e.pdf

Spohn, C., & Beichner, D. (2000). Is preferential treatment of female offenders a thing of the past? A multisite study of gender, race, and imprisonment. *Criminal Justice Policy Review, 11*(2), 149–184. Retrieved from http://cjp.sagepub.com/content/11/2/149.short

Spohn, C., & Holleran, D. (2000). The imprisonment penalty paid by young, unemployed black and hispanic male offenders. *Criminology, 38*(1), 281–306. doi:10.1111/j.1745-9125.2000.tb00891.x

Stacey, A., & Spohn, C. (2006). Gender and the social costs of sentencing: An analysis of sentences imposed on male and female offenders in three US district courts. *The Berkeley Journal of Criminal Law, 11*(1). Retrieved from http://heinonlinebackup.com/hol-cgi-bin/get_pdf.cgi?handle=hein.journals/bjcl11&section=9

Steffensmeier, D., & Allan, E. (1996). Gender and crime: Toward a gendered theory of female offending. *Annual Review of Sociology, 22*(1), 459–487. doi:10.1146/annurev.soc.22.1.459

Steffensmeier, D., & Demuth, S. (2006). Does gender modify the effects of race–Ethnicity on criminal sanctioning? Sentences for male and female white, black, and Hispanic defendants. *Journal of Quantitative Criminology, 22*(3), 241–261. doi:10.1007/s10940-006-9010-2

Steffensmeier, D., Kramer, J. H., & Streifel, C. (1993). Gender and imprisonment decisions. *Criminology, 31*(3), 411–446. doi:10.1111/j.1745-9125.1993.tb01136.x

Steffensmeier, D., Ulmer, J. T., & Kramer, J. H. (1998). The interaction of race, gender, and age in criminal sentencing: The punishment cost of being young, black, and male. *Criminology, 36*(4), 763–798; Retrieved from. 10.1111/j.1745-9125.1998.tb01265.x

Temkina, A., & Zdravomyslova, E. (2003). Gender studies in post-soviet society: Western frames and cultural differences. *Studies in East European Thought, 55*, 51–61. doi:10.1023/A:1021857831011

Tillyer, R., Hartley, R. D., & Ward, J. T. (2015). Differential treatment of female defendants: Does criminal history moderate the effect of gender on sentence length in federal narcotics cases? *Criminal Justice and Behavior, XX* (X), 1–19. doi:10.1177/0093854814560624

Titaev, K. (2014). Predvariyelnoe zakluchenie v rossiyskoy ugolovnoy justicii: Sociologicheskiy analiz veroyatnosti predvaritelnogo zaklucheniya i ego vlijanie na resheniya suda [Pretrial Detention in the Russian Criminal Justice]. *Economic Sociology, 15*(3), 88–113. doi:10.17323/1726-3247-2014-3-88-118

Ulmer, J. T. (2012). Recent developments and new directions in sentencing research. *Justice Quarterly, 29*(1), 1–40. doi:10.1080/07418825.2011.624115

Ulmer, J. T., & Bradley, M. (2006). Variation in trial penalties among serious violent offenses. *Criminology, 44*(3), 631–670. doi:10.1111/j.1745-9125.2006.00059.x

Visher, C. A. (1983). Gender, police arrest decisions, and notions of chivalry. *Criminology, 21*(1), 5–28. doi:10.1111/j.1745-9125.1983.tb00248.x

Volkov, V. (2014). *Socioeconomic status and sentencing disparities: Evidence from Russia's criminal courts.* ((IRL No. 1) IRL-Working Paper (Vol. 1)). Saint-Petrsburg.

Volkov, V. (2015). Legal and extralegal origins of sentencing disparities: Evidence from Russia's criminal courts. *SSRN Electronic Journal*, 1–32. doi:10.2139/ssrn.2629436

Zatz, M. (2000). The convergence of race, ethnicity, gender, and class on court decisionmaking: Looking toward the 21st century. *Criminal Justice*, 503–552. Retrieved from http://www.ncjrs.gov/App/abstractdb/AbstractDBDetails.aspx?id=185536

Zdravomyslova, O. (2003). *Semja i obschestvo: Gendernoe izmerenie rossijskoj transformacii* [Family and society: Gender evaluation of Russian transformation]. Moskow: Editorial URSS.

CRIMINOLOGY AND CRIMINAL JUSTICE IN RUSSIA

Appendix

Table A1. Code's regulation.

Article	Offense[15]	Bounds of prison term, years	
		Min.	Max.
111 p.1	Intentional infliction of a grave injury, which is hazardous for human life or which has involved the loss of sight, speech, hearing, or any organ or the loss of the organ's functions, or which has expressed itself in the indelible disfiguring of a human face, and also infliction of other harm which is dangerous to human life or which has involved an injury to a person's health, joined with considerable permanent loss of general ability to work by not less than one-third or by the full loss of an occupational capacity for work, which capacity was evident to the guilty person, or which has involved the interruption of pregnancy, mental derangement, or the victim's falling ill to drug addiction or toxicosis	2(since 2011– 0. 167)	8
112 p.1	Intentional infliction of a moderate personal injury, which is not hazardous to human life and which has not involved consequences referred to in Article 111 of the Criminal Code, but which has caused protracted injury to health or considerable stable loss of general capacity for work by not less than one-third	0. 167	3
158 p.1	Theft, that is, the secret larceny of other people's property	0. 167	2
158 p.2	Theft committed: a) by a group of persons by previous concert; b) with an illegal entry into premises or any other storehouse; c) with the infliction of considerable damage to a person; d) from clothes, the bag or any other hand luggage the victim has	0. 167	5
228 p.1	Illegal acquisition, storage, transportation, making or processing[16] of narcotic drugs, psychotropic substances or analogues thereof on a large scale, as well as illegal acquisition, storage, and transportation without the purpose of selling plants containing narcotics or psychotropic substances, or parts thereof containing narcotics or psychotropic substances on a large scale, without the purpose of sale	0. 167	3
228.1 p.1	Illegal making, sale or dispatch of narcotic drugs, psychotropic substances or analogues thereof, as well as illegal sale or dispatch of plants containing narcotics or psychotropic substances or parts thereof containing narcotics or psychotropic substances	4	8

Table A2. Descriptive statistics for the offenses.

Article of the Code	Share of sentenced among prosecuted persons	Total number of sentenced	Mean number of sentenced within a year	Share of females among sentenced	Share of incarcerated among sentenced	Share of females among sentenced to prison
111 p.1	0.97	99642	19928.4	0.24	0.43	0.13
112 p.1	0.52	50318	10063.6	0.05	0.16	0.03
158 p.1	0.71	300091	60018.2	0.21	0.21	0.15
158 p.2	0.77	502305	100461	0.13	0.32	0.09
228 p.1	0.98	198192	39638.4	0.09	0.24	0.09
228.1 p.1	0.99	29984	5996.8	0.20	0.73	0.21
Total	0.79	3355480	671096	0.15	0.30	0.10

CRIMINOLOGY AND CRIMINAL JUSTICE IN RUSSIA

Table A3. Average marginal effects of being incarcerated probit models (in/out decisions).

Type of crime	Violent: personal injury		Property: theft		Drugs: possession and dealing	
Models	(9)	(10)	(12)	(13)	(14)	(15)
Article of the Criminal Code	111 p.1	112 p.1	158 p.1	158 p.2	228 p.1	228.1 p.1
Female	−0.136**	−0.019	−0.024**	−0.043**	−0.003	−0.010
	(0.004)	(0.010)	(0.003)	(0.003)	(0.004)	(0.009)
Children	−0.029**	−0.014**	−0.015**	−0.024**	−0.013**	−0.000
	(0.003)	(0.003)	(0.002)	(0.002)	(0.002)	(0.009)
Female × children	0.002	−0.010	−0.011**	−0.016**	0.000	−0.001
	(0.007)	(0.015)	(0.004)	(0.004)	(0.006)	(0.012)
Married	−0.042**	−0.023**	−0.031**	−0.027**	−0.018**	−0.017*
	(0.003)	(0.004)	(0.002)	(0.002)	(0.002)	(0.008)
Female × married	−0.003	−0.003	0.006	0.006	−0.000	−0.005
	(0.007)	(0.017)	(0.005)	(0.005)	(0.006)	(0.015)
Observations	99642	50303	300085	502288	198188	29801

Legal and social controls, dummies of years, and regions are included. Clustered at court level standard errors are in parentheses. ** $p < 0.01$, * $p < 0.05$.

Table A4. Incarceration length decisions, OLS, and years.

Type of crime	Violent: personal injury		Property: theft		Drugs: possession and dealing	
Models	(16)	(17)	(18)	(19)	(20)	(21)
Article of the Code	111 p.1	112 p.1	158 p.1	158 p.2	228 p.1	228.1 p.1
Female	−0.375**	−0.245**	−0.092**	−0.219**	0.022	−0.056*
	(0.018)	(0.081)	(0.015)	(0.011)	(0.023)	(0.026)
Children	−0.078**	0.081*	0.050**	0.035**	0.014	−0.045*
	(0.015)	(0.033)	(0.013)	(0.009)	(0.012)	(0.020)
Female × children	0.245**	0.230	0.098**	0.148**	0.145**	0.107**
	(0.031)	(0.135)	(0.028)	(0.022)	(0.039)	(0.039)
Married	−0.044**	−0.004	0.023	0.032**	0.027*	−0.037
	(0.016)	(0.034)	(0.014)	(0.009)	(0.014)	(0.023)
Female × married	0.034	0.256	0.130**	0.090**	0.008	0.039
	(0.034)	(0.149)	(0.041)	(0.028)	(0.049)	(0.049)
Observations	43212	8151	61553	162557	46697	21797
R-squared	0.313	0.164	0.172	0.219	0.228	0.322

Legal and social controls, dummies of years, and regions are included. Clustered at court level standard errors are in parentheses. ** $p < 0.01$, * $p < 0.05$.

Female criminality in Russia: a research note from a penal colony

Oksana Kaplun ⓘ

ABSTRACT

This article assesses various factors contributing to fluctuating rates of female crime in Russia between 1991 and present. The author uses existing data and modern scientific literature regarding female crime in Russia as a framework for the study. The goal of this article, based on empirical research, is to show trends and tendencies of female crime specifically. The study was done in March 2013 in the Russian penal colony of Vladivostok. A total of 212 women aged between 18 and 64 years were interviewed. Ultimately, the study's findings will inform trends in female crime, and will contribute to the continued development of more effective crime prevention programmes in Russia.

Introduction

Female criminal behaviour has traditionally been perceived as a less serious problem than male criminal behaviour. However, despite the fact that women commit fewer crimes, the social consequences of these crimes are often worse relative to the social consequences experienced by men. As Ballinger pointed out, women commit far fewer crimes than men, but by breaking the law, women are not only committing a crime but also violating social norms and attitudes regarding the role of women and their expected behaviour (Ballinger, 2000). There are sufficient statistical data that show a steady rising trend in the dynamics of female crime since mid-1990s (Karpov, 2014; Shherbakova, 2007). According to the Federal Service for the Execution of Sentences in 2015, there were 52,157 female inmates staying in correctional facilities, such as penal colonies, prevention and treatment centres, and detention facilities (Federal Service for the Execution of Sentences, 2015). But little is known about the factors that may lead to female crime. Thus, the purpose of this study is to identify the main factors that contribute to female crime. Specifically, the research objectives of this study are (1) to analyse the female crime profile and (2) to examine the socio-economic position of female criminals and personal factors that may lead to their involvement in criminal activity.

Literature review

Although research on institutional population is limited in the Russian Federation (RF), some studies do provide valuable insight into female crime and further understanding of violence (Antonjan, 1992; Gilinsky, 2007; Kunts, 2010; Sinkov, 2011).

Shestakov (2006) found in a criminological study of spousal homicides in St. Petersburg (former Leningrad) that the majority of such crimes are committed by women following the pattern "family-conflict-crime." As a rule, a commission of a violent offence by a woman was preceded by a long-lasting conflict with a partner. Ilyashenko (2003) in his study of violent family

CRIMINOLOGY AND CRIMINAL JUSTICE IN RUSSIA

crimes came to a conclusion that "ongoing family conflicts" were the most commonly cited reason for such crimes, with 91.1% of ongoing immoral and abusive behaviour toward the victim being the trigger for nearly a third of them (28.7%). Repetskaya (2009) noted that female offenders reported that in 40% of cases, a homicide was committed as a response to violence or the threat of violence. The author also concluded that both women and men are equally victims of crimes committed by women. However, men more often become victims of physical abuse while women suffer from crimes in the economic sphere, such as fraud, embezzlement, etc. (Repetskaya, 2009).

An important point must be made that female violence in the family is not necessarily defensive in nature and in many cases women's behaviour is not that of a victim. Women are increasingly involved as a party to or initiator in fierce confrontations, and it is generally unclear what determines who will become a victim and a criminal in each particular case (Osipyan, 2011).

People who became the victims of women offenders were generally their acquaintances, friends, and neighbours with whom they often consumed alcohol (Repetskaya, 2009). It is also typical for women offenders to commit a similar repeated offence within a year after their release from a penitentiary facility where they served their first sentence (Stepanova & Yavchugovskaya, 2004). Family problems have an especially adverse effect on their lives, leading to the possibility of committing another crime. As an example, 50% of women offenders did not have a family at the time of committing a crime (Stepanova & Yavchugovskaya, 2001).

Although differing in their goals and data collection methods, these studies provide a better understanding of some of the various factors influencing female crime. This study aims to continue the same course of research to further pinpoint these factors.

Scope and nature of female crime in Russia

This study begins its analysis of the changes in the primary characteristics of female crime starting from 1997 to the year when the new Criminal Code of the RF came into effect. This was also when negative tendencies in the criminal activity of the population had become evident, which was related to changes in the political, economic, and social spheres in Russia (Shherbakova, 2007).

The analysis of the female crime trends in Russia from 1991, after the collapse of the Union of Soviet Socialist Republics, to present time allows for the distinction of several fluctuating periods of female criminal activity (Ilchenko & Khoroshilova, 2012). Between 1991 and 2000, there was an increase in the female crime rate in Russia (Figure 1). There was decline in the official number of female crimes only in the year of 1997, but this single year did not change the overall increasing trend in the female crime during this time period.

In Russia, this period is called "the boisterous 90s" as it is known for the near absence of social norms and the marked change in economic and moral norms as well (Shestakov, 2006). A lot of people not only lost their jobs during this time but also lost all possible means of financial support – delays in the payments of salaries and social benefits reached 6 or more months at some points, significantly impacting many individuals.

During this period, some people committed crimes to survive and to support their families, while others were driven by the incentive to make quick money, supported by the feeling of impunity and inaction of law enforcement authorities. This political and economic destabilisation lasted for a considerable period of time and shattered the welfare of society and women in particular (Volkova, 2001). During this time, the number of known female offenders increased 1.5 times and the percentage of women offenders, in relation to the total number of known offenders, decreased from 14.6% in 1997 to 17.0% in 2000 (Sinkov, 2011).

The second period (2001–2004) showed a downward trend in female crime. The lowering of the female crime level likely resulted from the decriminalisation of Article 200 of the Criminal Code of the RF (consumer fraud). Additionally, the lower statistics on a number of criminological indicators is associated with the difficulties of applying the new provisions of criminal law, criminal procedure legislation, and administrative legislation (Shcherbakova, 2007).

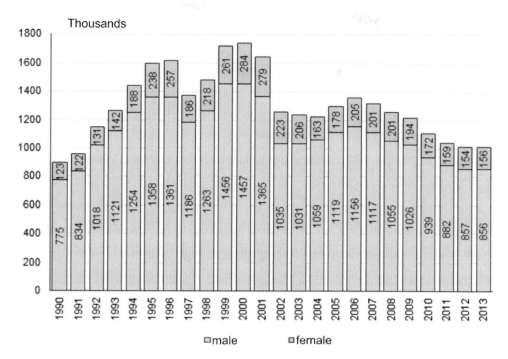

Figure 1. Scope of male and female crime in Russia. Source: http://demoscope.ru/.

During the third period (2005–2009), an increase in female crime was seen again. On the whole, over these years, the proportion of known women offenders grew by 1.4%. It can be estimated that in 2008–2009, one in seven offenders was female (Karpov, 2014).

The fourth period (2009 – present) is characterised by a steady decline in the total number of crimes committed in Russia. The tendency is equally true for both men and women offenders. Some explain this decrease in the crime rate by the changes in legislation along with a relative stability of socio-economic situation in Russia (http://demoscope.ru/). In 2014, the crime rate started to decline at a slower pace, and in 2015 there were some signs of an upward tendency, which came as the result of the current social and economic crisis in Russia.

Karpov notes that the statistical data surrounding these time periods does not include latent crimes which the police was not informed of or which, for some reason, were not registered (Karpov, 2014). Research shows that some 45–67% of convicted women committed additional crimes on top of those they were convicted for that remained unknown to the police (Sinkov, 2011). One of the most common latent crimes is the homicide of a newborn. According to some experts, between 30% and 50% of the registered infanticides remain unsolved (Makhmudova, 2007). The latency increases even more due to the fact that the birth and the homicide of the baby tend to be concealed by a family or partners. Consequently, it can be said that the official statistical data do not accurately reflect actual occurrence of female crime to the full extent.

Statistics on convicted women offenders

The tendency for criminalisation of the female population in Russia is reflected in the statistical data on convicted female inmates (male and female in Russia, 2015). This number reached a peak in 2001 when 170 thousand women were convicted (2001 saw a record number of convicted men as well). During the following years, however, the number of convicted female offenders was gradually declining.

Out of 13 kinds of punishments stipulated in the RF Criminal Code, one that was most widely imposed on women offenders was incarceration. Apart from this, women offenders are sentenced to a fine, deprivation of the right to hold certain positions or perform certain activities, compulsory works, reforming works, and imprisonment. However, the proportion of the aforementioned kinds of punishment in their total number is relatively small. For example, in 2012, the total number of punishment fines accounted for 20%, compulsory works for 11%, and reforming works for 6% (Karpov, 2014).

Methodology

Research location

The survey was conducted in a female penal colony in Primorsky region of Russia. Primorsky region is located in the Far East of Russia (Figure 2). The population is approximately 2,300,000 people, and its administrative centre is in the city of Vladivostok.

The majority of inmates of confinement facilities are based in adult penal colonies. The inmates of penal colonies are those who were sentenced to this type of confinement by court. Usually these are women who committed grave crimes as well as repeated crimes. On the territory of Primorsky region, there is only one standard regime penal colony for female convicts (IK-10), which was founded in 1942.

In this colony, inmates live in different buildings and are divided into various categories – the sick, mentally ill, and pensioners are accommodated separately and so are former law enforcement officers. Besides, those who are disciplined and show exemplary results, stick to the rules of the facility, and collaborate with the colony staff do not confront the disturbers of the colony order. Every penal colony building is a small fenced world of its own with its own supervisors. Women live in common rooms for 12–40 people and normally work in workshops (primarily sewing) located on the premises of the colony. The clothing factory in the IK-10 penal colony mainly specialises in manufacturing working clothes for special purposes – uniforms and accessories for military personnel, consumer goods, and governmental orders. The inmates must observe the colony rules and order and also obey the rules of the prison subculture (see more in http://www.aif.ru/society/people/na_vole_nas_nikto_ne_zhdet_fotozarisovki_iz_zhenskoy_kolonii). There is an evening (shift-type) general education school as well as a vocational school available for

Figure 2. Primorsky region of Russia. Source: http://www.primclub.ru/wp-content/uploads/2013/05/russia-primorsky.gif.

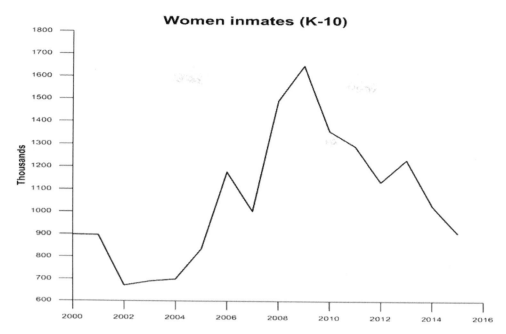

Figure 3. Women inmates in penal colony K-10 (Primorsky region of Russia).

attendance in IK-10 penal colony. The latter provides training for further obtaining qualifications to become a sewer and a light clothes tailor.

As for the total population of the penal colony IK-10, there were 898 female inmates in penal colony IK-10 in 2000, 1,355 in 2010, and 906 in 2015 (Figure 3). However, the decline in the number of the female inmates is more of a reflection of the amendments in the regulatory documents of the colony rather than lowering of the female crime level. Until 2013, the maximum allowed number of inmates in the colony was limited to 1,260 people, while from 2014 on it was reduced to 944 people. It is only safe to say that the colony has never experienced a deficit of incoming convicts and the number of its population has always been very close to maximum capacity.

The survey of this study, which was conducted in March 2013, was collected from 212 women aged between 18 and 64 years. The research was conducted with the financial support of the Presidents of the RF grant for young researchers. The project was managed by A. Lysova who selected the principal questions for the interview. The author of the article, O. Kaplun, obtained permission from the Federal Service for the Execution of Sentences to conduct the survey. However, at the last moment, the administration of the colony denied the author the access to the restricted area in the capacity of a researcher, so an anonymous opinion poll was included into a regular study, which was conducted by an in-house colony psychologist. Over 300 women were asked to answer the questions of the questionnaire, 212 of whom returned it filled out. Thus, the choice of the respondents was not random and this sampling cannot be considered representative of the population of female inmates of penitentiary facilities. However, the obtained information is of a certain value in terms of bringing to light the socio-economic position of women and personal problems that get them involved in criminal activity. The questionnaire in our project included 50 questions designed to analyse various aspects of women's lives and previous experiences. The data were entered into the system and processed with SPSS using methods of descriptive statistics and analysis.

Participants

Most women were kept in the penal colony for violent offences (40.7%) and drug-related crimes (41.1%). The remaining 18.2% of the female community had committed economic crimes. There is no legislative definition of the concept "economic crime" and this reflects "the complexity and multifaceted nature of this offence" (Mazhitova, 2011). In most cases, an economic crime is understood as a type of offence having property and commercial relations and economic rights of citizens, legal entities, and municipal and state formations as an object (Zolotukhin, 2012).

Article 22 of the Criminal Code of the RF gives the legally stipulated list of economic crimes which comprises several groups: (1) offences in business and other economic areas, such as fraud, misappropriation, and embezzlement; infliction of damage to property through deceit or breach of trust; illegal enterprise and banking; laundering proceeds of crime; (2) the manufacture and distribution of counterfeit money or financial credit documents, credit and debit cards, and other types of payment documents; (3) tax crimes: evasion of taxes, concealment of monetary resources or assets of a company or a private entrepreneur by means of which tax collection is to be effected (Volzhenkin, 2007).

In our research, we found the following age range of women in prison: up to 30 years – 39.5%, between 31 and 49 years – 51.9%, and 50 years and above – 8.6%. So, traditionally, the dominant group among women offenders is women over 30 years old. As few as 3.9% of the participants had a higher education, 2.6% had no education, and the remaining proportion had elementary school and vocational education. The majority of the participants of this study were not married (79%) (Table 1).

Results

Female crime profile

For the purposes of our research, we did not ask our respondents to specify the offence they committed. We asked them to put their offence into one of the following categories: a violent crime, a commercial crime, or a drug-related crime.

The results of our study showed that female inmates of the penal colony were mostly convicted for committing violent crimes. Women offenders having committed a homicide or infliction of bodily harm accounted for 42.1%. It should be noted that, although we did not ask that they specify the offence, 16.6% of women stated in the questionnaire at their own initiative that they had committed a homicide. Even though the rest of the women who had committed violent crimes did not specify the type of the crime, the proportion of women self-reporting to have committed a homicide was noteworthy. Women more often than men tended to commit violent

Table 1. Demographics of women in IK-10.

Variable	Description	(N/%)
Age (years)	1 = <30	39.5
	2 = 31–49	51.9
	3 = 50 and above	8.6
Education	1 = No education	2.6
	2 = School/vocation	93.5
	3 = Higher education	3.9
Type of crime	1 = Violent	42.1
	2 = Trafficking	31.6
	3 = Property	14.3
	4 = Other	12
Marriage	1 = Married	21
	2 = Not married	79
Residence	1 = Rural area	68.2
	2 = Cities	31.8

CRIMINOLOGY AND CRIMINAL JUSTICE IN RUSSIA

crimes related to conflicts at home, problems in family relationships, and personal feelings. Thirty per cent of crimes against life and health committed by women were family and home related. About one-third of the interviewed women initiated an attack and in 15% of all cases women were the only abusers in their families.

Additional evidence of abnormal trends in modern female crime is the increasing number of child abuse attempts. There has been an increase in the number of juvenile homicides with children in middle childhood and teenagers being victimised even more often than newborns. Most homicides of young children are committed through beating, poisoning, suffocation, drowning, and pushing the victim off of a high platform, such as a building or cliff.

It was revealed by the study that the second largest group of offences committed by women is those related to acquisition, possession, trafficking, manufacturing, and distribution of drugs. The results of our study showed that women offenders convicted of such crimes accounted for 31.67%. According to the results, about 70% of women offenders did not have a permanent source of income or a permanent job.

The third group of crimes included offences against property: theft, fraud, and embezzlement. Despite the relatively small proportion of such crimes – 14.3%, according to our study – many researchers note that their number is growing. For example, according to the data of Chikisheva (2011), between 2004 and 2010 in the Russian Far East, the number of frauds grew more than four times.

The number of real estate fraud cases shows the most significant growth among the crimes of such kind. As we see it, the major contributing factor here is the fact that a great number of women are engaged in the real estate business relative to men. Women work more frequently as real estate agents, public notaries, and clerks in state bodies performing official registration of real estate transactions and in passport offices.

Contributing factors and major causes of female crime

Empirical research conducted in the female penal colony revealed the following factors that affect female crime (Table 2):

(i) Social and economic conditions. One of the major factors contributing to female crime is unemployment. Unemployment is a strenuous experience in many respects. Being unemployed, even temporarily, is a shock that disturbs the normal flow of life. The absence of income impedes satisfaction of basic human needs of food and clothing. However, financial problems are not the only ones the unemployed have to face. Loss of job is a considerable stress. The state of instability arouses feelings of insecurity and anxiety, which are constantly

Table 2. Relationship between factors and type of crime.

Factors	Description	Violent crime (*N/*%)	Drags trafficking (*N/*%)	Property crime
Social and economic conditions	1 = Unemployed	39.5	68.1	46.2
	2 = Permanent job	49.2	7.0	52.2
	3 = Other (casual work)	11,3	24.9	1.6
Alcohol use	1 = Only women	14.2	10.4	7.8
	2 = Women and her partner	38	33.9	27.4
	3 = Only partner	42.8	47.9	43.6
	4 = Nobody	-	5.8	2.2
	5 = n/a	5	2	19
Social and cultural factors	1 = Domestic violence	27.5	10.6	0.9
	2 = Women were abusers	21.6	14.4	-
	3 = Abused in their childhood	52.2	22.7	12.1

growing until the person secures a job. In our study, the proportion of unemployed among the women offenders was 39.5%. The proportion of unemployed among the women who had been involved in illegal drug trafficking was even more and accounted for 68.1%. In addition, our findings demonstrate that the probability of committing a violent crime was higher for those penal colony female inmates who came from rural areas compared to urban citizens. It is important to expand education opportunities for rural area residents since low-educated women are more prone to committing crimes of violence, especially within their families.

(ii) Alcohol and drug addiction. Female alcoholism is one of the major factors contributing to female crime. The correlation between chronic alcohol addiction and inclination to commit various illegal acts was proven scientifically long ago (Dmitrieva, 2004; Repetskaya, 2009; Stepanova & Yavchugovskaya, 2001). As the research and the analysis of criminal cases show 60% of murderers as well as 20% of their victims were under the influence at the moment of committing the crime (Dmitrieva et al., 2004), it is determined that people with chronic alcohol addiction commit crimes against people, such as severe bodily injury, robbery, and disorderly conduct more often (Shcherbakova & Belaja, 2015; Stepanova & Yavchugovskaya, 2001).

According to the results, the majority of women who indicated that they drink alcohol regularly were convicted for committing violent crimes. In this group, 14.2% of women said they drank alcohol alone, 38% of the respondents stated that they drank together with their spouses, and another 42.8% indicated that their spouse or intimate partner was addicted to alcohol and it was the reason for disagreements and rows in their family. There were fewer alcohol addicts among women offenders convicted for other types of crimes. It is logical that for women convicted for drug-related crimes, drug addiction issue is more urgent; hence they skipped the questions in the questionnaire regarding alcohol use. In sum, according to the obtained data, about two-thirds of the female convicts were influenced by alcohol or narcotics at the moment of committing a crime and only 8% of the respondents said that none in their family used alcohol.

(iii) Social and cultural factors. These factors include low education level and, as a result, low qualification, low level of legal awareness, distorted morality, and legal culture. Other factors contributing to the growth of female crime are poorly organised leisure activities and low levels of culture, education, and qualification. The data obtained by our research suggests that a dysfunctional family and domestic abuse were among leading conditions pushing women towards crime. Thirty nine per cent of women offenders interviewed at the penal colony said that there was abuse in their families. It is important to note that in some cases a woman was the only abuser in the family with their husbands trying to calm them down and avoid a conflict, and in 36% of the cases women identified themselves as the initiators of the conflict.

Nearly all our respondents (87% of the female offenders) said that they suffered from domestic abuse. Women also shared that they were brought up in families where there were regular fights between their parents. The findings of this study indicate that women in the penal colony had a life background of physical and sexual abuse and trouble in the family.

Conclusion

In sum, women taking part in our research were serving their sentence for committing a rather narrow range of crimes. Our research showed that the female crime profile was represented by a little diversity of committed offences, with violent crimes accounting for the biggest proportion of them.

The major factors contributing to women committing a crime were their social and economic situation, alcohol and drug addiction as well as social and cultural factors. Poverty, poor living conditions, the absence of guaranteed state support in case of abuse, distrust in the police, and economic insecurity that are linked to increased female crime require the government to enforce and expand measures aimed at raising the living standards of people, especially those in rural areas. Additionally, taking into account the significance of violence as a means of solving a conflict present in the minds of many people, it is crucial to pay special attention to developing educational programmes focusing on raising legal and psychological awareness in women, promoting non-violent norms and values, and respect for the rights of every individual. In addition, the discharge of women after a long-term incarceration should come along with follow-up steps, such as reintegration into the labour market and search for a job. Considerable measures should be taken to make the process of adaptation and reintegration of women released from prison smoother.

ORCID

Oksana Kaplun http://orcid.org/0000-0002-1150-4269

References

Antonjan, J. M. (1992). *Crime between women* (pp. 256). Moscow: Rossiyskoe pravo.

Ballinger, A. (2000). *Dead woman walking; executed women in England and Wales 1900-1955* (pp. 102). Aldershot.

Chikisheva, N. A. (2011). *Women fraud: criminological and victimological characteristic.* (Abstract of Thesis). Vladivostok: Far Easter State University publishing.

Dmitrieva, T. B., Shostakovich, B. V., & Tkachenko, A. A. (2004). *A guide to Forensic Psychiatry.* Moscow: Publishing House «Medicine». 592 p.

Federal Service for the Execution of Sentences. (2015). *Brief characteristics of the penal system.* Retrieved October 20, 2015, from http://www.fsin.su/structure/inspector/iao/statistika/Kratkaya%20har-ka%20UIS/

Gilinsky, Y. I. (2007). Women in organized crime in Russia. In G. Fiandaca (Ed.), (pp. 300). New York, NY: Springer.

Ilchenko, O. Y., & Khoroshilova, A. A. (2012). Criminological characteristics of female crime. *Kriminologiya: Vchera, Segodnya, Zavtra, 26,* 67–70.

Ilyashenko, A. N. (2003). Victimological problems of violent crime in the family. *Law and Politics, 1*(37), 89–99.

Karpov, V. S. (2014). Criminal-legal measures applied to women criminals, practice and problems of application in the Russian Federation. *Aktual'nye Problemy Ekonomiki I Prava, 1*(29), 277–282.

Kunts, E. V. (2010). Women and youth deviant behavior as a subject of sociological and criminological issue. *Bulletin of the Chelyabinsk State University, 9,* 74–76.

Makhmudova, M. A. (2007). Problems of newborns killing by mothers: A regional perspective. *Questions of Juvenile Justice, 1,* 27–30.

Mazhitova, S. R. (2011). The problem of the "economic crime" definition. *Economic Crimes Bulletin of Chelyabinsk State University Issue, 35,* 49–53.

Osipyan, N. B. (2011). On the issue of peculiarities of female delinquency. *Psychology and Law, 2,* 11–21.

CRIMINOLOGY AND CRIMINAL JUSTICE IN RUSSIA

Repetskaya, A. L. (ed.). (2009). *Victimological Characteristics of Regional Crime and its Prevention* (pp. 304). Irkutsk: Baikal State University of Economics and Law Publishing.

Shcherbakova, L. M., & Belaja, O. P. (2015). Male and female criminal violence: A comparative analysis Criminology. *Journal of Baikal National University of Economics and Law, 2,* 69–75.

Shestakov, D. A. (2006). *Criminology: New approaches to crime* (pp. 344). St.Petersburg: Legal Center Press.

Shherbakova, L. M. (2007). *Female violent crime in modern Russia: Trends, determinants and prevention problems* (pp. 419). Stavropol.

Sinkov, D. V. (2011). Crime and punishment of women: Analysis of modern trends. *Kriminologicheskii Zhurnal BGUEP, 3*(17), 34–41.

Stepanova, I. B., & Yavchugovskaya, T. M. (2001). Features of criminological characteristics of female offenders. *Messenger of Ivanovo State University, 4,* 20–30.

Stepanova, I. B., & Yavchugovskaya, T. M. (2004). Criminological characteristic of women recidivism women. *Pravovedenie, 2,* 96–105.

Volkova, T. N. (2001). *Criminological and legal problems of female criminality in modern Russia* (Abstract of Thesis). Ryazan: Ryazan State University publishing.

Volzhenkin, B. V. (2007). *Crimes in the sphere of economic activity according criminal law in Russia* (pp. 763). St. Petersburg: Legal center Press.

Zolotukhin, A. P. (2012). Economic crime: Problems of criminal legal analysis. *Jurisprudence: past and Present, 11,* 113–119.

Index

accusatory bias 95–100, 102, 104, 106–7, 117
adjusted goodness-of-fit index (AGFI) 122
adversariality: "breaches" of 92; negotiations
    and 105; problem of asymmetry 105–6; threat
    to 106
advokatura 97, 106; Federal Law on 97; old bars'
    leadership of 97
age: bivariate analyses and 46; juvenile
    delinquency and 42, 46; range of women in
    prison 170; stereotypes and 142
Agenda of the Communist Party of the USSR 8
aggression: hostile (or expressive) 42;
    instrumental 42; *see also* violence
Albonetti, C. A. 142
Alexander II's Judiciary Reform of 1864 97
All-Russian Center of Public Opinion Research
    (WCIOM) 38, 114, 133n6
All-Union Institute of Juridical Sciences 8–9
American Society of Criminology's International
    Division 26
anomie theory 51
anomy theory 51–2
attitudes: juvenile delinquency and 43–4;
    towards social values, and juvenile
    delinquency 37–8

Ballinger, A. 165
Baltic Criminological Seminar 27
Bayley, David 56, 57, 66
behind-the-closet defence attorneys 102
Beljaeva, L. A. 39
bias: accusatory 95–100, 102, 104, 106–7, 117;
    economic 77; extralegal 75
bivariate analyses: juveniles' attitudes towards
    delinquency 46–9; juveniles' attitudes towards
    the society 45–9
Black, Donald 143
Blumberg, A. S. 95
"the boisterous 90s" 166
Borisenko, Elena 102
"bourgeois" criminology 9, 27
bourgeoisie consciousness 27
bourgeois society 97

Bright, S. B. 104
Burrage, M. 97

Caldwell, M. H. 103, 107
capitalist environment 27
case distribution system 104
Center of Deviantology (Sociology of Deviance)
    of the Sociological Institute of the Russian
    Academy of Sciences (St. Petersburg) 32
Cernkovich, S. A. 38
"checkmark system" *(palochnaya sistema)* 98
Chikisheva, N. A. 171
chronic alcohol addiction 172
civil claim 80
Cohen, S. 5
Cold War 8
collectivistic values 37
comparative goodness-of-fit index (CGFI) 122
confirmatory factor analysis (CFA) 123–4
conflict criminologists 30; *see also* criminologists
conflict of cultures 29
Congress of Soviets 132n1
Constitutional Court of Russia 117, 132n5
contemporary sociology 15
conventional value orientations 38
convicted women offenders 167–8
corridor defence attorneys 102
Cossack community 62
courtroom workgroups *see* workgroups in
    Russian criminal justice
Courts of Common Plea, USA 143
crime(s): bourgeoisie consciousness and 27;
    capitalist environment and 27; criminality and
    29; defined 10; drug-related 140, 142–3, 145,
    154–7; family-conflict- 165; globalization and
    29; "masculine" 145; political 97; prevention
    theory 11; property 153–6; rates and organic
    solidarity 51; recidivate 150; relationship
    between factors and type of 171; as social
    phenomenon 27
"Crime and Delinquency, Statistical Review" 32
Criminal Code of Russian Federation 1, 3, 30,
    141, 166, 170

INDEX

criminality: crime and 29; female *see* female criminality; as mental construct 29; as social construct 29; social control over 30

Criminal Procedural Code (CPC) reforms 113–14, 128; citizen attitudes about 115; criminal justice professionals and 114; criminal trial judge, role of 116–17; professional judge and 147; public approval ratings and 114

Criminal Procedure Code (CPC) 1, 8, 82

Criminal Procedure Code of Russian Federation 141

criminals: individual characteristics, studies on 27; marginal social status and 103

criminal sentencing: dependent variables and 150–1; gender and family ties and 140–58; gender order of Russian society 144; independent variables and 150–1; literature on gender disparity in 141–4; methods 149–50; modelling the sentencing process and data 147–8; overview 140–1; severity and leniency in 140–58; theoretical framework and hypotheses 144–7; *see also* sentencing

"Criminological Journal of Baikal State University of Economic and Law" 32

Criminological Research Institute of Lower Saxony 41

criminologists 7–8; on classification of offenders 11; concept of contradictions and 10; conflict *vs.* mainstream 30; Marxist approach adopted by 10; on socialist system 10; use of historical and dialectical materialism 9

criminology: as academic discipline 5; cultural 29; in post-Soviet Russia 2, 28–32; in Soviet Union 2; structural 29–30; studies/courses in Russia 12–14; teaching 32; typologies of 27; *see also* Russian criminology; *specific types*

"crisis of punishment" 30

cultural criminology 29

cultural values: comprehensive judicial reforms and 115; judgment of fairness of the judicial reform and 129; levels of importance of 127, 128; measuring 123–6; regression loadings for indicators of 123, 124; role in citizen acceptance and perceived fairness 113–32

cybercrime 29

Daly, K. 143

deepness period 39, 40, 51–2

defence attorneys 98; as "double-agent" 95; as effective negotiator 95; as effective negotiators 94–5; grounds for collusive behaviour of appointed 104–5; as mediators 94–5; as members of workgroups 99–101; organisational structure of criminal process and 100; pocket 102–5; pretrial workgroups and role of 95–101; problem of asymmetry 104–5; professional

situation of 98; trial workgroups and the role of 95–101; *see also* judges

delinquency *see* juvenile delinquency

demographic characteristics, and pretrial detention 80–1

The department of moral statistics 27

dependent variables: criminal sentencing and 150–1; juvenile delinquency and 42

dialectical materialism 10

domestic violence courts 143

downstream period 39–40, 51

druzhinniki 11, 58–9, 62, 70n4

druzhiny 57, 58–62, 70n2

Durkheim, Emile 51

economic bias 77

Eisenstein, J. 92–3

empirical criminological research 30–1

"The essentials of the Soviet criminology" 9

ethnicity: pretrial detention and 79

European Society of Criminology 12

European University at St. Petersburg, Russia 108n1

evil woman thesis 142

extenuating circumstances 80

Extra-Departmental Protection Directorate of the Ministry of Internal Affairs (UVVO) 63

extralegal bias 75

familial paternalism theory 143

"family based justice" 143

"family-conflict-crime" 165

family ties: criminal sentencing 140–58; drug crimes and 143; social control and 143

Federal Service for the Execution of Sentences 165, 169

female alcoholism 172

female crime: alcohol and drug addiction 172; contributing factors and major causes of 171–2; nature of 166–7; relationship between factors and type of 171; scope of 166–7; social and cultural factors 172; social and economic conditions 171–2

female crime profile 170–1

female criminality: contributing factors and major causes of 171–2; female crime profile 170–1; literature review 165–8; overview 165; scope and nature of female crime 166–7; statistics on convicted women offenders 167–8

female-favourable sentencing 142

female offenders 3

Feshbach, S. 42

Foundation of Public Opinion (FOM) 133n7

Fridrich-Ebert-Foundation 38

gender: criminal sentencing 140–58; descriptive statistics of dependent variables by 149; descriptive statistics of independent variables

INDEX

by 149; juvenile delinquency and 42; sentencing decisions and 143; sentencing in Finland and 143–4

gender disparity in sentencing 141–4

gender order of Russian society 144

Gilinskiy, Y. 27

glass ceiling 144

globalization, and crime 29

Gorbachev's "Perestroika" 27

Gorki experiment 60–1

group-value consistency 117–18

group-value theory 115

Gurinskaya, Anna 26

Haney, L. A. 142

hate crimes 29, 33

Heckman, J. J. 149

Hendley, K. 147

Hess, H. 29

hostile (or expressive) aggression 42

Ilyashenko, A. N. 165

Ilyina, L. V. 7

"imperial monopolists" 9

imprisonment, and pretrial detention 84–5

Independent Russian Institute for Social and National Problems 38

independent variables: criminal sentencing and 150–1; juvenile delinquency and 42–4

individualistic values 37; "competitor-centred" group and 50

inequality: problem of asymmetry 105–6; workgroups and 93

Ingelhart, Roland 43

inquisitive defence attorneys 102

Inside Plea Bargaining (Maynard) 94

Institute for Research of Crime Causes and Crime Prevention 27

Institute for the Rule of Law (IRL) 95–6, 108n1

Institute of Sociology of the Russian Academy of Sciences 38

instrumental aggression 42

instrumental liberal values 40

instrumental violence 36, 42, 45, 47, 50

instrumental violent delinquency 36

International Journal of Comparative and Applied Criminal Justice 26

International Society of Social Protection 28

International Union of Criminologists 7

Ivanov, L. O. 7

Jacob, H. 92

judges: chivalry or paternalistic attitudes of 142; institutional incentives of 107; judicial reform and 116–18; *see also* defence attorneys

judicial investigative remand: discussion and limitations 130–1; hypotheses testing

126–30; literature review and research question 115–18; measuring cultural values in Russia 123–5; measuring public opinion about the fairness of the judicial reforms 126; methodology 118–23; overview 113–15

judicial reforms: citizen support for 114–15; collectively-oriented individuals and 118; measuring public opinion about the fairness of 126; type of cultural values and judgment of fairness of 129; of XIX century 97

justice: family based 143; as a local phenomenon 93; slaughterhouse 104; social 141

juvenile delinquency: attitudes towards social values in Russia 37–8; attitudes towards society and 37; bivariate analyses and 45–9; criminological theories 51–2; dependent variables and 42; independent variables and 42–4; instrumental violence and 36; measuring 42; multivariate analyses 46–9; non-instrumental violence and 36; sample and questionnaire 41; social values and 36–52; socio-economic status (SES) and 43, 50–1; survey 41–9

Kaplun, O. 169

Karpov, V. S. 167

Khodorkovsky, Mikhail 140

Khodzhaeva, Ekaterina 108n2

Khrushchev's "Thaw" 27

kompromaty 65

Korzhakov, A. 65

Kramer, M. 141

Kruttschnitt, C. 143

Labeling Theory 27

Lapin, N. I. 39

latent classes 37

Law Department of Moscow State University and Sverdlovsk 9

leniency: in criminal sentencing 140–58; gender and 145–6; for parental offenders 146; towards defendants with children 155; towards women with children 151

Levada-Centre 38

Levin-Stankevich, B. L. 97

liberal values 40; instrumental 40; terminal 40

Lind, E. A. 115

literature: on gender disparity in sentencing 141–4; Russian judicial reform and 114–15; zero-acquittal policy of Soviet era 116

Logue, M. A. 143

"Lombrosianism" 8

Luban, D. 100

Lysova, A. 169

INDEX

mainstream criminologists 30

marriage: interaction effects of offender's sex and 154–6; punishment and 146–7

Marxist-Leninist ideology 8

Matza, D. 38

Maynard, D. W. 94, 100, 101

mechanical solidarity 51

Messner, S. F. 52

Ministry Internal Affairs (MVD) 32, 67

Ministry of Justice 97

MOB *(Militsia obshchestvennoi bezopasnosti)* 68

mobilisation period 39, 40, 52

modern anomy theory 52

multilateralization of policing 2; market-oriented approach to policing 64–5; order maintenance and 60–3; in post-Soviet Russia 56–70; private protection companies and 66–7; property rights protection and 63–4; since *perestroika* and *glasnost* 60–5; state law enforcement agencies and 67–70

multivariate analyses: juveniles' attitudes towards delinquency 46–9; juveniles' attitudes towards the society 46–9

negotiations: courtroom workgroups and the role of 92–5; layers of 100–1; lower layer of 100; meaning of 93–4; problem of asymmetry 105–6; social explanation of the nature of 91–2; structural 91; upper layer of 100

negotiators, defence attorneys as effective 94–5, 106

non-instrumental violence 36, 42, 45–6, 48, 50–1

non-instrumental violent delinquency 36

Novaja Gazeta ("New Newspaper") 31

NVivo software 108n5

Obschaya Gazeta ("Common Newspaper") 31

on duty defence attorneys 102

organic solidarity 51

organised crime 32

Orthodox Marxism 27

"The Oxford Handbook of Criminology" 29

Paneyakh, E. 99, 145

parasitising defence attorneys 102

Penitentiary Criminology 27

plea bargaining 80; courtroom workgroups and the role of negotiations 92–5; evidence from Russia 95–101; as norm 92; overview 91–2; pretrial and trial workgroups and the role of defence attorneys 95–101; problem of asymmetry 102–6; role of defence attorneys and the problem of asymmetry 91–108

pocket counsel/defence attorneys 102–5, 107

"pocket" practices 92, 102–5

policing: defined 56; market-oriented approach to 64–5; multilateralization *see* multilateralization

of policing; multilaterization of 2; unilateralism in Soviet 57–9

political regime: crime designing and 29; forms of policing and 70; role in criminalisation/decriminalisation 28

Political Regime and Criminality (Burlakov) 29

political science 15

"positivism" 8

post-Soviet Russia: criminal justice processes in 2; criminological theory development 28–30; criminology in 2, 28–32; criminology teaching 32; empirical criminological research 30–1; multilateralization of policing in 56–70

pretrial detention: demographic characteristics 80–1; ethnicity and 79; extralegal factors and 77; influence on sentence severity 85; introduction 74–5; likelihood of 82–3; likelihood of imprisonment and 84–5; research issues 75–7; role, in dismissal decisions 83–4; socio-economic status (SES) and 76; statistical analysis of data 78–80; "unemployed" status and 82

pretrial workgroups, and defence attorneys 95–101

private protection companies 66–7

problem of asymmetry 102–6; counsel from the pocket 102–4; grounds for collusive behaviour of appointed defence attorneys 104–5; negotiations, adversariality, and inequality 105–6

property rights protection 63–4

propiska 71n13

punishment individualisation 141

Putin, Vladimir 68–9

Rabovski, Julia 108n2

Radaev, V. 64, 66

Rand, R. 98

Reitler, A. K. 76

Repetskaya, A. L. 166

Research Institute of the General Prosecutor's Office of the Russian Federation 32

Research Institute of the MVD 32

retreatists 52

ritualists 52

RMSEA 122, 129

Rokeach, Milton 43

ROMIR (Center for Russian Public Opinion and Market Research) 133n6

Rosenfeld, R. 52

Russian Constitution 120

Russian Criminal Procedural Code 75; Article 60 77; Article 99 77; Article 111 81; Article 158 81; Article 228 81

Russian Criminological Association (RCA) 11–12, 27, 32

Russian criminology: of developed socialism 8–9; emergence and demise of 6–8; history 6–11;

INDEX

isolation of 14–15; overview 2, 6; in present time 11–14; relevance of 16–18; Soviet theory of crime 9–11; stages of development 27–8; Western theoretical approaches and 14; *see also* criminology
Russian judicial reforms *see* judicial reforms
Russian Revolution of 1917 7
Russian society, gender order of 144
Russian Soviet Federative Socialist Republic (RSFSR) 116–17, 133n8

"safeties" programme 65
Sakharov, A. 27
Saratov Centre for the Study of Organized Crime and Corruption 12
Saratov's Center of Research of Organized Crime and Corruption (Saratov) 32
Savolainen, J. 143
Scheerer, S. 29
Schneider, G.J. 32
school type, and juvenile delinquency 42–3
Schwartz, J. 118, 123, 144
self-policing mechanisms 2
sentencing 3; family-related factors 157–8; gender disparities in 143; pretrial detention and 74, 85; *see also* criminal sentencing
sentencing decisions: blameworthiness 142; family-related factors for 143; gender and 143; gender and family-related factors and 143; practical constraints and consequences 142; protection of the community 142; sex and 142
severity, in criminal sentencing 140–58
sex 143; parenthood dependent on 143; sentencing decisions and 142; as social characteristics of defendant 150–1; women as weaker 145
Shearing, Clifford 56, 57, 66
Sheley, J. 32
Shelley, L. 58
Shestakov, D. A. 165
"slaughterhouse justice" 104
social contradictions theory 10, 13, 14
social control: crime and 30; repressive 30; theory 143, 146
social dangerousness 10
social development: deepness period 39, 40, 51–2; downstream period 39–40, 51; mobilisation period 39, 40, 52; in Russia 39
social inequality 105
social justice 141
social values: delinquency of Russian youth and 36–52; excursus about change of 39–40; violence and 36; violent criminal behavior and 2; youth studies and attitudes towards 37–8
socio-economic status (SES): competitor-centred juveniles and 50; juvenile delinquency and 43, 50–1; pretrial detention and 76

Sociological institute of the Russian Academy of Sciences 31
Sociology of Violence (Committee Against Torture) 31
Solomon, P. H. 8, 99, 106
Soviet criminology *see* Russian criminology
special military courts 147
Spiridonov, L. 27
Spohn, C. 143
spousal homicides 165
Stacey, A. 143
State Institute for the Study of Crime and Criminal 7
state law enforcement agencies 67–70
Steffensmeier, D. 141, 144
St. Petersburg International Criminological Club 27
St. Petersburg International Criminology Club 12
street crimes 29
Streifel, C. 141
structural criminology 29–30
structural-equation modeling (SEM) techniques 122
subterranean value orientations 38
Sykes, G. M. 38

Tarnovsky, E. 27
terminal liberal values 40
terminal traditional values 40
theoretical criminology 11, 13
Tkachev, Governor 70–1n8
"Torture as Everyday Routine in Russia" 31
trial judges' authority 3
trial workgroups, and defence attorneys 95–101
Triandis, Harry 43
Tyler, T. R. 115
Tzar Alexander II 7

"unemployed" status, and pretrial detention 82
unilateralism in Soviet policing 57–9; illicit social practices and 58; regional political elites and 58; underground entrepreneurs and 59
Union of Forensic and Criminology Scholars 12
Uphoff, R. J. 95, 105

values 37; collectivistic 37; individualistic *see* individualistic values; instrumental liberal 40; liberal *see* liberal values; social *see* social values; terminal liberal 40; terminal traditional 40
violence: instrumental 36, 42, 45, 47, 50; non-instrumental 36, 42, 45–6, 48, 50–1; right-wing 32; *see also* aggression
"violence-managing agencies" 64–5
Volgograd State Educational University 41
Volkov, Vadim 64, 141, 158

INDEX

Western criminology 9, 10, 27
white-collar crime 29
Williams, Mariann 77
Workers' Detachments for Cooperation with the
  Police (ROSM or *Rabochii Otriad Sodeistviya
  Militsii*) 60
workgroups in Russian criminal justice:
  empirical data 95–6; goals of 92–3; plea
  bargaining and 92–5; pretrial 95–101;

professional situation of Russian advocates
  96–9; and the role of negotiations 92–5;
  Russian defence attorneys as members of
  99–101; trial 95–101

Yeltsin, Boris 58
"Youth of the New Russia" 38

Zhuikov, V. M. 114